Fixed Income Mathematics

Fixed Income Mathematics

Frank J. Fabozzi, CFA

Visiting Professor of Finance
Alfred P. Sloan School of Management
Massachusetts Institute of Technology
and
Managing Editor
The Journal of Portfolio Management

Probus Publishing Company
Chicago, Illinois

Library of Congress Cataloging-in-Publication Data

Fabozzi, Frank J.
      Fixed income mathematics.

      Includes index.
      1. Investments — Mathematics. 2. Business mathematics.
      3. Rate of return. I. Title
      HG4515.3.F23   1988   332.63'2'0151   88-15195
      ISBN 1-55738-007-4

Printed in the United States of America

BB

3   4   5   6   7   8   9   0

To my wife, Dessa

Contents

viii   Contents

Appendices

Preface

In recent years, participants in the fixed income markets have been introduced to new analytical frameworks for evaluating fixed income securities and new fixed income portfolio strategies. In discussing fixed income securities and strategies, we often hear terms such as *horizon return, duration, convexity, negative convexity, call-adjusted yield, call-adjusted duration, delta,* and *CPR*. What do they mean? Why are they useful in fixed income analysis?

Fixed Income Mathematics provides the tools needed to understand these concepts and their roles in evaluating fixed income securities and managing fixed income portfolios. It begins with the basic concepts of the mathematics of finance (the time value of money) and systematically builds on these, taking you through the most recent methodologies for evaluating fixed income securities with embedded options, such as callable corporate bonds, mortgage pass-through securities, and stripped mortgage-backed securities. The concepts are illustrated with numerical examples and graphs. The material is self-contained and requires only a basic knowledge of elementary algebra to understand.

Many of the chapters in this book are drawn from the lectures I delivered in my Fixed Income Seminar at the Sloan School of Management at MIT and my presentations to the sales personnel and bond traders at Bear Stearns & Co., as well as to other groups in Europe and Japan.

This book was written in conjunction with two other projects. First, *Fabozzi's Fixed Income Calculator*, a PC-based program that executes many of the calculations illustrated in this book, was developed jointly with SpectraSoft, Inc. Sample screen pages are shown in Appendix B of the book. Second, two videos were produced by VCA Teletronics/Financial Video Network (*Understanding Bond Pricing and Return Measures* and *Understanding Bond Price Volatility: Duration and Convexity*). Information about these products can be obtained from Probus Publishing.*

Acknowledgments

First and foremost, I wish to thank my wife Dessa for her patience and sacrifice of lost weekends so that I could complete this project. I hope that the royalties from this book will be sufficient for a long weekend vacation in the Caribbean. She was also kind enough to read several chapters of this book, taking every opportunity—*every opportunity*—to point out ways to improve the exposition. (I would have asked her to read all the chapters, but my ego is too fragile and divorce too high a price for improved exposition.)

I received helpful comments on portions of this book from the following individuals: Tom Bain (American National Bank in Terrell, Texas), Anand Bhattacharya (Underwood Neuhaus and Company), John Carlson (Security Pacific), Andrew Carron (The First Boston Corporation), Ravi Dattatreya (Prudential-Bache Capital Funding), Mark Dunetz (Kidder, Peabody), Menong Enverga (SpectraSoft), Matt Graves (First National Bank in Decatur, Illinois), Andrew Ho (Kidder, Peabody), Ken Ingram (Central Bank & Trust in Fort Worth, Texas), Mike Kinney (MidFirst S & L in Oklahoma City, Oklahoma), Dragomir Krgin (Merrill Lynch Capital Markets), James Mahoney (Kidder, Peabody), Luis Manalac (SpectraSoft), Matthew Mancuso (Bear Stearns), Fred Price (Bear Stearns), Larry Ng (SpectraSoft), Greg Rahe (American Home Savings in Edmond, Oklahoma), Sharmin Mossavar-Rahmani (Fidelity Management), Chuck Ramsey (Bear Stearns), Herman Sandler (Bear Stearns), Bruce Yablon (Bear Stearns), and Yu Zhu (Merrill Lynch Capital Markets).

Ed Rappa of Bear Stearns encouraged me and provided support at every step of this project. I am grateful to Stewart

---

* You might feel that this is all self-serving advertisement. You're right.

Myers, Chairman of the Department of Applied Economics, Finance, and Accounting at MIT, for giving me the opportunity to teach the Fixed Income Seminar.

Young Yim, my teaching assistant at MIT, read the book in its entirety and made helpful suggestions.

Last, but certainly not least, I give a special thanks to my secretary—Jean Marie DeJordy.

Frank J. Fabozzi

1
Introduction

At one time, not too long ago, the analysis of fixed income securities was relatively simple. In an economic environment that exhibited relatively stable interest rates, investors purchased fixed income securities with the intent of holding them to maturity. Yield to maturity could be used as a proxy measure of the relative value of fixed income securities. Risk was measured in terms of credit rating. When a fixed income security was callable, a second measure—yield to call—was used to assess its relative value. For a callable bond, the long-standing rule was that a conservative investor should use the lower of the yield to maturity and yield to call as a measure of the security's potential return.

Those days are gone today in an environment where interest rates fluctuate substantially. Why? Several factors rendered the traditional approach to fixed income analysis of limited value.

First, trading and portfolio strategies that require the sale of a fixed income security prior to maturity mean that a measure such as the yield to maturity is meaningless. The same holds for the yield to call. Also, since a fixed income security may not be held to maturity, some measure of risk that reflects its price volatility is needed.

Second, investors recognize that the only way to achieve a return equal to the yield to maturity is to reinvest the coupon payments. More specifically, to achieve the yield to maturity, an investor must reinvest the coupon payments at an interest rate equal to the yield to maturity. The impact on the return actually

1

realized by reinvesting the coupon payments at an interest rate less than the yield to maturity may not be trivial. The same is true for yield to call.

Third, the plain vanilla bond has been replaced by more complex fixed income security structures as investment bankers in the 1980s designed instruments to reduce the cost of debt for their clients. The securitization of mortgages introduces new instruments that cannot be analyzed by using the traditional methodology. Many of these new fixed income securities have options embedded in them. With the breakthroughs in option theory, frameworks have been developed for analyzing securities with embedded options.

In their now classic book, *Inside the Yield Book*, Sidney Homer and Martin Leibowitz were the first to clearly demonstrate the limitations of the conventional yield measures (yield to maturity and yield to call).[1] In addition, they documented the characteristics of bonds that bear upon their price volatility.

A measure of bond price volatility, popularly known as *duration*, was independently developed as far back as 1938 by Frederick Macaulay,[2] in 1945 by Paul Samuelson,[3] in 1946 by John Hicks,[4] and in 1952 by F.M. Redington.[5] The work of Lawrence Fisher and Roman Weil in 1971[6] showed the importance of duration for portfolio strategies.

In 1984 a paper written by Stanley Diller with the assistance of his Financial Strategies Group staff when he was em-

---

[1] Sidney Homer and Martin L. Leibowitz, *Inside the Yield Book* (Englewood Cliffs, N.J.: Prentice-Hall, 1972, and New York Institute of Finance, 1972), pp. 164-67.

[2] Frederick R. Macaulay, *Some Theoretical Problems Suggested by the Movement of Interest Rates, Bond Yields, and Stock Prices in the United States Since 1865* (New York: National Bureau of Economic Research, 1938).

[3] Paul A. Samuelson, "The Effect of Interest Rate Increases on the Banking System," *American Economic Review* (March 1945), pp. 16-27.

[4] John R. Hicks, *Value and Capital* (Oxford, Eng.: Clarendon Press, 1946).

[5] F. M. Redington, "Review of the Principle of Life Office Valuations," *Journal of the Institute of Actuaries* (1952), pp. 286-340.

[6] Lawrence Fisher and Roman Weil, "Coping with the Risk of Interest Rate Fluctuations and Returns to Bondholders from Naive and Optimal Strategies," *Journal of Business* (October 1971), pp. 408-431.

ployed at Goldman Sachs, particularly Ravi Dattatreya,[7] made two important contributions to our understanding of the price performance of a fixed income security. First, Diller demonstrated that yield and duration alone are not sufficient to assess the performance of a fixed income security. A third measure, convexity, is necessary. Second, he linked option theory and fixed income analysis, showing how the embedded option of a fixed income security will affect the performance of the security. Since then, several works have been published that incorporate and extend the concepts developed by Diller.

The objective of this book is to present the mathematics necessary to understand the latest methodologies for evaluating any fixed income security — those existing today and those that we will assuredly see in the future — and understanding the latest trading and portfolio strategies.

Overview of the Book

The basic foundations of the mathematics of finance are presented in the three chapters of Part I. Chapter 2 explains how to compute the future value of an investment. Chapter 3 shows how to calculate the present value of cash flows to be received (or paid) in the future. Since the price of any financial asset is the present value of the cash flows expected, it is essential to have a firm understanding of present value and its characteristics. The yield of any investment is explained in Chapter 4.

Bond pricing and return analysis are the subjects of Part II. Chapter 5 extends the present value analysis to bonds, showing how their price is determined. Conventional yield measures— yield to maturity and yield to call—which are simply applications of the yield measure reviewed in Chapter 4 are explained in Chapter 6. The potential sources of dollar return by investing in a bond are explained in Chapter 7. The conventional yield measures are then critically evaluated in terms of whether they properly account for each of these sources. After highlighting

---

[7] Stanley Diller, *Parametric Analysis of Fixed Income Securities* (New York: Financial Strategies Group, Goldman Sachs & Co., June 1984). Dr. Diller is currently the chief financial strategist at Bear Stearns & Co.

the deficiencies of the conventional yield measure, Chapter 8 describes a better measure of potential return—horizon return—that does take into consideration all sources of potential dollar return even if a bond is expected to be sold prior to the maturity date.

The price volatility of option-free bonds (i.e., bonds without embedded options) is covered in Part III. Price volatility properties of bonds, as well as the characteristics of bonds that affect their price volatility, are illustrated in Chapter 9. Several measures of bond price volatility—price value of a basis point, yield value of a price change, and duration—are described in Chapter 10. Chapter 11 explains the importance of convexity in explaining the potential price performance of a bond and how to calculate convexity.

The framework developed in Chapters 2 through 11 are then extended to fixed income securities with embedded options—callable corporate bonds, mortgages, mortgage pass-through securities, and stripped mortgage-backed securities—in Chapters 12–16. To understand how to evaluate fixed income securities with embedded options, Chapter 12 reviews the price and performance characteristics of interest rate options.

I
Time Value of Money

2
Future Value

The notion that money has a time value is one of the basic concepts in the analysis of any financial instrument. Money has a time value because of the opportunities for investing money at some interest rate. In the three chapters of Section I of this book, we review the three fundamental concepts involved in understanding the time value of money. In this chapter, we explain how the future value of an investment can be determined. In the next chapter, we will explain the procedure for determining how much money must be invested today (called the present value) in order to realize a specific amount in the future. Chapter 3 shows how to compute the yield on any investment.

Future Value of an Investment

Suppose an investor places $1,000 in a bank account and the bank agrees to pay interest of 7% a year. At the end of one year, the account will contain $1,070, that is, $1,000 of the original principal plus $70 of interest. Suppose that the investor decides to let the $1,070 remain in the bank account for another year and that the bank agrees to continue paying interest of 7% a year. The amount in the bank account at the end of the second year will equal $1,144.90, determined as follows:

Principal at beginning of year 2	$1,070.00
Interest for year 2 ($1,070 × .07)	74.90
Total in bank account	$1,144.90

In terms of our original $1,000 investment, the $1,144.90 represents the following:

Original investment at beginning of year 1	$1,000.00
Interest for year 1 ($1,000 × .07)	70.00
Interest for year 2 based on original investment	70.00
Interest for year 2 earned on interest for year 1 ($70 × .07)	4.90
Total	$1,144.90

The additional interest of $4.90 in year 2 above the $70 interest earned on the original principal of $1,000 is the interest on the interest earned in year 1.

After eight years, the $1,000 investment—if allowed to accumulate tax-free at an annual interest rate of 7%—will be $1,718.19, as shown below:

Beginning of year 1 original investment	$1,000.00
At the end of year 1 ($1,000.00 × 1.07)	$1,070.00
At the end of year 2 ($1,070.00 × 1.07)	$1,144.90
At the end of year 3 ($1,144.90 × 1.07)	$1,225.04
At the end of year 4 ($1,225.04 × 1.07)	$1,310.79
At the end of year 5 ($1,310.79 × 1.07)	$1,402.55
At the end of year 6 ($1,402.55 × 1.07)	$1,500.73
At the end of year 7 ($1,500.73 × 1.07)	$1,605.78
At the end of year 8 ($1,605.78 × 1.07)	$1,718.19

After eight years, $1,000 will grow to $1,718.19 if allowed to accumulate tax-free at an annual interest rate of 7%. We refer to the amount at the end of eight years as the *future value*.

Notice that the total interest at the end of eight years is $718.19. The total interest represents $560 of interest earned on the original principal ($70 × 8) plus $218.19 ($718.19 − $560) earned by the reinvestment of the interest.

Computing the Future Value of an Investment

To compute the amount that $1,000 will grow to at the end of eight years if interest is earned at an annual interest rate of 7%, $1,000 can be multiplied by 1.07 eight times, as shown below:

$$\$1,000 \ (1.07) \ (1.07) \ (1.07) \ (1.07) \ (1.07) \ (1.07) \ (1.07) \ (1.07)$$
$$= \$1,718.19$$

A shorthand notation for this calculation is

$$\$1,000 \ (1.07)^8 = \$1,718.19.$$

In general, the notation $(1.07)^N$ means that 1.07 should be multiplied N times. The N is called the exponent of the expression. Most pocket calculators have a function key that computes a number raised to some exponent.

To generalize the formula further, suppose $1,000 is invested for N periods at an annual interest rate of i (expressed as a decimal). Then, the future value N periods from now can be expressed as follows:

$$\$1,000 \ (1 + i)^N$$

For example, if $1,000 is invested for four years at an annual interest rate of 10% ($i = .10$), then it will grow to $1,464.10:

$$\$1,000 \ (1.10)^4$$
$$= \$1,000 \ (1.4641)$$
$$= \$1,464.10.$$

The expression $(1 + i)^N$ is the amount to which $1 will grow at the end of N years if an annual interest rate of i is earned. This expression is called the *future value of $1*. By multiplying the future value of $1 by the original principal, the future value of the original principal can be determined.

For example, we just demonstrated that the future value of $1,000 invested for four years at an annual interest rate of 10% would be $1,464.10. The future value of $1 is $1.4641. Therefore, if instead of $1,000, $50,000 is invested, the future value would be

$$\$50,000 \ (1.4641) = \$73,205.00.$$

We can generalize the formula for the future value as follows:

$$FV = P \ (1 + i)^N$$

where
  FV = Future value ($);
  P = Original principal ($);
  i = Interest rate (in decimal form);
  N = number of years.

The following five illustrations show how to apply the future value formula.

Illustration 2-1.   A pension fund manager invests $10 million in a financial instrument that promises to pay 8.7% per year for five years. The future value of the $10 million investment is $15,175,665, as shown below:

$$P = \$10,000,000;$$
$$i = .087;$$
$$N = 5$$

$$FV = \$10,000,000 \ (1.087)^5$$
$$= \$10,000,000 \ (1.5175665)$$
$$= \$15,175,665.$$

Illustration 2-2.   A life insurance company receives a premium of $10 million, which it invests for five years. The investment promises to pay an annual interest rate of 9.25%. The future value of $10 million at the end of five years is $15,563,500, as shown below:

$$P = \$10,000,000;$$
$$i = .0925;$$
$$N = 5$$

$$FV = \$10,000,000 \ (1.0925)^5$$
$$= \$10,000,000 \ (1.5563500)$$
$$= \$15,563,500.$$

Illustration 2-3. Suppose that a life insurance company has guaranteed a payment of $14 million to a pension fund four years from now. If the life insurance company receives a premium of $11 million and can invest the entire premium for four years at an annual interest rate of 6.5%, will it have sufficient funds from this investment to meet the $14 million obligation?

The future value of the $11 million investment at the end of four years is $14,151,130, as shown below:

$$P = \$11,000,000;$$
$$i = .065;$$
$$N = 4$$

$$FV = \$11,000,000 \ (1.065)^4$$
$$= \$11,000,000 \ (1.2864664)$$
$$= \$14,151,130.$$

Since the future value is expected to be $14,151,130, the life insurance company will have sufficient funds from this investment to satisfy the $14 million obligation to the pension fund.

Illustration 2-4. The portfolio manager of a tax-exempt fund is considering investing $400,000 in an instrument that pays an annual interest rate of 5.7% for four years. At the end of four years, the portfolio manager plans to reinvest the proceeds for three more years and expects that, for the three-year period, an annual interest rate of 7.2% can be earned. The future value of this investment is $615,098, as shown below.

Future value of the $400,000 investment for four years at 5.7%:

$$P = \$400{,}000;$$
$$i = .057;$$
$$N = 4$$

$$FV = \$400{,}000 \ (1.057)^4$$
$$= \$400{,}000 \ (1.248245)$$
$$= \$499{,}298.$$

Future value of $499,298 reinvested for three years at 7.2%:

$$i = .072;$$
$$N = 3$$

$$FV = \$499{,}298 \ (1.072)^3$$
$$= \$499{,}298 \ (1.231925)$$
$$= \$615{,}098.$$

Illustration 2-5. Suppose that the portfolio manager in the previous illustration has the opportunity to invest the $400,000 for seven years in an instrument that promises to pay an annual interest rate of 6.15%. Is this alternative a more attractive investment than the one analyzed in the previous illustration?

The future value of $400,000 seven years from now is $607,435:

$$P = \$400{,}000;$$
$$i = .0615;$$
$$N = 7$$

$$FV = \$400{,}000 \ (1.0615)^7$$
$$= \$400{,}000 \ (1.518588)$$
$$= \$607{,}435.$$

Assuming that both investments have the same default risk, the investment in the previous illustration will provide a greater future value at the end of seven years *if* the expectation of the portfolio manager—concerning the annual interest rate at which the rolled-over funds can be reinvested—is realized.

Fractional Periods

In our illustrations, we have computed the future value for whole years. The future value formula, however, is the same if an investment is made for part of a year. Most pocket calculators can accommodate fractional exponents.

For example, suppose that $100,000 is invested for seven years and three months. Since three months is 0.25 of one year, N in the future value formula is 7.25. Assuming an annual interest rate of 5%, the future value of $100,000 invested for seven years and three months is $142,437, as shown below:

$$P = \$100,000;$$
$$i = .05;$$
$$N = 7.25$$

$$FV = \$100,000 \ (1.05)^{7.25}$$
$$= \$100,000 \ (1.424369)$$
$$= \$142,437.$$

Compounding More than One Time Per Year

An investment may pay interest more than one time per year. For example, interest may be paid semiannually, quarterly, monthly, weekly, or daily. Our future value formula can handle interest payments that are made more than once per year. This is done by adjusting the annual interest rate and the exponent. The annual interest rate is adjusted by dividing by the number of times that interest is paid per year. The exponent, which represents the number of years, is adjusted by multiplying the number of years by the number of times interest is paid per year.

Mathematically, we can express the future value when interest is paid m times per year as follows:

$$FV = P \ (1 + i)^n$$

where
   i = *annual* interest rate divided by m;
   n = number of interest payments ($= N \times m$).

Illustration 2-6.   Suppose that a portfolio manager invests $1 million in an investment that promises to pay an annual interest rate of 6.4% for six years. Interest on this investment is paid semiannually. The future value is $1,459,340, as shown below:

$$P = \$1,000,000;$$
$$m = 2;$$
$$i = .032 \ (= .064/2);$$
$$N = 6;$$
$$n = 12 \ (6 \times 2)$$

$$FV = \$1,000,000 \ (1.032)^{12}$$
$$= \$1,000,000 \ (1.459340)$$
$$= \$1,459,340.$$

If interest is paid only once per year, the future value would be $1,450,941 instead of $1,459,340. The higher future value when interest is paid semiannually reflects the more frequent opportunity for reinvesting the interest paid.

Illustration 2-7.   Suppose that in the previous illustration, interest is paid quarterly rather than semiannually. The future value is $1,463,690, as shown below:

$$P = \$1,000,000;$$
$$m = 4;$$
$$i = .016 \ (= .064/4);$$
$$N = 6;$$
$$n = 24 \ (6 \times 4)$$

$$FV = \$1,000,000 \ (1.016)^{24}$$
$$= \$1,000,000 \ (1.463690)$$
$$= \$1,463,690.$$

The future value is greater than if interest is paid semiannually.

Future Value of an Ordinary Annuity

Suppose that an investor expects to receive $10,000 a year from some investment for each of the next five years starting one year

Exhibit 2-1
Future Value of an Ordinary Annuity of $10,000 Per Year for 5 Years

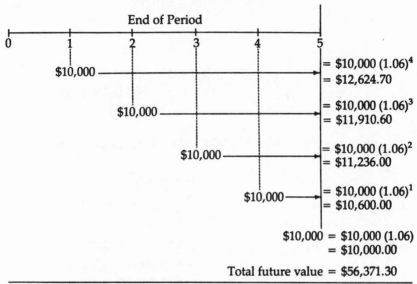

Total future value = $56,371.30

from now. Each time the investor receives the $10,000 he plans to invest it. Let's assume that the investor can earn an annual interest rate of 6% each time $10,000 is invested. How much money will the investor have at the end of five years?

Our future value formula makes it simple to determine how much each $10,000 investment will grow to. This calculation is shown below, and illustrated graphically in Exhibit 2-1.

Future value of the first $10,000, received one year from now:

$$P = \$10,000; i = .06; N = 4.$$

Notice that N is 4 since the first payment of $10,000 will be invested from the beginning of year two (or end of year one) until the end of year five.

$$
\begin{aligned}
FV \text{ of first } \$10,000 &= \$10,000 \ (1.06)^4 \\
&= \$10,000 \ (1.262470) \\
&= \$12,624.70
\end{aligned}
$$

Future value of the second $10,000, received two years from now:

$$P = \$10,000;$$
$$i = .06;$$
$$N = 3.$$

$$
\begin{aligned}
FV \text{ of second } \$10,000 &= \$10,000\,(1.06)^3 \\
&= \$10,000\,(1.191060) \\
&= \$11,910.60
\end{aligned}
$$

Future value of the third $10,000, received three years from now:

$$P = \$10,000;$$
$$i = .06;$$
$$N = 2.$$

$$
\begin{aligned}
FV \text{ of third } \$10,000 &= \$10,000\,(1.06)^2 \\
&= \$10,000\,(1.123600) \\
&= \$11,236.00
\end{aligned}
$$

Future value of the fourth $10,000, received four years from now:

$$P = \$10,000;$$
$$i = .06;$$
$$N = 1.$$

$$
\begin{aligned}
FV \text{ of fourth } \$10,000 &= \$10,000\,(1.06)^1 \\
&= \$10,000\,(1.06) \\
&= \$10,600.00
\end{aligned}
$$

Future value of the last $10,000, received five years from now:

$$P = \$10,000;$$
$$i = .06;$$
$$N = 0.$$

$$
\begin{aligned}
FV \text{ of fifth } \$10,000 &= \$10,000\,(1.06)^0 \\
&= \$10,000\,(1.00) \\
&= \$10,000.00
\end{aligned}
$$

Notice that since the last payment is received at the end of the fifth year, it will not be invested. Therefore, its future value will be simply $10,000.

If we total all the future values, we obtain:

Future value of first $10,000	$ 12,624.70
Future value of second $10,000	11,910.60
Future value of third $10,000	11,236.00
Future valueof fourth $10,000	10,600.00
Future value of fifth $10,000	10,000.00
Total future value	$ 56,371.30

The total future value of $56,371.30 is composed of the five payments of $10,000, or $50,000, plus $6,371.30 of interest earned by investing the $10,000 annual payments.

When the same amount of money is received (or paid) periodically, it is referred to as an *annuity*. When the first receipt (or payment) occurs one period from now, it is referred to as an *ordinary annuity*.

Computing the Future Value of an Annuity

In Chapter 8, you will need to know how to compute the future value of an ordinary annuity. Of course, the procedure we just followed—whereby we computed the future value of each investment—can be used. Fortunately, there is a formula that can be used to speed up this computation. The formula is

$$FV = A \left[\frac{(1 + i)^N - 1}{i} \right]$$

where
   A = amount of the annuity ($);
   i = annual interest rate (in decimal).

The term in the square brackets is the *future value of an ordinary annuity of $1 per year*. Multiplying the future value of an ordinary annuity of $1 by the amount of the annuity produces the future value of an ordinary annuity of any amount.

For example, in the previous example, in which $10,000 is invested each year for the next five years, starting one year from now, we have:

$$A = \$10,000;$$
$$i = .06;$$
$$N = 5;$$

therefore,

$$FV = \$10,000 \left[\frac{(1.06)^5 - 1}{.06} \right]$$

$$= \$10,000 \left[\frac{1.3382256 - 1}{.06} \right]$$

$$= \$10,000 \, (5.63710)$$

$$= \$56,371.$$

This value agrees with our earlier calculations.

Illustration 2-8.   Suppose that a portfolio manager purchases $5 million of par value of 10-year bonds that promise to pay 8% interest per year.[1] The price of the bonds is $5 million. The interest payment is made once per year by the issuer; the first annual interest payment will be made one year from now. How much will the portfolio manager have if she (1) holds the bonds until they mature 10 years from now and (2) can reinvest the annual interest payments at an annual interest rate of 6.7%?

The amount that the portfolio manager will have at the end of 10 years will be equal to:

(1)   the $5 million when the bonds mature;
(2)   10 annual interest payments of $400,000 (.08 × $5 million)
(3)   the interest earned by investing the annual interest payments.

We can determine the sum of (2) and (3) by applying the formula for the future value of an ordinary annuity. In this

---

[1] Eurodollar bonds, for example, pay coupon interest once per year.

illustration, the annuity is $400,000 per year (.08 × $5,000,000). Therefore,

$$A = \$400,000;$$
$$i = .067;$$
$$N = 10$$

$$FV = \$400,000 \left[\frac{(1.067)^{10} - 1}{.067} \right]$$

$$= \$400,000 \left[\frac{1.912688 - 1}{.067} \right]$$

$$= \$400,000 \, [13.62221]$$
$$= \$5,448,884.$$

The future value of the ordinary annuity of $400,000 per year for 10 years invested at 6.7% is $5,448,884. Since $4,000,000 of this future value represents the total annual interest payments made by the issuer and invested by the portfolio manager, $1,448,884 ($5,448,884 - $4,000,000) must be the interest earned by reinvesting the annual interest payments. Therefore, the total amount that the portfolio manager will have at the end of 10 years by making the investment will be:

Par (maturity) value	$5,000,000
Interest payments	4,000,000
Interest on reinvestment of interest payments	1,448,884
Total	$10,448,884

As you will see in Chapter 8, it will be necessary to determine the total future amount at the end of the portfolio manager's investment horizon to assess the relative value of a bond.

Future Value of an Ordinary Annuity when Payments Occur More than Once Per Year

We can easily generalize the future value of an ordinary annuity to handle situations in which payments are made more than one time per year. For example, instead of assuming that an investor receives and then invests $10,000 per year for five years, starting one year from now, suppose that the investor receives $5,000 every six months for five years, starting six months from now.

The general formula for the future value of an ordinary annuity when payments occur m times per year is

$$FV = A \left[\frac{(1 + i)^n - 1}{i} \right]$$

where
A = Amount of the annuity ($);
i = Annual interest rate divided by m (in decimal).
$n = N \times m$.

The value in the square brackets is the *future value of an ordinary annuity of $1 per period.*

Illustration 2-9. Let's rework the analysis for the bonds in Illustration 2-8 assuming that the interest is paid every six months, the first payment to be received and invested six months from now. The interest payment every six months is $200,000. The future value of the 20 semiannual interest payments of $200,000 to be received plus the interest earned by investing the interest payments is found as follows:

$A = \$200,000$;
$m = 2$;
$i = .0335\ (.067/2)$;
$n = 20\ (10 \times 2)$

$$FV = \$200,000 \left[\frac{(1.0335)^{20} - 1}{.0335} \right]$$

$$= \$200,000 \left[\frac{1.932901 - 1}{.0335} \right]$$

$$= \$200,000\ [27.84779]$$

$$= \$5,569,558.$$

Since the interest payments are equal to $4,000,000, the interest earned on the interest payments invested is $1,569,558. Because of the more frequent reinvestment of the interest payments received, the interest of $1,569,558 earned by investing the interest payments exceeds the interest earned if interest is paid only one time per year, that is, $1,448,884 (see Illustration 2-8).

The total amount that the portfolio manager will have at the end of 10 years by making the investment will be

Par (maturity) value	$ 5,000,000
Interest payments	4,000,000
Interest on reinvestment of interest payments	1,569,558
Total	$10,569,558

Summary

In this chapter we have explained how to compute the future value of an investment. The formulas that we introduced are summarized in Exhibit 2-2.

Exhibit 2-2

Summary of Formulas for Future Value Computations

(1) Future value of an investment made for N years:

$$FV = P\,(1 + i)^N,$$

where

    FV = Future value (\$);
    P = Original principal (\$);
    i = Interest rate (in decimal form);
    N = Number of years.

(2) Future value of an investment made for n periods:

$$FV = P\,(1 + i)^n,$$

where

    i = *Annual* interest rate divided by m;
    m = Number of payments per year;
    n = Number of periods ($= N \times m$).

(3) Future value of an ordinary annuity for N years:

$$FV = A \left[\frac{(1 + i)^N - 1}{i} \right],$$

where

    A = Amount of the annuity (\$)
    i = Annual interest rate (in decimal).

(4) Future value of an ordinary annuity for n periods:

$$FV = A \left[\frac{(1 + i)^n - 1}{i} \right],$$

where

    A = Amount of the annuity (\$)
    m = Number of payments per year
    i = Annual interest rate divided by m (in decimal)
    n = Number of periods ($N \times m$).

3
Present Value

In the previous chapter, we illustrated how to compute the future value of an investment. In this chapter, we will illustrate how to work the process in reverse; that is, given the future value of an investment, we will illustrate how to determine the amount of money that must be invested today in order to realize that future value. The amount of money that must be invested today is called the *present value*. Since, as we shall explain later in this chapter, the price of *any* financial instrument is the present value of its expected cash flows, it is necessary to understand present value in order to be able to price a fixed income instrument.

Present Value of an Amount to be Received in the Future

Recall from the previous chapter that the future value of a sum invested for N years can be expressed as

$$FV = P (1 + i)^N,$$

where
> FV = Future value ($);
> P = Original principal ($);
> i = Interest rate (in decimal form);
> N = Number of years;
> $(1 + i)^N$ = Future value of $1 invested at i for N years.

What we are interested in is how to determine the amount of money that must be invested today, earning an interest rate of i for

N years, in order to produce a specific future value. This can be done by solving the future value formula for P, the original principal:

$$P = FV \left[\frac{1}{(1 + i)^N} \right].$$

Instead of using P in the above formula, we shall denote the present value as PV. Therefore, the present value formula can be rewritten as

$$PV = FV \left[\frac{1}{(1 + i)^N} \right].$$

The term in the square brackets is equal to the present value of $1; that is, it indicates how much must be set aside today, earning an interest rate of i, in order to have $1 N years from now.

The process of computing the present value is also referred to as *discounting*. Therefore, the present value is sometimes referred to as the *discounted value*, and the interest rate is referred to as the *discount rate*.

The following four illustrations demonstrate how to compute the present value.

Illustration 3-1. A pension fund manager knows that he must satisfy a liability of $9 million six years from now. Assuming that an annual interest rate of 7.5% can be earned on any sum invested today, the pension fund manager must invest $5,831,649 today in order to have $9 million six years from now, as shown below:

$$FV = \$9,000,000;$$
$$i = .075;$$
$$N = 6$$
$$PV = \$9,000,000 \left[\frac{1}{(1.075)^6} \right]$$
$$= \$9,000,000 \left[\frac{1}{1.543302} \right]$$
$$= \$9,000,000 \, (.647961)$$
$$= \$5,831,649.$$

Illustration 3-2.   Suppose that in the previous illustration the pension fund manager could earn 8.3% instead of 7.5%; then the present value of the $9 million to be paid six years from now would be $5,577,912, as shown below:

$$FV = \$9,000,000;$$
$$i = .083;$$
$$N = 6$$

$$PV = \$9,000,000 \left[\frac{1}{(1.083)^6} \right]$$

$$= \$9,000,000 \left[\frac{1}{1.613507} \right]$$

$$= \$9,000,000 \,(.619768)$$

$$= \$5,577,912$$

Illustration 3-3.   Suppose a money manager has the opportunity to purchase a financial instrument that promises to pay $800,000 four years from now. The price of the financial instrument is $572,000. Should the money manager invest in this finanical instrument if she wants a 7.8% annual interest rate?

To answer this, the money manager must determine the present value of the $800,000 to be received four years from now. The present value is $592,400, as shown below:

$$FV = \$800,000;$$
$$i = .078;$$
$$N = 4$$

$$PV = \$800,000 \left[\frac{1}{(1.078)^4} \right]$$

$$= \$800,000 \left[\frac{1}{1.350439} \right]$$

$$= \$800,000 \,(.740500)$$

$$= \$592,400.$$

Since the price of the financial instrument is only $572,000, the money manager will realize more than a 7.8% annual interest rate if the financial instrument is purchased and the issuer pays

$800,000 four years from now. In the next chapter, we'll show you how to compute the annual interest rate that the money manager would realize.

Another way of looking at the problem faced by this money manager is by asking how much the $572,000 would grow to in four years if invested at 7.8%. Using the formula for the future value of an investment, we find that the future value is $772,451, as shown below:

$$P = \$572{,}000;$$
$$i = .078;$$
$$N = 4$$

$$FV = \$572{,}000 \ (1.078)^4$$
$$= \$572{,}000 \ (1.350439)$$
$$= \$772{,}451.$$

A $572,000 investment would grow to only $772,451. Yet, an investment of $572,000 in the financial instrument would produce $800,000 four years from now. Consequently, the financial instrument offers more than a 7.8% annual interest rate. The present value of $592,400 tells the money manager that as long as she pays no more than $592,400, an annual interest rate of at least 7.8% will be earned from this investment.

Illustration 3-4. Instead of promising $800,000 four years from now, suppose that the financial instrument in the previous illustration promised to pay $800,000 five years from now. Assume that the money manager still wants an annual interest rate of 7.8%. Is the investment still attractive if it is selling for $572,000?

As shown below, the present value of the $800,000 five years from now is $549,536:

$$FV = \$800{,}000;$$
$$i = .078;$$
$$N = 5$$
$$PV = \$800{,}000 \left[\frac{1}{(1.078)^5} \right]$$
$$= \$800{,}000 \left[\frac{1}{1.455733} \right]$$
$$= \$800{,}000 \ (.686920)$$
$$= \$549{,}536.$$

Since the present value is less than the price of $572,000, the financial instrument offers an annual interest rate that is less than 7.8%.

Present Value for a Fractional Period

If a future value is to be received or paid over a fractional part of a year, the number of years is adjusted accordingly. For example, if $1,000 is to be received nine years and three months from now and the interest rate is 7%, the present value is determined as follows:

$$FV = \$1,000;$$
$$i = .07;$$
$$N = 9.25 \text{ years (3 months is .25 years)}$$

$$PV = \$1,000 \left[\frac{1}{(1.07)^{9.25}} \right]$$

$$= \$1,000 \left[\frac{1}{1.86982} \right]$$

$$= \$1,000 \, (.53481)$$

$$= \$534.81.$$

Properties of the Present Value

There are two properties of the present value that you should recognize.

First, for a given future value at a specified time in the future, the higher the interest rate (or discount rate), the lower the present value. To see this, compare the present value in Illustration 3-1 to that in Illustration 3-2. When the annual interest rate increased from 7.5% to 8.3%, the present value of the $9 million needed six years from now decreased from $5,831,649 to $5,577,912. The reason that the present value decreases as the interest rate increases should be easy to understand. The higher the interest rate that can be earned on any sum invested today, the less has to be invested today to realize a specified future value.

The second property of the present value is that for a given interest rate (discount rate), the further into the future the future value will be received, the lower the present value. This is demonstrated in Illustrations 3-3 and 3-4. When the amount of $800,000 is to be received four years from now, the present value is $592,536; however, if the $800,000 is to be received five years from now, the present value declines to $549,536. The reason is that the further into the future a given future value is to be received, the more opportunity there is for interest to accumulate. The result is that fewer dollars have to be invested.

Present Value of a Series of Future Values

In most applications in investment management and asset/liability management, a financial instrument will offer a series of future values or a financial institution will have multiple liabilities in the future. To determine the present value of a series of future values, the present value of each future value must first be computed. Then, the present values are added together to obtain the present value of the series of future values. This procedure is demonstrated in the following three illustrations.

Illustration 3-5.   A pension fund manager knows that the following liabilities must be satisfied:

Years from now	Liability
1	$200,000
2	340,000
3	500,000
4	580,000

Suppose that the pension fund manager wants to invest a sum of money that will satisfy this liability stream. Let's assume that any amount that can be invested today can earn an annual interest rate of 8.5%. How much must be invested to satisfy this liability stream?

The answer is the present value of the liability stream. Consequently, the present value of each liability must be calculated and the results totaled, as shown below.

Years from now	Future value of liability	Present value of $1 at 8.5%	Present value of liability
1	$200,000	0.921659	$184,332
2	340,000	0.849455	288,815
3	500,000	0.782908	391,454
4	580,000	0.721574	418,513

Total present value = $1,283,114

The present value of $1,283,114 means that if this sum is invested today at an annual interest rate of 8.5%, it will provide sufficient funds to satisfy the liability stream.

For those who must be convinced that this is true, let's look at what would happen if $1,283,114 is invested at 8.5% in a bank account and at the end of each year enough money is withdrawn from the bank account to satisfy the liability.

(1) Year	(2) Amount at beginning of year	(3) Interest at 8.5% [.086 × (2)]	(4) Withdrawn to pay liability	(5) Amount at end of year [(2) + (3) (4)]
1	$1,283,114	$109,065	$200,000	$1,192,179
2	1,192,179	101,335	340,000	953,514
3	953,514	81,049	500,000	534,563
4	534,563	45,437	580,000	0

As can be seen from the above computations, the $1,283,114 investment will provide enough money to pay the liability stream. At the end of the fourth year (after the last liability is paid), there is no money left in the account.

Illustration 3-6. An investor is considering the purchase of a financial instrument that promises to make the following payments:

Years from now	Promised payment by issuer
1	$ 100
2	100
3	100
4	100
5	1,100

This financial instrument is selling for $1,243.83. Assume that the investor wants a 6.25% annual interest rate on this investment. Should the investor purchase this investment?

To answer this question, the investor first must compute the present value of the future amounts that are expected to be received, as follows:

Years from now	Future value of payment	Present value of $1 at 6.25%	Present value of payment
1	$ 100	0.9412	$ 94.12
2	100	0.8858	88.58
3	100	0.8337	83.37
4	100	0.7847	78.47
5	1,100	0.7385	812.35

Total present value = $1,156.89

Since the present value of the series of future values promised by the issuer of this financial instrument is less than the price of $1,243.83, the investor would earn an annual interest rate of less than 6.25%. Thus, the financial instrument is unattractive.

Present Value of an Ordinary Annuity

When the same amount of money is received or paid each year, the series is referred to as an annuity. When the first payment must be received or paid one year from now, the annuity is called an *ordinary annuity*. When the first payment or receipt is immediate, the annuity is called an *annuity due*. In all the applications discussed in this book, we shall deal with ordinary annuities.

Of course, one way to compute the present value of an ordinary annuity is to follow the procedure explained in the previous section: compute the present value of each future value and then total the present values. Fortunately, there is a formula that can be employed to compute—in one step—the present value of an ordinary annuity:

$$PV = A \left[\frac{1 - \left[\frac{1}{(1 + i)^N} \right]}{i} \right]$$

where

A = Amount of the annuity ($).

The term in the brackets is the *present value of an ordinary annuity of $1 for N years.*

The following two illustrations show how to apply this formula.

Illustration 3-7. An investor has the opportunity to purchase a financial instrument that promises to pay $500 a year for the next 20 years, beginning one year from now. The financial instrument is being offered for a price of $5,300. The investor seeks an annual interest rate of 5.5% on this investment. Should the investor purchase this financial instrument?

Since the first payment is to be received one year from now, the financial instrument is offering a 20-year annuity of $500 per year. The present value of this ordinary annuity is calculated as follows:

$$A = \$500;$$
$$i = .055;$$
$$N = 20$$

$$PV = \$500 \left[\frac{1 - \left[\frac{1}{(1.055)^{20}} \right]}{.055} \right]$$

$$= \$500 \left[\frac{1 - \left[\frac{1}{2.917757} \right]}{.055} \right]$$

$$= \$500 \left[\frac{1 - .342729}{.055} \right]$$

$$= \$500 \, (11.950382)$$

$$= \$5,975.19$$

Since the present value of an ordinary annuity of $500 per year when discounted at 5.5% exceeds the price of the financial instrument ($5,300), this financial instrument offers an annual interest rate in excess of 5.5%. Therefore, it is an attractive investment for this investor.

Illustration 3-8.   In Illustration 3-6 we computed the present value of a financial instrument that offered $100 a year for four years and $1,100 at the end of the fifth year. This payment series is equivalent to an ordinary annuity of $100 a year for *five* years and a future-value payment of $1,000 five years from now. Viewing the payments of the financial instrument in this way, let's compute the present value.

The present value of an ordinary annuity of $100 per year for five years at an annual interest rate of 6.25% is

$$A = \$100;$$
$$i = .0625;$$
$$N = 5$$

$$PV = \$100 \left[\frac{1 - \left[\frac{1}{(1.0625)^5} \right]}{.0625} \right]$$

$$= \$100 \left[\frac{1 - \left[\frac{1}{1.354081} \right]}{.0625} \right]$$

$$= \$100 \left[\frac{1 - .738508}{.0625} \right]$$

$$= \$100 \ (4.1838)$$
$$= \$418.38.$$

The present value of the $1,000 to be received five years from now is $738.51, as shown below:

$$FV = \$1,000;$$
$$i = .0625;$$
$$N = 5$$

$$PV = \$1,000 \left[\frac{1}{(1.0625)^5} \right]$$

$$= \$1,000 \left[\frac{1}{1.354081} \right]$$

$$= \$1,000 \,(.738508)$$

$$= \$738.51.$$

The present value of the series offered by this financial instrument is then:

Present value of ordinary annuity of $100 for five years at 6.25%	$ 418.38
Present value of $1,000 five years from now at 6.25%	738.51
Total present value	$1,156.89

This agrees with the computation in Illustration 3-6.

Perpetual Annuity: Special Case

So far we have shown how to compute the present value of an ordinary annuity over a specific time period. Suppose, instead, that the annuity will last forever. This is called a *perpetual annuity*. The formula for a perpetual annuity is[1]

$$PV = \frac{A}{i}.$$

Illustration 3-9. An investor can purchase for $1,000 a financial instrument that promises to pay $80 per year forever. The investor wants an annual interest rate of 10% from this investment. Is this investment attractive to the investor?

---

[1] The formula is derived from the formula for the present value of an ordinary annuity. As the number of years gets very large, the value of $1/(1+i)^N$ approaches zero. The numerator in the brackets is then equal to 1, producing the above formula for the present value of a perpetual annuity.

The present value of the $80 perpetual annuity is equal to $800, as shown below:

$$A = \$80;$$
$$i = .10$$
$$PV = \frac{\$80}{.10}$$
$$= \$800.$$

Since the $1,000 price for the financial instrument is greater than the present value of the perpetual annuity ($800), the investment offers an annual interest rate that is less than 10%; therefore, it is not an attractive investment, given the minimum annual interest rate required by the investor.

Present Value When the Frequency Is More Than Once Per Year

In the computations of the present value, we have assumed that the future value is to be received or paid once each year. In practice, the future value may be received or paid more than once per year. In this situation, the formulas for the present value given earlier in this chapter must be modified in two ways. First, the annual interest rate is divided by the frequency per year.[2] For example, if the future values are received or paid semiannually, the annual interest rate is divided by 2; if quarterly, the annual interest rate is divided by 4. Second, the number of periods after which the future value will be received or paid must be adjusted by multiplying the number of years by the frequency per year.

The general formula for the present value of a future sum is

$$PV = FV \left[\frac{1}{(1 + i)^n} \right],$$

---

[2] Technically, this is not the proper way for adjusting the annual interest rate. For example, an 8% annual interest rate is not equal to a quarterly interest rate of 2%. However, in the computation of the yield on bonds, the market has adopted a convention that embodies this approach. This will be made clearer in the next two chapters.

where
- i = Periodic interest rate [annual interest rate (in decimal) divided by m];
- m = Frequency of receipt or payment of the future value;
- n = Number of periods [number of years (N) times m].

Illustration 3-10. An investor is considering the purchase of a financial instrument that promises to make the following payments every three months (quarterly):

Period (three months)	Promised payments
1	$1,000
2	1,200
3	1,500
4	1,700
5	1,800
6	2,000

If the investor seeks an annual interest rate of 12% from this investment, what is the most that the investor should pay for it?

The most that the investor should pay in order to earn an annual interest rate of at least 12% is the present value of the future payments promised. As shown below, the present value is $8,212.79.

Periods from now	Future value of payment	Present value of $1 at 3.0% *	Present value of payment
1	$1,000	.97087	$ 970.87
2	1,200	.94260	1,131.12
3	1,500	.91514	1,372.71
4	1,700	.88849	1,510.43
5	1,800	.86261	1,552.70
6	2,000	.83748	1,674.96

Total present value = $8,212.79

*.12 annual interest rate divided by 4.

When the present value of an ordinary annuity is sought, the general formula is

$$PV = A \left[\frac{1 - \left[\dfrac{1}{(1 + i)^N} \right]}{i} \right]$$

where
A = Amount of the annuity (in dollars *per period*).

Illustration 3-11.   In Illustration 3-6, we computed the present value of the following series of future amounts, assuming an annual interest rate of 6.25%:

Years from now	Promised payment by issuer
1	$ 100
2	100
3	100
4	100
5	1,100

Instead of annual payments, let's assume that the payments are made by the issuer every six months, in the following way:

Six month periods from now	Promised payment by issuer
1	$ 50
2	50
3	50
4	50
5	50
6	50
7	50
8	50
9	50
10	1,050

This is equivalent to an ordinary annuity of $50 per six-month period for 10 six-month periods and $1,000 to be paid 10 six-month periods from now. Notice that the $1,000 is treated on the same time-period basis as the annuity.

The present value of the ordinary annuity, for

A = $50;
m = 2 (that is, payments every six months);
i = .03125 (.0625 annual interest rate divided by 2);
n = 10 (5 years times 2);

is

$$PV = \$\,50 \left[\frac{1 - \left[\frac{1}{(1.03125)^{10}} \right]}{.03125} \right]$$

$$= \$\,50 \left[\frac{1 - \left[\frac{1}{1.360315} \right]}{.03125} \right]$$

$$= \$\,50 \left[\frac{1 - .735124}{.03125} \right]$$

$$= \$\,50 \quad (8.4760)$$

$$= \$423.80.$$

The present value of the $1,000 to be received after 10 six-month periods, for

FV = $1,000;
m = 2 (that is, payments every six months);
i = .03125 (.0625 annual interest rate divided by 2);
n = 10 (5 years times 2);

is

$$PV = \$1{,}000 \left[\frac{1}{(1.03125)^{10}} \right]$$

$$= \$1{,}000 \left[\frac{1}{1.360315} \right]$$

$$= \$1{,}000 \quad (.735124)$$

$$= \$735.12.$$

The present value of the future value series offered by the financial instrument is then:

Present value of ordinary annuity of $50 for 10 six-month periods at .03125	$ 423.80
Present value of $1,000 after 10 six-month periods at .03125%	735.12
Total present value	$1,158.92

Notice that because the payments are made more often, the present value of the future payments has increased from $1,156.89 to $1,158.92.

Illustration 3-12.   Suppose a banker agrees to make a $100,000 30-year loan to an individual to purchase a home. Under the terms of the loan, the monthly payments to be made by the individual will all be the same. The annual interest rate that the banker charges for the loan is 12%. How much must the fixed monthly payment be in order for the banker to realize an annual interest rate of 12%?

We can employ the formula for the present value of an ordinary annuity to determine the fixed monthly payment. The banker wants to receive an annuity of some fixed monthly amount such that the present value of that ordinary annuity, at an annual interest rate of 12%, is $100,000. In the formula for the present value of an ordinary annuity, the number of monthly payments is 360 (30 years times 12) and the interest rate is 1% (12% divided by 12). Therefore, we know the following:

$$\$100,000 = A \left[\frac{1 - \left[\frac{1}{(1.01)^{360}} \right]}{.01} \right]$$

The unknown is A, the monthly annuity or monthly loan payment. We can solve for A as follows:

$$\$100{,}000 = A \left[\frac{1 - \left[\dfrac{1}{35.949641} \right]}{.01} \right]$$

$$= A \left[\frac{1 - .0278167}{.01} \right]$$

$$= A \quad (97.21833)$$

Solving for A,

$$A = \left[\frac{\$100{,}000}{97.21833} \right] = \$1{,}028.61.$$

Therefore, the fixed monthly payment must be $1,028.61.

Pricing Any Financial Instrument

The price of any financial instrument is equal to the present value of the cash flows *expected* from investing in the financial instrument. Determining the price, therefore, requires the following input:

(1) Estimation of the expected cash flows, and
(2) Determination of the appropriate interest rate or discount rate so that the present value of the cash flows can be computed.

The cash flow in any period is simply the difference between the cash inflow and cash outflow from investing in the financial instrument. The expected cash flows of some financial instruments are simple to compute; for others, the task is not as simple. The determination of the interest rate or discount rate reflects the required yield for financial instruments with *comparable* risk. As we introduce the various bonds throughout this book, we'll show how to formulate the cash flows and discount rate.

Summary

In this chapter we explained how to compute the present value of amounts to be received in the future or payments to be made in the future. A summary of the formulas used in this chapter to compute present values is presented in Exhibit 3-1.

Exhibit 3-1

Summary of Formulas for Computing the Present Value

(1) Present value of a future value N years from now:

$$PV = FV \left[\frac{1}{(1 + i)^N} \right],$$

where
PV = Present value ($);
FV = Future value ($);
i = Interest rate (in decimal form);
N = Number of years.

(2) Present value of a future value n periods from now:

$$PV = FV \left[\frac{1}{(1 + i)^n} \right],$$

where
i = Periodic interest rate [annual interest rate (in decimal) divided by m];
m = Frequency of receipt or payment of the future value;
n = Number of periods [number of years (N) times m].

(3) Present value of an ordinary annuity for N years:

$$PV = A \left[\frac{1 - \left[\frac{1}{(1 + i)^N} \right]}{i} \right],$$

where
A = Amount of the annuity ($).

(4) Present value of an ordinary annuity for n periods:

$$PV = A \left[\frac{1 - \left[\frac{1}{(1 + i)^n} \right]}{i} \right],$$

where
   A = Amount of the annuity (in dollars) per period;
   i = Periodic interest rate [annual interest rate (in decimal) divided by m].

(5) Present value of a perpetual annuity:

$$PV = \frac{A}{i}.$$

4
Yield
(Internal Rate
of Return)

In the previous chapter we showed how to use the present value to determine whether a financial instrument provided a minimum annual interest rate specified by an investor. For example, if the present value of the promised future value payments of some financial instrument selling for $944.14 is $1,039.57, then the investment offers an annual interest rate greater than 9%. But how much greater? What rate of return or yield will the investor earn by buying the financial instrument for $944.14? The purpose of this chapter is to explain how the yield on any investment can be computed.

Computing the Yield on Any Investment

The yield on any investment is computed by determining the interest rate that will make the present value of the cash flow from the investment equal to the price of the investment. Mathematically, the yield on any investment, y, is the interest rate that will make the following relationship hold:

$$p = \frac{C_1}{(1+y)^1} + \frac{C_2}{(1+y)^2} + \frac{C_3}{(1+y)^3} + \cdots + \frac{C_N}{(1+y)^N}$$

43

where
   C_t = cash flow in year t;
   p = price;
   N = number of years.

The individual terms that are being summed on the right-hand side of the above relationship are the present values of the cash flow. The yield calculated from the above relationship is also called the *internal rate of return*.

   Alternatively, using the capital Greek letter sigma to denote summation, the above expression can be rewritten as

$$p = \sum_{t=1}^{N} \frac{C_t}{(1+y)^t}.$$

   Solving for the yield (y) requires a trial-and-error procedure. The objective is to find the interest rate that will make the present value of the cash flows equal to the price. Exhibit 4-1 explains the trial-and-error procedure. The following two illustrations demonstrate how it is carried out.

Illustration 4-1.   A financial instrument offers the following annual payments:

Years from now	Promised annual payments (Cash flow to investor)
1	$ 2,000
2	2,000
3	2,500
4	4,000

Suppose that the price of this financial instrument is $7,704. What is the yield or internal rate of return offered by this financial instrument?

   To compute the yield, we must try different interest rates until we find one that makes the present value of the cash flows

Exhibit 4-1
Step-by-Step Summary of Yield Computation
for Any Investment

Objective: Find the interest rate that will make the present value of the cash flows equal to the price of the investment.

Step 1: Select an interest rate.

Step 2: Compute the present value of each cash flow, using the interest rate selected in Step 1.

Step 3: Total the present value of the cash flows found in Step 2.

Step 4: Compare the total present value found in Step 3 with the price of the investment and:

if the total present value of the cash flows found in Step 3 is equal to the price of the investment, the interest rate is the yield.

if the total present value of the cash flows found in Step 3 is greater than the price of the investment, the interest rate used is not the yield. Go back to Step 1 and use a higher interest rate.

if the total present value of the cash flows found in Step 3 is less than the price of the investment, the interest rate used is not the yield. Go back to Step 1 and use a lower interest rate.

equal to $7,704 (the price of the financial instrument). Trying an annual interest rate of 10% gives the following present value:

Years from now	Promised annual payments (Cash flow to investor)	Present value of cash flow at 10%
1	$ 2,000	$ 1,818
2	2,000	1,652
3	2,500	1,878
4	4,000	2,732
	Total present value =	$ 8,080

Since the present value computed using a 10% interest rate exceeds the price of $7,704, a higher interest rate must be tried. If a 14% interest rate is assumed, the present value is $7,348, as shown below:

Years from now	Promised annual payments (Cash flow to investor)	Present value of cash flow at 14%
1	$ 2,000	$ 1,754
2	2,000	1,538
3	2,500	1,688
4	4,000	2,368
	Total present value =	$ 7,348

At 14%, the present value of the cash flows exceeds the price of the financial instrument. Therefore, a lower interest rate must be tried. Using a 12% interest rate:

Years from now	Promised annual payments (Cash flow to investor)	Present value of cash flow at 12%
1	$ 2,000	$ 1,786
2	2,000	1,594
3	2,500	1,780
4	4,000	2,544
	Total present value =	$ 7,704

The present value of the cash flow is equal to the price of the financial instrument when a 12% interest rate is used. Therefore, the yield is 12%.

Although the formula for the yield is based on annual cash flows, the formula can be generalized to any number of periodic payments in a year. The generalized formula for determining the yield is

$$p = \frac{C_1}{(1+y)^1} + \frac{C_2}{(1+y)^2} + \frac{C_3}{(1+y)^3} + \cdots + \frac{C_n}{(1+y)^n}$$

where

C_t = cash flow in period t;
n = number of periods.

In shorthand notation, this can be expressed as

$$p = \sum_{t=1}^{n} \frac{C_t}{(1+y)^t} .$$

Keep in mind that the yield computed is now the yield for the period. That is, if the cash flows are semiannual, the yield is a semiannual yield. If the cash flows are monthly, the yield is a monthly yield. The annual interest rate is computed by multiplying the yield for the period by the appropriate factor (m).

Illustration 4-2. In Illustration 3-11 of the previous chapter (page 36), an investor considered purchasing a financial instrument that promised the following *semiannual* cash flows:

10 payments of $50 every six months
$1,000 10 six month periods from now

Suppose the price of this financial instrument is $1,243.88. At the 6.5% annual interest rate sought by the investor, the present value of the cash flows is equal to $1,158.92; thus, the financial instrument would not be an attractive investment for this investor. What yield is this financial instrument offering?

The yield can be computed by a trial-and-error procedure, as summarized in the table below:

Annual interest rate	Semi-annual interest rate	Present value of 10 six-month payments of $50*	Present value of $1,000 10 six-month periods from now**	Total present value
6.000%	3.000%	$ 426.51	$ 744.09	$ 1,160.60
5.500	2.750	432.00	762.40	1,194.40
5.000	2.500	437.60	781.20	1,218.80
4.500	2.225	443.31	800.51	1,243.83

*$50 × present value of an ordinary annuity of $1 for 10 periods.
**$1,000 × present value of $1 10 periods from now.

As can be seen from the calculation, when a semiannual interest rate of 2.250% is used to find the present value of the cash flows, the present value is equal to the price of $1,243.83. Hence, 2.250% is the six month yield. Doubling this yield gives the annual interest rate of 4.5%. This agrees with what we said earlier: this financial instrument is unattractive because it offers a yield that is less than the 6.5% annual interest rate specified by the investor.

Illustration 4-3.   Suppose that the financial instrument analyzed in the previous illustration is selling for $944.14 instead of $1,243.83. What is the yield offered on this financial instrument at this lower price?
    The table below shows the calculation of the yield:

Annual interest rate	Semi-annual interest rate	Present value of 10 six-month payments of $50*	Present value of $1,000 10 six-month periods from now**	Total present value
9.000%	4.500%	$ 395.64	$ 643.93	$ 1,039.57
9.500	4.750	390.82	628.72	1,019.54
10.000	5.000	386.09	613.91	1,000.00
10.500	5.250	381.44	599.49	980.93
11.000	5.500	376.88	585.43	962.31
11.500	5.750	372.40	571.74	944.14

*$50 × present value of an ordinary annuity of $1 for 10 periods.
**$1,000 × present value of $1 10 periods from now.

An interest rate of 5.75% equates the present value of the cash flows to the price of the financial instrument; hence, 5.75% is the six-month yield, and 11.50% is the annual interest rate.

Illustration 4-4. A 30-year mortgage for $50,000 was originated today. The mortgage requires that the homeowner (borrower) pay $349.60 each month for 360 months. The manager of a mortgage portfolio has the opportunity to purchase this mortgage today for $43,449. What is the yield offered by this series of mortgage payments?

The computations below show that the monthly yield is 0.75% (0.0075):

Annual interest rate	Monthly interest rate	Present value of 360 monthly payments of $349.60*
7.50%	0.6250%	$ 50,000
8.00	0.6667	47,643
8.50	0.7083	45,469
9.00	0.7500	43,449

*349.60 × present value of an ordinary annuity of $1 for 360 periods

Since the monthly yield is 0.7500%, the annual interest rate is 9.0%.

Notice that the annual interest on the mortgage must be 7.50% because it is the monthly yield of 0.6250% that equates the present value of the monthly payments to the amount borrowed by the homeowner, $50,000.

Illustration 4-5. Issuers of financial instruments must determine the cost of the funds they obtain. The cost of funds, referred to as the *all-in-cost of funds,* is just the interest rate that will equate the present value of the cash payments that the issuer must pay the security holders to the net proceeds received at the time of issuance. That is, the all-in-cost of funds is the internal rate of return.

Suppose that an issuer agrees to make the following payments to security holders every six months:

30 payments every six months of $1 million
$20 million 30 six month periods from now.

At the time of issuance, the issuer received net proceeds of
$19,696,024. The all-in-cost of funds for this issue is 5.10% semian-
nually, as shown below:

Annual interest rate	Semi-annual interest rate	Present value of 30 six-month payments of $1 million*	Present value of $20 million 30 six-month periods from now**	Total present value
10.000%	5.000%	$ 15,372,451	$ 4,627,549	$ 20,000,000
10.100	5.050	15,285,221	4,561,927	19,847,148
10.200	5.100	15,198,759	4,497,265	19,696,024

*1 million × present value of an ordinary annuity of $1 for 30 periods
**20 million × present value of $1 30 periods from now

Yield Calculation When There Is Only One Cash Flow

There is a special case when it is not necessary to go through the
time-consuming trial-and-error procedure to determine the yield.
This is the case where there is only one cash flow provided by the
investment. We'll introduce the formula by means of an illustration.

Illustration 4-6.   A financial instrument that can be purchased for
$6,805.82 promises to pay $10,000 five years from now. The yield
is the interest rate that will make $6,805.82 grow to $10,000 in five
years. That is, we are looking for the value of y that will satisfy the
following relationship:

$$\$10,000 = \$6,805.82 \, (1 + y)^5.$$

We can solve this equation as follows. Dividing both sides by
$6,805.82:

$$\frac{\$10,000}{\$6,805.82} = (1 + y)^5$$

$$1.46933 = (1 + y)^5.$$

Taking the 5th root of both sides:

$$(1.46933)^{1/5} = (1 + y)$$
$$(1.46933)^{.20} = (1 + y)$$
$$1.0800 = (1 + y).$$

Subtracting 1 from both sides:

$$1.0800 - 1 = y.$$
$$.08 = y.$$

Hence, the yield on this investment is 8%.

It is not necessary to go through all the steps in Illustration 4-6 to compute the yield. The following formula is consistent with those steps:

$$y = (\text{Future value per dollar invested})^{1/n} - 1 ,$$

where

n = Number of periods until the cash flow will be received;

$$\frac{\text{Future value}}{\text{per dollar invested}} = \frac{\text{Cash flow from investment}}{\text{Amount invested (or price)}}.$$

Illustration 4-7. An investment offers a payment 20 years from now of $84,957. The price of the investment is $20,000. The yield for this investment is 7.50%, as shown below:

$$n = 20$$

$$\frac{\text{Future value}}{\text{per dollar invested}} = \frac{\$84,957}{\$20,000} = 4.24785$$

$$y = (4.24785)^{1/20} - 1$$
$$= 1.07499 - 1$$
$$= .074999 \text{ or } 7.5\% .$$

Illustration 4-8.   In Illustration 2-8, we computed how many dollars would be available to a portfolio manager if he invests $5 million (the par value) in bonds that mature in 10 years and promise to pay an annual interest rate of 8%. The interest is assumed to be paid once per year, and these payments are assumed to be reinvested at an annual interest rate of 6.7%. We calculated that at the end of 10 years, the portfolio manager would have $10,448,884, consisting of $5 million in par value, $4 million in annual interest payments, and the balance, $1,448,884, from interest earned on the reinvestment of the annual interest payments.

The yield on this investment based on the portfolio manager's expectations can be computed by finding the yield that will make a $5 million investment grow to $10,448,884 in 10 years. Since we have reduced the problem to that of an investment that provides the portfolio manager with one cash flow, the yield can be found as follows:

$$n = 10 \ (= N)$$

$$\text{Future value per dollar invested} = \frac{\$10,448,884}{\$ 5,000,000} = 2.08978$$

$$\begin{aligned} y &= (2.08978)^{1/10} - 1 \\ &= 1.07649 - 1 \\ &= .07649 \text{ or } 7.65\% \ . \end{aligned}$$

Annualizing Yields

So far throughout this book, we have annualized interest rates by simply multiplying by the frequency of payments per year. We called the resulting rate the annual interest rate. For example, if we computed a semiannual yield, we annualized it by multiplying by 2. Alternatively, if we had an annual interest rate and wanted to use a semiannual interest rate, we divided by 2.

The procedure given for computing the annual interest rate, given a periodic (weekly, monthly, quarterly, semiannual, etc.) interest rate is not correct. To see why, suppose that $100 is invested for one year at an annual interest rate of 8%. At the end of one year, the interest is $8. Suppose, instead, that $100 is invested for one year at an annual interest rate of 8%, but interest is paid semiannually at 4% (one-half the annual interest rate). The interest at the end of one year is found by first calculating the future value of $100 at the end of one year:

$$\$100 \ (1.04)^2$$
$$= \$100 \ (1.0816)$$
$$= \$108.16$$

Interest is therefore $8.16 on a $100 investment. The interest rate or yield on the $100 investment is therefore 8.16% ($8.16/$100). The 8.16% is called the *effective annual yield*.

Investors who are familiar with certificates of deposit offered by banks and thrifts should recognize the difference between the annual interest rate and effective annual yield. Typically, both of these interest rates are quoted for a certificate of deposit, the higher interest rate being the effective annual yield.

To obtain the effective annual yield associated with a periodic interest rate, the following formula can be used:

Effective annual yield = $(1 + \text{Periodic interest rate})^m - 1$
where
m = Frequency of payments per year.

For example, in the previous example, the periodic yield is 4% and the frequency of payments is twice per year. Therefore,

$$\text{Effective annual yield} = (1.04)^2 - 1$$
$$= 1.0816 - 1$$
$$= .0816 \text{ or } 8.16\%$$

If interest is paid quarterly, then the periodic interest rate is 2% (8%/4), and the effective annual yield is 8.24%, as shown below:

$$\text{Effective annual yield} = (1.02)^4 - 1$$
$$= 1.0824 - 1$$
$$= .0824 \text{ or } 8.24\%$$

We can also determine the periodic interest rate that will produce a given annual interest rate. For example, suppose we wanted to know what quarterly interest rate would produce an effective annual yield of 12%. The following formula can be used:

Periodic interest rate = $(1 +$ Effective annual yield$)^{1/m} - 1$.

Applying this formula to determine the quarterly interest rate to produce an effective annual yield of 12%, we find:

$$
\begin{aligned}
\text{Periodic interest rate} &= (1.12)^{1/4} - 1 \\
&= 1.0287 - 1 \\
&= .0287 \text{ or } 2.87\%.
\end{aligned}
$$

Summary

In this chapter we explained how to compute the yield on any investment, given the expected cash flows and the price. The yield is the interest rate that will make the present value of the cash flows equal to the price of the financial instrument. The yield computed in this manner is also called the internal rate of return. We also demonstrated how to compute the effective annual yield of an investment. A summary of the formulas introduced in this chapter is provided in Exhibit 4-2.

Exhibit 4-2
  Summary of Yield (Internal Rate of Return) Formulas

(1) Yield (or internal rate of return) on any investment from which the cash flows are received annually is the interest rate that will make the following relationship hold:

$$p = \frac{C_1}{(1+y)^1} + \frac{C_2}{(1+y)^2} + \frac{C_3}{(1+y)^3} + \cdots + \frac{C_N}{(1+y)^N}$$

or

$$p = \sum_{t=1}^{N} \frac{C_t}{(1+y)^t}.$$

where
  y = Yield;
  C_t = Cash flow in year t;
  p = Price;
  N = Number of years.

(2) Yield (or internal rate of return) on any investment from which the cash flows are received periodically is the interest rate that will make the following relationship hold:

$$p = \frac{C_1}{(1+y)^1} + \frac{C_2}{(1+y)^2} + \frac{C_3}{(1+y)^3} + \cdots + \frac{C_n}{(1+y)^n}$$

or

$$p = \sum_{t=1}^{n} \frac{C_t}{(1+y)^t}.$$

where
  C_t = Cash flow in period t;
  n = Number of periods.

Exhibit 4-2 continued.

(3) Yield (internal rate of return) on an investment in which there is only one cash flow received n periods from now:

$$y = (\text{Future value per dollar invested})^{1/n} - 1$$

where

n = Number of periods when cash flow will be received;

$$\frac{\text{Future value}}{\text{per dollar invested}} = \frac{\text{Cash flow from investment}}{\text{Amount invested (or price)}}.$$

(4) Effective annual yield associated with a periodic interest rate:

$$\text{Effective annual yield} = (1 + \text{Periodic interest rate})^m - 1$$

where

m = Frequency of payments per year.

(5) Periodic interest rate consistent with an effective annual yield:

$$\text{Periodic interest rate} = (1 + \text{Effective annual yield})^{1/m} - 1$$

II
Bond Pricing and Return Analysis

5
The Price
of a Bond

In Chapter 3 we explained that the price of any financial instrument is equal to the present value of the expected cash flow. The interest rate or discount rate used to compute the present value depends on the yield offered on comparable securities in the market. In this chapter we shall explain how to compute the price of a noncallable bond. After we review the price characteristics of call options in Chapter 12, we will discuss the pricing of callable bonds and mortgage pass-through securities in Chapters 13 and 16, respectively.

Determining the Cash Flows

The first step in determining the price of a bond is to determine its cash flows. The cash flows of a noncallable bond consist of (1) periodic coupon interest payments to the maturity date and (2) the par (or maturity) value at maturity. While the periodic coupon payments can be made over any time period during the year (weekly, monthly, quarterly, semiannually, or annually), most bonds issued in the United States pay coupon interest semiannually. In our illustrations, we shall assume that the coupon interest is paid semiannually. Also, to simplify the analysis, we shall assume that the next coupon payment for the bond will be made exactly six months from now. Later in the chapter we generalize the pricing model to allow for a coupon payment that is more or less than six months from now.

Consequently, the cash flows for a noncallable bond consist of an annuity (that is, the fixed coupon interest paid every six months) and the par or maturity value. For example, a 20-year bond with a 9% (4.5% per six months) coupon rate and a par or maturity value of $1,000 has the following cash flows:

$$\text{Semiannual coupon interest} = \$1,000 \times .045$$
$$= \$45;$$
$$\text{Maturity value} = \$1,000.$$

Therefore, there are 40 semiannual cash flows of $45, and a $1,000 cash flow 40 six-month periods from now.

Notice the treatment of the par value. It is *not* treated as if it is received 20 years from now. Instead, it is treated on a consistent basis with the coupon payments, which are semiannual.

Determining the Required Yield

The interest rate or discount rate that an investor wants from investing in a bond is called the *required yield*. The required yield is determined by investigating the yields offered on comparable bonds in the market. By comparable, we mean noncallable bonds of the same credit quality and the same maturity.[1]

The required yield is typically specified as an annual interest rate. When the cash flows are semiannual, the convention is to use one-half the annual interest rate as the periodic interest rate with which to discount the cash flows. As explained at the end of the previous chapter, a periodic interest rate that is one-half the annual yield will produce an effective annual yield that is greater than the annual interest rate.

Pricing a Bond

Given the cash flows of a bond and the required yield, we have all the necessary data to price the bond. The price of a bond is the

---

[1] In Chapter 10, we introduce a measure of interest rate risk known as duration. Instead of talking in terms of a bond with the same maturity as being comparable, we recast the analysis in terms of the same duration.

present value of the cash flows, and it can be determined by adding

(1) The present value of the semiannual coupon payments

and

(2) The present value of the par or maturity value.

In general, the price of a bond can be computed from the following formula:

$$p = \frac{c}{(1+i)^1} + \frac{c}{(1+i)^2} + \frac{c}{(1+i)^3} + \cdots + \frac{c}{(1+i)^n} + \frac{M}{(1+i)^n},$$

where

p = Price ($);
c = *Semiannual* coupon payment ($);
M = Maturity value;
n = Number of periods (number of years times 2);
i = Periodic interest rate (required yield divided by 2) (in decimal).

Since the semiannual coupon payments are equivalent to an ordinary annuity, the present value of the coupon payments, that is, the present value of

$$p = \frac{c}{(1+i)^1} + \frac{c}{(1+i)^2} + \frac{c}{(1+i)^3} + \cdots + \frac{c}{(1+i)^n},$$

can be expressed

$$c \left[\frac{1 - \left[\frac{1}{(1+i)^n} \right]}{i} \right].$$

This formula is the same as the formula for the present value of an ordinary annuity for n periods introduced in Chapter 3 (see Exhibit 3-1). Instead of using A to represent the annuity, we have used c, the semiannual coupon payment.

Illustration 5-1. Compute the price of a 9% coupon bond with 20 years to maturity and a par value of $1,000 if the required yield is 12%.

The cash flows for this bond are as follows:

(1)   40 semiannual coupon payments of $45 and
(2) $1,000 40 six-month periods from now.

The semiannual or periodic interest rate is 6%.
The present value of the 40 semiannual coupon payments of $45 discounted at 6% is $677.08, as shown below:

$$c = \$45;$$
$$n = 40;$$
$$i = .06.$$

$$\$45 \left[\frac{1 - \left[\frac{1}{(1.06)^{40}} \right]}{.06} \right]$$

$$= \$45 \left[\frac{1 - \left[\frac{1}{10.28572} \right]}{.06} \right]$$

$$= \$45 \left[\frac{1 - .097222}{.06} \right]$$

$$= \$45 \, (15.04630)$$
$$= \$677.08.$$

The present value of the par or maturity value 40 *six-month periods* from now discounted at 6% is $97.22, as shown below:

$$M = \$1,000;$$
$$n = 40$$
$$i = .06.$$

$$\$1,000 \left[\frac{1}{(1.06)^{40}} \right]$$

$$= \$1,000 \left[\frac{1}{10.28572} \right]$$

$$= \$1,000 \, (.097222)$$
$$= \$97.22.$$

The price of the bond is then equal to the sum of the two present values:

Present value of coupon payments	$ 677.08
Present value of par (maturity) value	97.22
Price	$ 774.30

Illustration 5-2. Compute the price of the bond in Illustration 5-1, assuming that the required yield is 7%.

The cash flows are unchanged, but, the periodic interest rate is now 3.5% (7%/2).

The present value of the 40 semiannual coupon payments of $45 discounted at 3.5% is $960.98, as shown below:

$$c = \$45;$$
$$n = 40;$$
$$i = .035.$$

$$\$45 \left[\frac{1 - \left[\frac{1}{(1.035)^{40}} \right]}{.035} \right]$$

$$= \$45 \left[\frac{1 - \left[\frac{1}{3.95926} \right]}{.035} \right]$$

$$= \$45 \left[\frac{1 - .252572}{.035} \right]$$

$$= \$45 \, (21.35509)$$
$$= \$960.98.$$

The present value of the par or maturity value of $1,000 40 *six-month periods from now* discounted at 3.5% is $252.57, as shown below:

$$M = \$1,000;$$
$$n = 40;$$
$$i = .035.$$

$$\$1,000 \left[\frac{1}{(1.035)^{40}} \right]$$

$$= \$1,000 \left[\frac{1}{3.95926} \right]$$

$$= \$1,000 \, (.252572)$$

$$= \$252.57.$$

The price of the bond is then equal to the sum of the two present values:

Present value of coupon payments	$ 960.98
Present value of par (maturity) value	252.57
Price	$1,213.55

Illustration 5-3.   Compute the price of the bond in Illustration 5-1, assuming that there are 16 years to maturity rather than 20 years. (Assume that the required yield is still 12%.)

The cash flows for this bond are as follows:

(1) 32 semiannual coupon payments of $45;
(2) $1,000 32 six-month periods from now.

The semiannual or periodic interest rate is 6%.

The present value of the 32 semiannual coupon payments of $45 discounted at 6% is

$$c = \$45;$$
$$n = 32;$$
$$i = .06.$$

$$\$45 \left[\frac{1 - \left[\frac{1}{(1.06)^{32}} \right]}{.06} \right]$$

$$= \$45 \left[\frac{1 - \left[\frac{1}{6.45339} \right]}{.06} \right]$$

$$= \$45 \left[\frac{1 - .154957}{.06} \right]$$

$$= \$45 \, (14.08404)$$

$$= \$633.78.$$

The present value of the par or maturity value *32 six-month periods from now* discounted at 6% is:

$$M = \$1,000;$$
$$n = 32;$$
$$i = .06.$$

$$\$1,000 \left[\frac{1}{(1.06)^{32}} \right]$$

$$= \$1,000 \left[\frac{1}{6.45339} \right]$$

$$= \$1,000 \,(.154957)$$

$$= \$154.96.$$

The price of the bond is then equal to the sum of the two present values:

Present value of coupon payments	$ 633.78
Present value of par (maturity) value	154.96
Price	$ 788.74.

Illustration 5-4.   Compute the price of a 14 year bond with a 9% coupon rate assuming that the required yield is 7%.

The cash flows for this bond are as follows:

(1) 28 semiannual coupon payments of $45;
(2) $1,000 28 six-month periods from now

The periodic interest rate is 3.5%.

The present value of the 28 semiannual coupon payments when discounted at 3.5% is

$$c = \$45;$$
$$n = 28;$$
$$i = .035.$$

$$\$45 \left[\frac{1 - \left[\frac{1}{(1.035)^{28}} \right]}{.035} \right]$$

$$= \$45 \left[\frac{1 - \left[\frac{1}{2.62017} \right]}{.035} \right]$$

$$= \$45 \left[\frac{1 - .381655}{.035} \right]$$

$$= \$45 \, (17.66700)$$

$$= \$795.02.$$

The present value of the par or maturity value *28 six-month periods from now* discounted at 3.5% is

$$M = \$1,000;$$
$$n = 32;$$
$$i = .035.$$

$$\$1,000 \left[\frac{1}{(1.035)^{28}} \right]$$

$$= \$1,000 \left[\frac{1}{2.62017} \right]$$

$$= \$1,000 \, (.381654)$$

$$= \$381.65.$$

The price of the bond is then equal to the sum of the two present values:

Present value of coupon payments	$ 795.02
Present value of par (maturity) value	381.65
Price	$1,176.67

Relationship Between Required Yield and Price at a Given Point in Time

The price of an option-free bond changes in the direction opposite to the change in the required yield. The reason is that the price of the bond is the present value of the cash flows. As the required yield increases, the present value of the cash flows decreases; hence, the price decreases. The opposite is true when

Exhibit 5-1
Price/Yield Relationship for a 20-Year, 9% Coupon Bond

Required yield (%)	Present value of 40 coupon payments (*)	Present value of par value in 40 periods (**)	Price of bond
5	$1,129.62	$372.43	$1,502.05
6	1,040.16	306.56	1,346.72
7	960.98	252.57	1,213.55
8	890.67	208.29	1,098.96
9	828.07	171.93	1,000.00
10	772.16	142.05	914.21
11	722.08	117.46	839.54
12	677.08	97.22	774.30
13	636.55	80.54	717.09
14	599.93	66.78	666.71

* Computed as follows:

$$\$45 \left[\frac{1 - \left[\frac{1}{(1 + i)^{40}} \right]}{i} \right],$$

where i is one-half the required yield.

**Computed as follows:

$$\$1,000 \left[\frac{1}{(1 + i)^{40}} \right],$$

where i is one-half the required yield.

the required yield decreases: the present value of the cash flows increases and, therefore, the price of the bond increases.

We can see this by comparing the price of the 20-year, 9% coupon bond that we priced in Illustrations 5-1 and 5-2. When the required yield is 12%, the price of the bond is $774.30. If, instead, the required yield is 7%, the price of the bond is $1,213.55. Exhibit 5-1 shows the price of the bond for required yields from 5% to 14% for the 20-year, 9% coupon bond.

Exhibit 5-2

Price/Yield Relationship

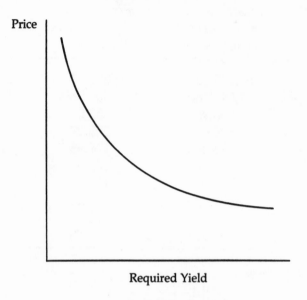

If we graphed the price/yield relationship for any noncallable bond, we would find that it has the "bowed" shape shown in Exhibit 5-2. This shape is referred to as *convex*. The convexity of the price/yield relationship has important implications for the investment properties of a bond. We've devoted Chapter 11 to examine this relationship more closely.

The Relationship Between Coupon Rate, Required Yield and Price

For a bond issue at a given point in time, the coupon rate and the term to maturity for the issue are fixed. Consequently, as yields in the marketplace change, the only variable that an investor can change to compensate for the new yield required in the market is the price of the bond. As we saw in the previous section, as the required yield increases (decreases), the price of the bond decreases (increases).

Generally, when a bond is issued, the coupon rate is set at approximately the prevailing yield in the market.[2] The price of the bond will then be approximately equal to its par value. For example, in Exhibit 5-1, we see that when the required yield is equal to the coupon rate, the price of the bond is its par value ($1,000). Consequently, we have the following properties:

When the coupon rate equals the required yield, then the price equals the par value.

When the price equals the par value, then the coupon rate equals the required yield.

When yields in the marketplace rise above the coupon rate at *a given point in time*, the price of the bond has to adjust so that the investor can realize some additional interest. This adjustment is accomplished by having the bond's price fall below the par value. The difference between the par value and the price is a capital gain and represents a form of interest to the investor to compensate for the coupon rate being lower than the required yield. When a bond sells below its par value, it is said to be selling at a *discount*. We can see this in Exhibit 5-1. When the required yield is greater than the coupon rate of 9%, the price of the bond is always less than the par value ($1,000). Consequently, we have the following properties:

When the coupon rate is less than the required yield, then the price is less than the par value.

When the price is less than the par value, then the coupon rate is less than the required yield.

Finally, when the required yield in the market is below the coupon rate, the price of the bond must sell above its par value. This occurs because investors who would have the opportunity to purchase the bond at par would be getting a coupon rate in excess of what the market would require. As a result, investors would bid up the price of the bond because its yield is attractive. It will be bid up to a price that offers the required yield in the market. A bond whose price is above its par value is said to be

---

[2] The exception is an original-issue deep-discount bond such as a zero-coupon bond. We'll discuss zero coupon bonds later in this chapter.

selling at a *premium*. Exhibit 5-1 shows that for a required yield less than the coupon rate of 9%, the price of the bond is greater than its par value. Consequently, we have the following properties:

When the coupon rate is greater than the required yield, then the price is greater than the par value.

When the price is greater than the par value, then the coupon rate is greater than the required yield.

Time Path of a Bond

If the required yield is unchanged between the time the bond is purchased and the maturity date, what will happen to the price of the bond? For a bond selling at par value, the coupon rate is equal to the required yield. As the bond moves closer to maturity, the bond will continue to sell at par value. Thus, for a bond selling at par, its price will remain at par as the bond moves toward the maturity date.

The price of a bond will *not* remain constant for a bond selling at a premium or a discount. This can be seen for a discount bond by comparing the price found in Illustration 5-1 to that found in Illustration 5-3. In both illustrations the bond has a 9% coupon rate and the investor has a required yield of 12%. In Illustration 5-1, the maturity of the bond is 20 years, while in Illustration 5-3 the maturity is 16 years. With 20 years to maturity, the price of the bond is $774.30. Four years later, when the bond has 16 years remaining to maturity, the price of the bond increases to $788.14. For all discount bonds the following is true: as the bond moves toward maturity its price will increase if *the required yield* does not change.

Exhibit 5-3 shows the price of the 20-year, 9% coupon bond as it moves toward maturity, assuming that the required yield remains at 12%. The price of the bond is decomposed into the present value of the coupon payments and the present value of the par value. Notice that as the bond moves toward maturity, there are fewer coupon payments that will be received by the bondholder. The present value of the coupon payments decrease. Since the maturity date is closer, however, the present value of the par value increases. The increase in the present

Exhibit 5-3
Time Path of the Price of a Discount Bond: 20-Year,
9% Coupon, 12% Required Yield

Years remaining to maturity	Present value of coupon payments of $45 at 6%	Present value of par value at 6%	Price of bond
20	$677.08	$ 97.22	$ 774.30
18	657.94	122.74	780.68
16	633.78	154.96	788.74
14	603.28	195.63	798.91
12	564.77	256.98	811.75
10	516.15	311.80	827.95
8	454.77	393.65	848.42
6	377.27	496.97	874.24
4	279.44	627.41	906.85
2	155.93	792.09	948.02
1	82.50	890.00	972.50
0	0.00	1,000.00	1,000.00

value of the par value is greater than the decline in the present value of the coupon payments, resulting in a price increase. Exhibit 5-4 graphically portrays the time path of a bond selling at a discount.

For a bond selling at a premium, the price of the bond declines as it moves toward maturity. Illustrations 5-2 and 5-4 show this property for a 9% coupon bond for which the required yield is 7%. When the bond has 20 years to maturity, its price is $1,213.55. Six years later, when the bond has 14 years remaining to maturity, the price of the bond declines to $1,176.67.

The time path of the 20-year, 9% coupon bond selling to yield 7% is shown in Exhibit 5-5. As the bond moves toward maturity, the present value of the coupon payments decreases and the present value of the par value increases. Unlike a bond selling at a discount, the increase in the present value of the par value is not sufficient to offset the decline in the present value of the coupon payments. As a result, the price of a bond selling at a

Exhibit 5-4
Time Path of a Discount Bond, Assuming No Change in Required Yield

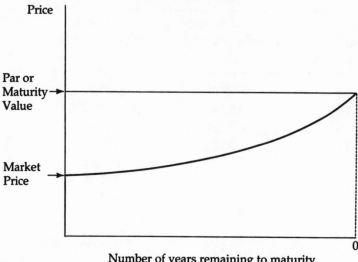

Number of years remaining to maturity

Exhibit 5-5
Time Path of the Price of a Premium Bond: 20-Year, 9% Coupon, 7% Required Yield

Years remaining to maturity	Present value of coupon payments of $45 at 3.5%	Present value of par value at 3.5%	Price of bond
20	$960.98	$ 252.57	$ 1,213.55
18	913.07	289.83	1,202.90
16	858.10	332.59	1,190.69
14	795.02	381.65	1,176.67
12	722.63	437.96	1,160.59
10	639.56	502.57	1,142.13
8	544.24	576.71	1,120.95
6	434.85	661.78	1,096.63
4	309.33	759.41	1,068.74
2	165.29	871.44	1,036.73
1	85.49	933.51	1,019.00
0	0.00	1,000.00	1,000.00

Exhibit 5-6
**Time Path of a Premium Bond, Assuming No Change
in Required Yield**

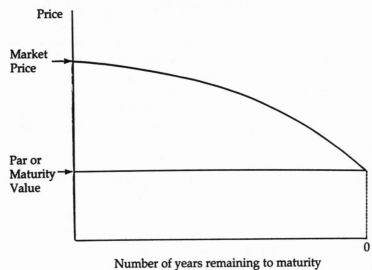

Number of years remaining to maturity

premium decreases over time if the required yield does not change. A graphical depiction of the time path of any premium bond is presented in Exhibit 5-6.

Analysis of Bond Price Changes

In managing a portfolio, a money manager will be concerned with investigating the expected performance of a bond over an investment horizon based on certain assumptions about the future direction of interest rates. We'll demonstrate how this is done in Chapter 8. Doing so will require that we be able to analyze the way a bond's price will change under a specified set of assumptions.

The price of a bond will change for one or more of the following three reasons:

(1) A change in the required yield due to changes in the credit quality of the issuer;

(2) A change in the maturity of the bond as it moves toward maturity without any change in the required yield (that is, the time path of the bond);

(3) A change in the required yield due to a change in the yield on comparable bonds (that is, a change in the yield required by the market).

Predicting the change in an issue's credit quality before that change is recognized by the market is one of the challenges of investment management. For purposes of our illustrations below, let's suppose that the issue's credit quality is unchanged, so that we can focus on the last two reasons.

It is informative to separate the effect of the change in price due to the time path of a bond from that of the change due to a change in the required yield. The next two illustrations show how this is done.

Illustration 5-5. Suppose that a money manager purchases a 20-year, 9% coupon bond at a price of $774.30 to yield 12%. The money manager expects to hold this bond for four years, at which time the money manager believes that the required yield on comparable 16-year bonds will be 8%. On the basis of the money manager's expectations, we can investigate what will happen to the price of the bond four years from now.

After this bond is held for four years, it becomes a 16-year bond. If the required yield for a 16-year bond is 8%, the price of the bond four years from now will be $1,089.37.[3] The price of this bond is therefore expected to increase by $315.07 ($1,089.37 − $744.30). Not all of the price change, however, is due to the decline in market yield. If the required yield remained at 12%, the price of the bond in four years would have increased to $788.74, an increase of $14.44 ($788.74 − $744.30). Therefore, we can decompose the expected price change after four years as follows:

Price change due to the time path of a discount bond	$ 14.44
Price change due to the change in the required yield	300.63
Total price change	$ 315.07

---

[3] The price is determined as follows:

Present value of 32 coupon payments at 4%	$ 804.31
Present value of par (maturity) value at 4%	285.06
Price	$1,089.37

Illustration 5-6. Suppose that a money manager is considering the purchase of a 20-year, 9% coupon bond selling at $1,213.55 to yield 7%. If the money manager purchases this bond, she expects to hold it for six years, at which time she expects that the required yield on 14-year bonds may be 11%. What would be the price performance of this bond based on the money manager's expectations?

The price of a 14-year, 9% coupon bond if an 11% required yield is assumed is $858.79.[4] If the required yield remained at 7%, however, the price of a 14-year bond with a coupon rate of 9% would be $1,176.67 (see Exhibit 5-5). The price change can be broken down as follows:

Price change due to the time path of a discount bond	– $ 36.88
Price change due to the change in the required yield	– $317.88
Total price change	– $354.76

The Price of a Zero-Coupon Bond

So far we have determined the price of coupon-bearing bonds. There are bonds that do not make any periodic coupon payments. Instead, the investor realizes interest by the difference between the maturity value and the purchase price.

The pricing of a zero-coupon bond is no different from the pricing of a coupon bond: its price is the present value of the expected cash flows. In the case of a zero-coupon bond, the only cash flow is the maturity value. Therefore, the formula for the price of a zero-coupon bond that matures N years from now is

$$p = M \left[\frac{1}{(1 + i)^n} \right],$$

---

[4] The price is determined as follows:

Present value of 28 coupon payments at 5.5%	$ 635.46
Present value of par (maturity) value at 5.5%	223.32
Price	$ 858.79

where

p = Price;
M = Maturity value;
i = Periodic interest rate (annual interest rate / 2);
N = Number of years;
n = $2 \times N$.

Pay particular attention to the number of periods used in the pricing of a zero-coupon bond. Although an issue may mature in N years, the number of six-month periods is used in the exponent, and the periodic interest rate is the required yield divided by 2. The reason is that the pricing of a zero-coupon bond must be made consistent with the pricing of a coupon bond. Recall that with a coupon bond the present value of the par or maturity value is computed using twice the number of years to maturity. Therefore, we handle the maturity value for the zero-coupon bond the same way.

Illustration 5-7. Compute the price of a zero coupon bond that matures 10 years from now if the maturity value is $1,000 and the required yield is 8.6%.
   The price is determined as follows:

$$M = \$1,000;$$
$$i = .043 \ (.086/2);$$
$$N = 10;$$
$$n = 20 \ (2 \times 10);$$
$$p = \$1,000 \left[\frac{1}{(1.043)^{20}} \right]$$
$$= \$1,000 \left[\frac{1}{2.321059} \right]$$
$$= \$1,000 \ (.43083)$$
$$= \$430.83.$$

Illustration 5-8. Compute the price of a seven-year, zero-coupon bond with a maturity value of $100,000 if the required yield is 9.8%.
   The price is $51,185.06, as shown below:

$$M = \$100,000;$$
$$i = .049 \ (.098/2);$$
$$N = 7;$$
$$n = 14 \ (2 \times 7);$$

$$p = \$100,000 \left[\frac{1}{(1.049)^{14}} \right]$$

$$= \$100,000 \left[\frac{1}{1.953695} \right]$$

$$= \$100,000 \ (.5118506)$$
$$= \$51,185.06.$$

Price Quotes

In all but our last illustration, we have assumed that the maturity or par value of the bond is $1,000. A bond can take on any maturity or par value. Consequently, when quoting a bond price, traders quote the price as a percentage of par value.

A bond selling at par is quoted as 100, meaning 100% of its par value. A bond selling at a discount will be selling for less than 100; a bond selling at a premium will be selling for more than 100. The following examples illustrate how a price quote is converted into a dollar price.

Price quote (1)	Converted to a decimal (2) [= (1)/100]	Par value (3)	Dollar price (4) = [(2)×(3)]
95	.9500000	$1,000	$950.00
95 1/2	.9550000	100,000	95,500.00
98 1/4	.9825000	5,000	4,912.50
80 1/8	.8012500	10,000	8,012.50
74 1/32	.7403125	1,000,000	740,312.50
100	1.0000000	10,000	10,000.00
103	1.0300000	1,000	1,030.00
106 3/4	1.0675000	500,000	533,750.00
108 3/8	1.0837500	25,000	27,093.75
111 11/32	1.1134375	100,000	111,343.75

For some securities a unique market convention has been adopted for quoting prices. For example, for Treasury notes and bonds, a quote of "95-5," "95.5," or "95:05" means 95% plus 5/32, the number following the hyphen, decimal, or colon representing the number of 32nds. So for a $100,000 par value Treasury note or bond, a quote of 95-5 or 95.5 or 95:05 indicates a dollar price of $95,156.25, as shown below:

$$95\frac{5}{32}\% = 95.15625\% = .9515625;$$

then

$$\$100,000 \times .9515625 = \$95,156.25.$$

Corporate and municipal bonds are frequently quoted in eighths rather than 32nds.

Determining the Price When the Settlement Date Falls Between Coupon Periods

In our illustrations, we assumed that the next coupon payment is six months away. This means that settlement occurs on the day after a coupon date. Typically, an investor will purchase a bond between coupon dates so that the next coupon payment is less than six months away. To compute the price, we have to answer the following three questions:

(1) How many days are there until the next coupon payment?

(2) How should we determine the present value of cash flows received over fractional periods?

(3) How much must the buyer compensate the seller for the coupon interest earned by the seller for the fraction of the period that the bond was held?

The first question is the "day-count" question. The second is the "compounding" question. The last question asks how accrued interest is determined. Below we address these questions.

Day Count

Market conventions for each type of bond dictate the answer to the first question: the number of days until the next coupon payment.

For Treasury coupon securities, a nonleap year is assumed to have 365 days. The number of days between settlement and the next coupon payment is therefore the actual number of days between the two dates. The day count convention for a coupon-bearing Treasury security is said to be "actual/actual," which means "the actual number of days in a month/actual number of days in the coupon period." For example, consider a Treasury bond whose last coupon payment was on March 1; the next coupon would be six months later on September 1. Suppose this bond is purchased with a settlement date of July 17. The actual number of days between July 17 (the settlement date) and September 1 (the date of the next coupon payment) is 46 days (the actual number of days in the coupon period is 184), as shown below:

July 17 to July 31	14 days
August	31 days
September 1	1 day
	46 days

In contrast to the "actual/actual" day count convention for coupon-bearing Treasury securities, for corporate and municipal bonds and agency securities, the day count convention is "30/360." That is, each month is assumed to have 30 days and each year 360 days. For example, suppose that the security in our previous example is not a coupon-bearing Treasury security but instead either a coupon-bearing corporate bond, municipal bond, or agency security. The number of days between July 17 and September 1 is as shown below:

Remainder of July	13 days
August	30 days
September 1	1 day
	44 days

There are financial calendars available that provide the day count between settlement and the next coupon payment. Most money managers, however, use software programs that will furnish this information.

Compounding

Once the number of days between the settlement date and the next coupon date is determined, the present value formula must be modified to take into account that the cash flows will not be received six months (one full period) from now. The "Street" convention is to compute the price as follows:

(1) Determine the number of days in the coupon period.
(2) Compute the following ratio:

$$w = \frac{\text{number of days between settlement and next coupon payment}}{\text{number of days in the coupon period}}.$$

For a corporate bond, municipal bond, and agency security, the number of days in the coupon period will be 180, since a year is assumed to have 360 days. For a coupon-bearing Treasury security, the number of days is the actual number of days. The number of days in the coupon period is called the *basis*.

(3) Determine the first cash flow which is w times the semiannual coupon payment.
(4) For a bond with n coupon payments remaining to maturity, the price is:

$$p = \frac{w \times c}{(1+i)^w} + \frac{c}{(1+i)^{1+w}} + \frac{c}{(1+i)^{2+w}} + \cdots$$
$$+ \frac{c}{(1+i)^{n-1+w}} + \frac{M}{(1+i)^{n-1+w}}$$

where
p = Price ($);
c = *Semiannual* coupon payment ($);
M = Maturity value;
n = Number of coupons payments remaining;
i = Periodic interest rate (required yield divided by 2) (in decimal).

The period (exponent) in the formula for determining the present value can be expressed generally as $t - 1 + w$. For example, for the first cash flow, the period is $1 - 1 + w$, or simply w. For the second cash flow it is $2 - 1 + w$, or simply $1 + w$. If the bond has 20 coupon payments remaining, the period is $20 - 1 + w$, or simply $19 + w$.

Illustration 5-9. Suppose that a corporate bond with a coupon rate of 10% maturing March 1, 1994, is purchased with a settlement date of July 17, 1988. What would the price of this bond be if it is priced to yield 6.5%?

The next coupon payment will be made on September 1, 1988. Since the bond is a corporate bond, based on a 30/360 day count convention, there are 44 days between the settlement date and the next coupon date. The number of days in the coupon payment is 180 days. Therefore,

$$w = \frac{44}{180} = .24444.$$

The number of coupon payments remaining, n, is 12. The semi-annual interest rate is 3.25% (6.5%/2). The first coupon payment will be

$$.24444 \times \$5 = \$1.222.$$

The calculation based on the formula for the price is given in Exhibit 5-7. The price of this corporate bond is 116.2797. Because corporate bonds are frequently quoted in eighths, however, the price would be rounded accordingly. Since two eighths equals 0.25, 116 and two eighths will equal 116.25. For three eighths, the price would be 116.375. Since the price we computed is closer to 116.25, the bond price would be 116.25.

Had the hypothetical bond been a Treasury bond rather than a corporate bond, the price would have been expressed in terms of 32nds. In the illustrations used throughout this book, we will not round off the price.

Exhibit 5-7

Price Calculation When a Bond
is Purchased Between Coupon Payments

Period	Cash flow per $100 of par	Present value of $1 at 3.25%	Present value of cash flow
0.24444	$1.222	$0.992212	$1.212704
1.24444	5.000	0.960980	4.804902
2.24444	5.000	0.930731	4.653658
3.24444	5.000	0.901435	4.507175
4.24444	5.000	0.873060	4.365303
5.24444	5.000	0.845579	4.227896
6.24444	5.000	0.818963	4.094815
7.24444	5.000	0.793184	3.965922
8.24444	5.000	0.768217	3.841087
9.24444	5.000	0.744036	3.720181
10.24444	5.000	0.720616	3.603081
11.24444	105.000	0.697933	73.28300
		Total	$116.2797

Accrued Interest and the Total Payment

The buyer must compensate the seller for the portion of the next coupon interest payment the seller has earned but will not receive from the issuer because the issuer will send the next coupon payment to the buyer. This amount is called *accrued interest* and depends on the number of days from the last coupon payment to the settlement date.[5] The accrued interest is computed as follows:

$$AI = c \left[\frac{\text{Number of days from last coupon payment to settlement date}}{\text{Number of days in coupon period}} \right],$$

where

AI = Accrued interest ($);

c = Semiannual coupon payment ($).

---

[5] Accrued interest is not computed for all bonds. No accrued interest is computed for bonds in default or income bonds. A bond that trades without accrued interest is said to be traded "flat."

Illustration 5-10. Let's continue with the hypothetical corporate bond in Illustration 5-9. Since the number of days between settlement (July 17, 1988) and the next coupon payment (September 1, 1988) is 44 days and the number of days in the coupon period is 180, the number of days from the last coupon payment date (March 1, 1988) to the settlement date is 136 (180 - 44). The accrued interest per $100 of par value is

$$AI = \$5 \ \frac{136}{180} \ = \$3.777778$$

Illustration 5-11. If the bond in the previous illustration were a Treasury bond rather than a corporate, the accrued interest would have been computed as follows. The number of days in the coupon period would be based on the actual number of days. Between March 1 and September 1 the actual number of days is 184. The actual number of days between March 1 and July 17 is 138. Accrued interest per $100 of par value is then

$$AI = \$5 \ \frac{138}{184} \ = \$3.75$$

The *total payment* (also called the *invoice price* or *proceeds*) that the buyer must remit to the seller is the price plus accrued interest.

Illustration 5-12. For our hypothetical corporate bond, the total payment per $100 of par value the buyer would remit to the seller would be the price of $116.25 (the rounded price) plus accrued interest of $3.777778, or $120.02778. If $1 million of par value had been purchased, the cost to the buyer would be as follows:

Price	$1,162,500.00
Accrued interest	37,777.78
Total payment	$1,200,277.78

Summary

In this chapter we have shown how to determine the price of a noncallable bond. The price is simply the present value of the bond's expected cash flows, the discount rate being equal to the yield offered on comparable bonds. For a noncallable bond, the cash flows are the coupon payments and the par value or maturity value. For a zero-coupon bond, there are no coupon payments: the price is equal to the present value of the maturity value, where the number of periods used to compute the present value is double the number of years. Exhibit 5-8 summarizes the pricing formulas presented in this chapter.

The higher (lower) the required yield, the lower (higher) the price of a bond. Therefore, a bond's price changes in the direction opposite to the change in the required yield. When the coupon rate is equal to the required yield, the bond will sell at its par value. When the coupon rate is less (greater) than the required yield, the bond will sell for less (more) than its par value. A bond selling below (above) its par value is said to be selling at a discount (premium).

Over time, the price of a bond will change. Assuming the credit quality of the issuer is unchanged, the price change can be broken down into an amount attributed to a change in the required yield and an amount attributed to the time path of the bond.

Exhibit 5-8

Summary of Pricing Formulas

(1) Price of a noncallable bond when next coupon payment is six months away:

$$p = \frac{c}{(1+i)^1} + \frac{c}{(1+i)^2} + \frac{c}{(1+i)^3} + \cdots + \frac{c}{(1+i)^n} + \frac{M}{(1+i)^n} \ ,$$

where
    p = Price ($);
    c = *Semiannual* coupon payment ($);
    M = Maturity value;
    n = Number of periods (number of years times 2);
    i = Periodic interest rate (required yield divided by 2) (in decimal).

(2) Present value of the coupon payments:

$$c \ \frac{1 - \left[\dfrac{1}{(1+i)^n}\right]}{i} \ .$$

(3) Price of a zero-coupon bond:

$$p = M \ \left[\frac{1}{(1+i)^n}\right]$$

where
    N = Number of years;
    $n = 2 \times N.$

(4) Price of a bond purchased between coupon payments with n coupon payments remaining:

$$p = \frac{w \times c}{(1+i)^w} + \frac{c}{(1+i)^{1+w}} + \frac{c}{(1+i)^{2+w}} + \cdots$$

$$+ \frac{c}{(1+i)^{n-1+w}} + \frac{M}{(1+i)^{n-1+w}}$$

Exhibit 5-8 continued.

where

n = Number of coupons payments remaining;

i = Periodic interest rate (required yield divided by 2) (in decimal).

$$w = \frac{\text{Number of days between settlement and next coupon payment}}{\text{Number of days in the coupon period}}$$

(5) Accrued interest

$$AI = c \left[\frac{\text{Number of days from last coupon payment to settlement date}}{\text{Number of days in coupon period}} \right]$$

where

AI = Accrued interest ($).

(6) Total payment = Price + Accrued interest.

6
Conventional Yield Measures for Bonds

In the previous chapter, we explained how to compute the price of a bond, given the required yield. In this chapter, we'll show how to compute various yield measures for a bond, given its price. We focus here on three conventional yield measures commonly quoted by dealers and traders: (1) current yield, (2) yield to maturity, and (3) yield to call. While these yield measures are commonly used by bond market participants, their usefulness in assessing the relative value of a bond over some specified investment horizon is questionable. In the next chapter we critically evaluate these yield measures; in Chapter 8 we suggest a yield measure that is more useful for determining the potential return by investing in a bond.

Current Yield

The current yield relates the *annual* coupon interest to the market price. The formula for the current yield is

$$\text{Current yield} = \frac{\text{Annual dollar coupon interest}}{\text{Price}}.$$

Illustration 6-1.   The current yield for an 18-year, 6% coupon bond selling for $700.89 is 8.56%, as shown below

$$\text{Annual dollar coupon interest} = \$1{,}000 \times .06$$
$$= \$60;$$

$$\text{Current yield} = \frac{\$60}{\$700.89} = .0856 \text{ or } 8.56\%.$$

Illustration 6-2.   The current yield for a 19-year, 11% coupon bond selling for $1,233.64 is 8.92%, as shown below:

$$\text{Annual dollar coupon interest} = \$1{,}000 \times .11$$
$$= \$110$$

$$\text{Current yield} = \frac{\$110}{\$1{,}233.64} = .0892 \text{ or } 8.92\%.$$

The current yield considers only the coupon interest and no other source of return that will affect an investor's yield. For example, in Illustration 6-1, no consideration is given to the capital gain that the investor will realize when the bond matures; in Illustration 6-2, no recognition is given to the capital loss that the investor will realize when the bond matures.

Yield to Maturity

In Chapter 4 we explained how to compute the yield or internal rate of return on any investment. The yield is the interest rate that will make the present value of the cash flows equal to the price (or initial investment). The yield to maturity is computed in the same way as the yield; the cash flows are those that the investor would realize by holding the bond to maturity. For a semiannual-pay bond in which the next coupon payment will be received six months from now, the yield to maturity is computed by solving the following relationship for y:

$$p = \frac{c}{(1 + y)^1} + \frac{c}{(1 + y)^2} + \frac{c}{(1 + y)^3} + \cdots + \frac{c}{(1 + y)^n} + \frac{M}{(1 + y)^n},$$

where

  p = Price ($);
  c = *Semiannual* coupon interest ($);
  M = Maturity value ($);
  n = Number of periods (number of years × 2);
  y = One-half the yield to maturity.

For a semiannual-pay bond, doubling the interest rate or discount rate (y) gives the yield to maturity.

Using the Greek letter sigma to denote summation, the above relationship can be expressed as follows:

$$p = \sum_{t=1}^{n} \frac{c}{(1+y)^t} + \frac{M}{(1+y)^n}.$$

Recall from Chapter 4 that the computation of the yield requires a trial-and-error procedure. The next two illustrations show how to compute the yield to maturity for a bond.

Illustration 6-3. In Illustration 6-1 we computed the current yield for an 18-year, 6% coupon bond selling for $700.89. The maturity or par value for this bond is $1,000. The yield to maturity for this bond is 9.5%, as shown below:

  Cash flows for the bond:

  (1) 36 coupon payments of $30 every six months and
  (2) $1,000 36 six-month periods from now.

To get y, different interest rates must be tried until one is found that makes the present value of the cash flows equal to the price of $700.89. Since the coupon rate on the bond is 6% and the bond is selling at a discount, the yield must be greater than 6%.[1] Exhibit 6-1 shows the present value of the cash flows of the bond for periodic interest rates from 3.25% to 4.75% (corresponding to annual interest rates from 6.5% to 9.50%, respectively). As can be seen from this exhibit, when a 4.75% interest rate is used, the present value of the cash flows is $700.89. Therefore, y is 4.75%, and the yield to maturity is 9.50%.

---

[1] See page 69 of Chapter 5.

Exhibit 6-1

Computation of Yield to Maturity for an 18-Year, 6% Coupon Bond Selling at $700.89

Objective: Find—by trial and error—the semiannual interest rate that will make the present value of the following cash flows equal to $700.89:

36 coupon payments of $30 every six months;
$1,000 36 six-month periods from now.

Annual interest rate	Semi-annual rate	Present value of 36 payments of $30 (*)	Present value of $1,000 36 periods from now (**)	Present value of cash flows
6.50%	3.25%	$ 631.20	$ 316.20	$ 947.40
7.00	3.50	608.71	289.83	898.54
7.50	3.75	587.42	265.72	853.14
8.00	4.00	567.25	243.67	810.92
8.50	4.25	548.12	223.49	771.61
9.00	4.50	529.98	205.03	735.01
9.50	4.75	512.76	188.13	700.89

*

$$\$30 \left[\frac{1 - \left[\dfrac{1}{(1 + \text{Semiannual interest rate})^{36}} \right]}{\text{Semiannual interest rate}} \right].$$

**

$$\$1,000 \left[\frac{1}{(1 + \text{Semiannual interest rate})^{36}} \right].$$

Illustration 6-4. In Illustration 6-2 we computed the current yield for a 19-year, 11% coupon bond selling for $1,233.64. The maturity or par value for this bond is $1,000. The yield to maturity for this bond is 8.50%, as shown below:

Cash flows for the bond:

(1)   38 coupon payments of $55 every six months and
(2) $1,000 38 six-month periods from now.

Exhibit 6-2
Computation of Yield to Maturity for a 19-Year, 11% Coupon Bond Selling at $1,233.64

Objective: Find—by trial and error—the semiannual interest rate that will make the present value of the following cash flows equal to $1,233.64:

38 coupon payments of $55 every six months;
$1,000 38 six-month periods from now.

Annual interest rate	Semi-annual rate	Present value of 38 payments of $55 (*)	Present value of $1,000 38 periods from now (**)	Present value of cash flows
6.00%	3.00%	$1,237.09	$325.23	$1,562.32
6.50	3.25	1,190.36	296.60	1,486.96
7.00	3.50	1,146.26	270.56	1,416.82
7.50	3.75	1,104.60	246.86	1,351.46
8.00	4.00	1,065.23	225.29	1,290.52
8.50	4.25	1,028.00	205.64	1,233.64

*

$$\$55 \left[\frac{1 - \left[\dfrac{1}{(1 + \text{Semiannual interest rate})^{38}} \right]}{\text{Semiannual interest rate}} \right].$$

**

$$\$1,000 \left[\frac{1}{(1 + \text{Semiannual interest rate})^{38}} \right].$$

We are looking for the interest rate y that will make the present value of the cash flows equal to $1,233.64 (the price of the bond). Since the bond is selling at a premium and the coupon rate is 11%, the yield must be less than 11%.[2] Exhibit 6-2 shows the present value of the cash flows of the bond for periodic

---

[2] See page 69 of Chapter 5.

interest rates from 3.00% to 4.25% (corresponding to annual interest rates from 6.0% to 8.50%, respectively). The present value of the cash flows is equal to the price when a 4.25% interest rate is used. The value for y is therefore 4.25%. Doubling 4.25% produces the yield to maturity of 8.50%.

The yield to maturity considers not only the current coupon income but any capital gain or loss that the investor will realize by *holding the bond to maturity*. The yield to maturity also considers the timing of the cash flows.

Yield to Maturity for a Zero Coupon Bond

In Chapter 4, we explained that when there is only one cash flow, it is much easier to compute the yield on an investment. A zero coupon bond is characterized by a single cash flow resulting from an investment. Consequently, the following formula, presented in Chapter 4 (Exhibit 4-2), can be applied to compute the yield to maturity for a zero coupon bond:

$$y = \text{(Future value per dollar invested)}^{1/n} - 1$$

where

y = One-half the yield to maturity;

$$\text{Future value per dollar invested} = \frac{\text{Maturity value}}{\text{Price}}.$$

Once again, doubling y gives the yield to maturity. *Remember that the number of periods used in the formula is double the number of years.*

Illustration 6-5. The yield to maturity for a zero coupon bond selling for $274.78 with a maturity value of $1,000, maturing in 15 years, is 8.8%, as computed below:

$$\text{Future value per dollar invested} = \frac{\$1,000.00}{\$274.78}$$

$$n = 30 \ (15 \times 2);$$
$$y = (3.639275)^{1/30} - 1$$
$$= (3.639275)^{.033333} - 1$$
$$= 1.044 - 1$$
$$= .044 \text{ or } 4.4\%.$$

Doubling 4.4% gives the yield to maturity of 8.8%.

Computing the Yield to Maturity When the Settlement Date Falls Between Coupon Payments

In the last chapter we explained how to compute the total payment (invoice price) to be paid when the settlement date for a bond lies between coupon payments. The yield to maturity for a bond when the settlement date falls between coupons is the interest rate that will make the present value of the cash flows equal to the total payment. That is, for a semiannual-pay bond with n coupon payments remaining, we must solve the following relationship for y:

$$tp = \frac{w \times c}{(1+y)^w} + \frac{c}{(1+y)^{1+w}} + \frac{c}{(1+y)^{2+w}} + $$

$$ + \frac{c}{(1+y)^{n-1+w}} + \frac{M}{(1+y)^{n-1+w}} ,$$

where

tp = Total payment ($) (price plus accrued interest);
c = *Semiannual* coupon payment ($);
M = Maturity value;
n = Number of coupons payments remaining;
y = One-half yield to maturity;
$w = \dfrac{\text{Number of days between settlement and the next coupon payment}}{\text{Number of days in the coupon period}}$.

Doubling y gives the yield to maturity.

Using the Greek letter sigma to denote summation, the formula can be expressed as follows:

$$tp = \frac{w \times c}{(1+y)^w} + \sum_{t=2}^{n} \frac{c}{(1+y)^{t-1+w}} + \frac{M}{(1+y)^{n-1+w}} .$$

Illustration 6-6. Suppose that a 10% coupon corporate bond maturing on March 1, 1994, is selling for 115 with a July 17, 1988, settlement. The cash flow for this bond per $100 of par value, and the corresponding periods they will be received, were shown in Illustration 5-9 of the previous chapter to be:

Period	Cash flow
.24444	$ 1.2222
1.24444 through 10.2444	$ 5.0000
11.24444	$ 105.0000

In Illustration 5-10 of the previous chapter, we showed that the accrued interest is $3.777778. Since the assumed price is $115, the total payment is $118.777778. The semiannual interest rate that will make the present value of the cash flows equal to the total payment of $118.777778 is 3.3735%. Doubling the semiannual interest rate gives a yield to maturity of 6.747%.

Illustration 6-7. Had the bond in Illustration 6-6 been a Treasury bond rather than a corporate, the cash flows for the bond would be as follows:

Number of days from settlement to next coupon payment = 46; Number of days in coupon period = 184;

$$w = \frac{46}{184} = .25;$$

First cash flow per $100 par value = .25 × $5 = 1.250.

The cash flows for this bond per $100 of par value and the corresponding periods they will be received are as follows:

Period	Cash flow
.25	$ 1.25
1.25 through 10.25	$ 5.00
11.25	$ 105.00

In Illustration 5-11 of Chapter 5 we showed that the accrued interest per $100 of par value is $3.75. The total payment is then $118.75, assuming a price of 115. The interest rate that will make the present value of the cash flow equal to $118.75 is 3.374%. The yield to maturity is then 6.748%.

Relationship Between Coupon Rate, Current Yield,
and Yield to Maturity

The following relationship should be recognized between the coupon rate, current yield, and yield to maturity:

Bond selling at	Relationship
Par	Coupon rate = Current yield =Yield to maturity
Discount	Coupon rate < Current yield < Yield to maturity
Premium	Coupon rate > Current yield >Yield to maturity

The relationship for discount and premium bonds can be verified from the illustrations presented earlier in this chapter.

Problem with the Annualizing Procedure

As we pointed out in Chapter 4, multiplying a semiannual interest rate by 2 will give an underestimate of the effective annual yield. The proper way to annualize the semiannual yield is by applying the following formula presented in Chapter 4 (see Exhibit 4-2):

Effective annual yield = $(1 + \text{Periodic interest rate})^k - 1$,
where
k = Number of payments per year.

For a semiannual-pay bond, the formula can be modified as follows:

Effective annual yield = $(1 + \text{Semiannual interest rate})^2 - 1$
or
Effective annual yield = $(1 + y)^2 - 1$.

For example, in Illustration 6-3, the semiannual interest rate is 4.75%, and the effective annual yield is 9.73%, as shown below:

$$\text{Effective annual yield} = (1.0475)^2 - 1$$
$$= 1.0973 - 1$$
$$= .0973 \text{ or } 9.73\%.$$

Although the proper way for annualizing a semiannual interest rate is given in the formula above, the convention adopted in the bond market is to double the semiannual interest rate. The yield to maturity computed in this manner — doubling the semiannual yield — is called a *bond equivalent yield*. In fact, this convention is carried over to yield calculations for other types of fixed income securities.[3]

Comparing Yield to Maturity on Annual Pay
and Semiannual Pay Bonds

While Treasury, corporate, and municipal bonds issued in the United States are semiannual-pay bonds, Eurodollar fixed rate bonds are annual-pay bonds. The yield to maturity on an annual pay security such a Eurodollar fixed rate bond is just the interest rate that will make the present value of the annual cash flows equal to the total payment (invoice price). To convert the yield to maturity of an annual pay-bond to a yield to maturity on a bond equivalent basis, the following formula should be used:

Yield to maturity on a bond equivalent basis
$$= 2\left[(1 + \text{Yield to maturity})^{1/2} - 1\right].$$

Illustration 6-8.   Suppose the yield to maturity on a Eurodollar fixed rate bond is 9%. The yield to maturity for this bond on a bond equivalent basis is

$$2\left[(1.09)^{1/2} - 1\right]$$
$$= 2\,(1.0440 - 1)$$
$$= .088 \text{ or } 8.8\%$$

Notice that the yield to maturity on a bond equivalent basis will be less than the yield to maturity computed for an annual-pay bond.

---

[3] For example, in Chapter 16, we shall discuss the yield calculations for mortgage pass-through securities. The periodic interest rate is computed on a monthly basis. To compute an annual yield, the practice is first to compute an effective semiannual yield as follows:

Effective semiannual yield $= (1 + \text{Monthly interest rate})^6 - 1$.

Then the effective semiannual yield is doubled.

Yield to Call

For a callable bond, investors also compute another yield (or internal-rate-of-return) measure, the *yield to call*. The cash flows for computing the yield to call are those that would result if the issue were called on its first call date. The yield to call is the interest rate that will make the present value of the cash flows if the bond is held to the first call date equal to the price of the bond (or total payment).

Mathematically, the yield to call can be expressed as follows for a bond on which the next coupon payment will be due six months from now:

$$p = \frac{c}{(1+y)^1} + \frac{c}{(1+y)^2} + \frac{c}{(1+y)^3} + \cdots + \frac{c}{(1+y)^{n^*}} + \frac{CP}{(1+y)^{n^*}} ,$$

where

p = Price ($);
c = *Semiannual* coupon interest ($);
CP = Call price ($);
n^* = Number of periods until first call date (number of years × 2);
y = One-half the yield to call.

For a semiannual-pay bond, doubling the interest rate (y) gives the yield to call.

Alternatively, the above relationship can be expressed as follows:

$$p = \sum_{t=1}^{n^*} \frac{c}{(1+y)^t} + \frac{CP}{(1+y)^{n^*}} .$$

The next two illustrations show how the yield to call is computed.

Illustration 6-9. In Illustrations 6-1 and 6-3 we computed the current yield and yield to maturity for an 18-year, 6% coupon bond selling for $700.89. Suppose that this bond is callable in five years at $1,030. The cash flows for this bond if it is called in five years are:

Exhibit 6-3
Computation of Yield to Call for an 18-Year, 6% Coupon Bond, Callable in 5 Years at $1,030, Selling at $700.89

Objective: Find—by trial and error—the semiannual interest rate that will make the present value of the following cash flows equal to $700.89:

10 coupon payments of $30 every six months;
$1,030 10 six-month periods from now.

Annual interest rate	Semi-annual rate	Present value of 10 payments of $30 (*)	Present value of $1,030 10 periods from now (**)	Present value of cash flows
11.20%	5.60%	$225.05	$597.31	$822.36
11.70	5.85	222.38	583.35	805.73
12.20	6.10	219.76	569.75	789.51
12.70	6.35	217.19	556.50	773.69
13.20	6.60	214.66	543.58	758.24
13.70	6.85	212.18	531.00	743.18
14.20	7.10	209.74	518.73	728.47
14.70	7.35	207.34	506.78	714.12
15.20	7.60	204.99	495.12	700.11

*
$$\$30 \left[\frac{1 - \left[\dfrac{1}{(1 + \text{Semiannual interest rate})^{10}} \right]}{\text{Semiannual interest rate}} \right].$$

**
$$\$1,030 \left[\frac{1}{(1 + \text{Semiannual interest rate})^{10}} \right].$$

(1) 10 coupon payments of $30 every six months and
(2) $1,030 in 10 six-month periods from now.

The value for y that we seek is the one that will make the present values of the cash flows equal to $700.89. From Exhibit 6-3 it can be seen that when y is 7.6%, the present value of the cash flows is $700.11, which is close enough to $700.89 for our purposes. Therefore, the yield to call on a bond equivalent basis is 15.2% (double the periodic interest rate of 7.6%).

Illustration 6-10. In Illustrations 6-2 and 6-4 we computed the current yield and yield to maturity for a 19 year, 11% coupon bond selling for $1,233.64. Suppose that this bond is callable in six years at $1,055. If the bond is called on the first call date, the cash flows for this bond would be:

(1) 12 coupon payments of $55 every six months and
(2) $1,055 in 12 six-month periods from now.

Exhibit 6-4 shows the present value of the cash flows for several interest rates. The interest rate that equates the present value of the cash flows to the price of $1,233.64 is approximately 3.55% Therefore, the yield to call on a bond equivalent basis is 7.1%.

Other Yield-to-Call Measures

Other yield-to-call measures are used by some investors. Each is just a calculation of an internal rate of return. *Yield to par call* assumes that the call price used in the calculation is the par value. *Yield to worst* is the minimum yield (internal rate of return) based on a calculation of yield to call for all possible call dates and the yield to maturity.

Yield (Internal Rate of Return) for a Portfolio

The yield for a portfolio of bonds is not simply the average or weighted average of the yield to maturity of the individual bond issues in the portfolio. It is computed by determining the cash flows for the portfolio and determining the interest rate that will make the present value of the cash flows equal to the market value of the portfolio.[4]

---

[4] In Chapter 10 we shall discuss the concept of duration. A good approximation to the yield for a portfolio can be obtained by using duration to weight the yield to maturity of the individual bonds in the portfolio.

Exhibit 6-4
Computation of Yield to Call for a 19-Year, 11% Coupon Bond, Callable in 6 Years at $1,055, Selling at $1,233.64

Objective: Find—by trial and error—the semiannual interest rate that will make the present value of the following cash flows equal to $1,233.64:

12 coupon payments of $55 every six months;
$1,000 12 six-month periods from now.

Annual interest rate	Semi-annual rate	Present value of 12 payments of $55 (*)	Present value of $1,055 12 per-iods from now (**)	Present value of cash flows
5.10%	2.55%	$562.47	$779.87	$1,342.34
5.60	2.80	554.06	757.42	1,311.48
6.10	3.05	545.84	735.66	1,281.50
6.60	3.30	537.79	714.58	1,252.37
7.10	3.55	529.92	694.15	1,224.07
7.60	3.80	522.22	674.35	1,196.57

*
$$\$55 \left[\frac{1 - \left[\dfrac{1}{(1 + \text{Semiannual interest rate})^{12}} \right]}{\text{Semiannual interest rate}} \right].$$

**
$$\$1,055 \left[\frac{1}{(1 + \text{Semiannual interest rate})^{12}} \right].$$

Illustration 6-11.   Consider the following three-bond portfolio:[5]

Bond	Coupon rate	Maturity	Par value	Price value	Yield to maturity
A	7.0%	5 years	$10,000,000	$ 9,209,000	9.0%
B	10.5%	7 years	$20,000,000	$20,000,000	10.5%
C	6.0%	3 years	$30,000,000	$28,050,000	8.5%

[5] To simplify the illustration, it is assumed that the coupon payment date is the same for each bond

The portfolio's total market value is $57,259,000. The cash flow for each bond in the portfolio and for the whole portfolio is given below:

Period cash flow received	Bond A	Bond B	Bond C	Portfolio
1	$350,000	$1,050,000	$900,000	$2,300,000
2	350,000	1,050,000	900,000	2,300,000
3	350,000	1,050,000	900,000	2,300,000
4	350,000	1,050,000	900,000	2,300,000
5	350,000	1,050,000	900,000	2,300,000
6	350,000	1,050,000	30,900,000	32,300,000
7	350,000	1,050,000	—	1,400,000
8	350,000	1,050,000	—	1,400,000
9	350,000	1,050,000	—	1,400,000
10	10,350,000	1,050,000	—	11,400,000
11	—	1,050,000	—	1,050,000
12	—	1,050,000	—	1,050,000
13	—	1,050,000	—	1,050,000
14	—	21,050,000	—	21,050,000

To determine the yield (internal rate of return) for this three-bond portfolio, the interest rate that makes the present value of the cash flows shown in the last column of the table above equal to $57,259,000 (the total market value of the portfolio) must be found. If an interest rate of 4.77% is used, the present value of the cash flows will equal $57,259,000. Doubling 4.77% gives 9.54%, which is the yield on the portfolio on a bond equivalent basis.

Summary

In this chapter we have explained three conventional yield measures: (1) current yield, (2) yield to maturity, and (3) yield to call. Exhibit 6-5 summarizes the formulas presented in this chapter to calculate these yield measures. The shortcomings of these measures for evaluating the potential return from owning a bond are explained in the next chapter.

Exhibit 6-5
Summary of Formulas for Conventional Yield Measures

(1) Current yield:

$$\text{Current yield} = \frac{\text{Annual dollar coupon interest}}{\text{Price}}$$

(2) Yield to maturity for a bond with a coupon payment due six months from now — solve for y:

$$p = \frac{c}{(1+y)^1} + \frac{c}{(1+y)^2} + \frac{c}{(1+y)^3} + \cdots + \frac{c}{(1+y)^n} + \frac{M}{(1+y)^n}$$

or

$$p = \sum_{t=1}^{n} \frac{c}{(1+y)^t} + \frac{M}{(1+y)^n},$$

where
  p = Price;
  c = *Semiannual* coupon interest ($);
  M = Maturity value ($);
  n = Number of periods (number of years $\times 2$);
  y = One-half the yield to maturity.

For a semiannual-pay bond,

$$\text{Yield to maturity} = 2 \text{ times } y.$$

(3) Yield to maturity for a zero coupon bond:

$$y = (\text{Future value per dollar invested})^{1/n} - 1,$$

where
  y = One-half the yield to maturity;

$$\text{Future value per dollar invested} = \frac{\text{Maturity value}}{\text{Price}}$$

$$\text{Yield to maturity} = 2 \text{ times } y.$$

(4) Yield to maturity when the settlement date is between coupon payments — solve for y:

$$tp = \frac{w \times c}{(1 + y)^w} + \frac{c}{(1 + y)^{1 + w}} + \frac{c}{(1 + y)^{2 + w}} + \cdots$$

$$+ \frac{c}{(1 + y)^{n - 1 + w}} + \frac{M}{(1 + y)^{n - 1 + w}}$$

or

$$tp = \frac{w \times c}{(1 + y)^w} + \sum_{t = 2}^{n} \frac{c}{(1 + y)^{t - 1 + w}} + \frac{M}{(1 + y)^{n - 1 + w}},$$

where

    tp = Total payment (\$) (price plus accrued interest);
    c = *Semiannual* coupon payment (\$);
    M = Maturity value;
    n = Number of coupons payments remaining;
    y = One-half yield to maturity;

    $w = \dfrac{\text{Number of days between settlement and the next coupon payment}}{\text{Number of days in the coupon period}}.$

Yield to maturity = 2 times y.

(5) Yield to call — solve for y:

$$p = \frac{c}{(1 + y)^1} + \frac{c}{(1 + y)^2} + \frac{c}{(1 + y)^3} + \cdots + \frac{c}{(1 + y)^{n^*}} + \frac{CP}{(1 + y)^{n^*}}$$

or

$$p = \sum_{t = 1}^{n^*} \frac{c}{(1 + y)^t} + \frac{CP}{(1 + y)^{n^*}},$$

where

    p = Price (\$);
    c = *Semiannual* coupon interest (\$);
    CP = Call price (\$);
    n^* = Number of periods until first call date (number of years $\times$ 2);
    y = One-half the yield to call.

Exhibit 6-5 continued.

For a semiannual-pay bond,

$$\text{Yield to call} = 2 \text{ times } y.$$

(6) Yield to worst:

Lowest of (yield to maturity; all possible yields to call).

7
Potential Sources
of Dollar Return

To make an intelligent decision about the attractiveness of a bond, an investor must be able to measure the potential yield from owning it. This requires an understanding of the potential sources of dollar return from investing in a bond and then converting the total dollar return from all sources into a yield measure that can be used to compare different bonds.

The purpose of this chapter is threefold: (1) to explain the potential sources of dollar return, (2) to examine the characteristics of a bond that affect its dollar return, and (3) to analyze whether the conventional measures of yield discussed in Chapter 6 appropriately account for the potential sources of dollar return. In the next chapter, we'll present a measure of yield that is more useful to an investor in evaluating the relative value of bonds.

Potential Sources of Dollar Return

When an investor owns a bond, the dollar return that he expects to receive takes the form of the periodic interest payments made by the issuer (that is, the coupon interest payments) and any capital appreciation realized when the bond is sold. For example, suppose that an investor buys a 20-year, 7% coupon bond with a par value of $1,000 for $816. If this investor expects to hold this bond until it matures, he will receive 40 coupon interest payments of $35, one every six months, and at the end of 20 years he will receive $1,000 for the bond he purchased for $816. This will result in a capital gain of $184. Consequently, an investor who buys this bond and holds it to maturity expects a return in the form of 40 semiannual coupon interest payments of $35 and a capital gain of $184.

There is, however, another potential source for a bond's dollar return that may not be recognized by many investors. This source is the interest income that can be realized by reinvesting the coupon interest payments. For example, when an investor receives the first $35 coupon interest payment from the bond issuer, he must do something with that money. If he invests the money in another instrument for the next 19.5 years, this reinvestment will add to the return from holding the bond. This is also true for the second coupon interest payment of $35, which can be invested for 19 years, and subsequent coupon interest payments. This potential source of return is referred to as the *interest-on-interest* component of a bond's dollar return.

You might expect that since the interest-on-interest component is ignored by most individual investors, it cannot be terribly important. In fact, for certain bonds, the interest-on-interest component can comprise more than 50% of a bond's potential dollar return.

Conventional Measures and the Three Potential Sources of a Bond's Dollar Return

To summarize what we have said so far, an investor who purchases a bond can expect to receive a dollar return from one or more of the following sources:

(1) The periodic interest payments made by the issuer (that is, the coupon interest payments),

(2) Any capital gain (or capital loss which reduces the dollar return) when the bond matures or is sold, and

(3) Income from reinvestment of the periodic interest payments (the interest-on-interest component).

Any measure of a bond's potential yield should consider each of the three potential sources of return. Do the three conventional bond measures (current yield, yield to maturity, and yield to call) take into account these three potential sources of return?

The current yield considers only the coupon interest payments. No consideration is given to any capital gain (or loss) or interest on interest.

The yield to maturity takes into account coupon interest and any capital gain (or loss). It also considers the interest-on-interest component; however, implicit in the computation of the yield to maturity is the assumption that the coupon payments can be reinvested at the computed yield to maturity. The yield to maturity, therefore, is a *promised* yield. That is, the promised yield to maturity will be realized if (1) the bond is held to maturity and (2) the coupon interest payments are reinvested at the yield to maturity. If either (1) or (2) does not occur, the actual yield realized by an investor can be greater than or less than the yield to maturity.

For example, for our 20-year, 7% coupon bond selling at $816, the yield to maturity is 9%. Thus, if an investor buys this bond, holds it to maturity and reinvests each semiannual coupon payment at 9% until the maturity date, the promised yield to maturity of 9% at the time of purchase will be realized. We'll demonstrate this in the next section.

Although the yield to maturity does consider the interest-on-interest component of a bond's potential dollar return, the assumption that the coupon interest payments can be reinvested at the yield to maturity is not very realistic. For example, in October 1981, an investor could have purchased an investment grade coupon bond offering a yield to maturity of 17%. To realize that promised yield, each coupon payment had to be reinvested at a rate of interest equal to 17%. In recent years, however, yields on investment grade bonds have not been anything near this rate. Thus, it is unlikely that a 17% yield would be realized by the investor by holding the bond to maturity.

The yield to call also takes into account all three potential sources of return. In this case, the assumption is that the coupon payments can be reinvested at the yield to call. Therefore, it suffers from the same drawback concerning the implicit assumption of the reinvestment rate of the coupon interest payments.

Computation of the Interest-on-Interest Component of a Bond's Dollar Return

The interest-on-interest component can represent a substantial portion of a bond's potential return. In this section we shall explain how to determine the contribution of the interest-on-interest component.

The portion of the potential total dollar return from coupon interest and interest on interest can be computed by using the formula for the future value of an annuity (see Exhibit 2-2 of Chapter 2):

$$FV = A \left[\frac{(1+i)^n - 1}{i} \right]$$

where
A = Amount of the annuity ($);
m = Number of payments per year;
i = Annual interest rate divided by m (in decimal);
n = Number of periods ($N \times m$).

For purposes of computing the coupon interest and interest on interest for a bond paying semiannual coupon interest,

A = *Semiannual* coupon interest ($);
m = 2;
i = *Semiannual* reinvestment rate (in decimal);
n = Double the number of years to maturity.

Letting

c = *Semiannual* coupon interest ($)
and
r = *Semiannual* reinvestment rate (in decimal),

we can rewrite the formula for the future value of an annuity for computing the coupon interest plus interest on interest, as

Coupon interest
plus $= c \left[\dfrac{(1+r)^n - 1}{r} \right].$
interest on interest

The total coupon interest is found by multiplying the semi-annual coupon interest by the number of periods; that is,

$$\text{Total coupon interest} = n \times c.$$

The interest-on-interest component is then the difference between the coupon interest plus interest on interest and the total coupon interest. Mathematically, this can be expressed as

$$\text{Interest on interest} \ = c \left[\frac{(1 + r)^n - 1}{r} \right] - n \times c .$$

The reinvestment rate assumed for the yield to maturity is the yield to maturity.

The three illustrations that follow demonstrate the application of the above formulas, as well as the importance of the interest-on-interest component as a source of potential return from a bond.

Illustration 7-1. Suppose that an investor is considering purchasing a seven-year issue selling at par ($1,000) and having a coupon rate of 9%. Since this bond is selling at par, the yield to maturity is 9%.

Remember that a yield to maturity of 9% as conventionally computed means a 4.5% semiannual yield.[1] If an investor is promised a yield of 4.5% for 14 six-month periods (seven years) on a $1,000 investment, the amount at the end of 14 six-month periods should be[2]

$$\$1,000 \ (1.045)^{14} = \$1,852 .$$

Since the investment is $1,000, the total dollar return that the investor expects is $852.

Let's look at the total dollar return from holding this bond to maturity. The total dollar return comes from two sources:

---

[1] See Chapter 6, page 96.

[2] This is just an application of the future value of $1 formula, Chapter 2, page 9.

(1) Coupon interest of $45 every six months for seven years, and

(2) Interest earned from reinvesting the semiannual coupon interest payments at 4.5%.

Since the bond is selling at par, no capital gain will be realized by holding the bond to maturity.

For this bond:

$$c = \$45;$$
$$m = 2;$$
$$r = .045 \ (= .09/2);$$
$$n = 14 (= 7 \times 2)$$

Coupon interest
plus $= \$45 \left[\dfrac{(1.045)^{14} - 1}{.045} \right]$
interest on interest

$$= \$45 \left[\frac{1.8519 - 1}{.045} \right]$$

$$= \$45 \ (18.9321)$$
$$= \$852 \ .$$

Notice that the total dollar return for this bond is the same as that which we computed for an investment of $1,000 for 14 six-month periods at 4.5%.

The total coupon interest is $14 \times \$45 = \$630$.

The interest-on-interest component is then $222, as shown below:

$$\text{Interest on interest} \ = \$45 \left[\frac{(1.045)^{14} - 1}{.045} \right] - 14 \ (\$45)$$

$$= \$852 - \$630$$
$$= \$222.$$

Interest on interest as a percentage of total dollar return is

$$\frac{\$222}{\$852} = 26\%.$$

For this seven-year, 9% coupon bond selling at par to offer a yield to maturity of 9%, 26% of this bond's total dollar return must come from reinvesting the coupon payments at a simple annual interest rate of 9%.

Illustration 7-2. Suppose that an investor is considering a 20-year, 7% coupon bond selling for $816. The yield to maturity for this bond is 9%.

First, let's consider how much the total dollar return should be for an investment of $816 for 40 six-month periods if the semi-annual yield is 4.5%. The total future amount would be $4,476, because

$$\$816 \ (1.045)^{40} = \$4,746.$$

Since the investment is $816, the total dollar return should be $3,930.

Now let's look at the $816 investment in the bond. The total dollar return from holding this bond to maturity comes from all three sources:

(1) Coupon interest of $35 every six months for 20 years,
(2) Interest earned from reinvesting the semiannual coupon interest payments at 4.5%, and
(3) A capital gain of $184 (= $1,000 − $816).

For this bond;

$$c = \$35;$$
$$m = 2;$$
$$r = .045 \ (= .09/2);$$
$$n = 40 \ (= 20 \times 2).$$

Coupon interest plus interest on interest

$$= \$35 \left[\frac{(1.045)^{40} - 1}{.045} \right]$$

$$= \$35 \left[\frac{5.8164 - 1}{.045} \right]$$

$$= \$35 \ (107.031)$$

$$= \$3,746.$$

The total coupon interest is 40 × $35 = $1,400.

The interest-on-interest component is then $2,346, as shown by the following calculation:

$$\text{Interest on interest} = \$35 \left[\frac{(1.045)^{40} - 1}{.045} \right] - 40 \, (\$35)$$

$$= \$3,746 - \$1,400$$
$$= \$2,346.$$

The total dollar return is then:

Total coupon interest	$1,400
Interest on interest	2,346
Capital gain	184
Total	$3,930

Once again, the total dollar return is the same as that which would be expected from investing $816 for 40 six-month periods at 4.5%. The percentage breakdown of the total dollar return is

Total coupon interest	35%
Interest on interest	60%
Capital gain	5%

Hence, for this bond, the interest-on-interest component must comprise 60% of total dollar return if the investor is to realize a 9% yield to maturity.

Illustration 7-3.   The two previous illustrations have shown the computation of the interest-on-interest component for a bond selling at par (Illustration 7.1) and a bond selling at a discount (Illustration 7.2), both with a yield to maturity of 9%. Now let's consider a bond selling at a premium with a yield to maturity of 9%. Suppose an investor is considering a 12% coupon bond with 25 years to maturity selling for $1,296. The yield to maturity is 9%.

The total dollar return from holding this bond to maturity is composed of

(1) Coupon interest of $60 every six months for 25 years,
(2) Interest earned from reinvesting the semiannual coupon interest payments at 4.5%, and
(3) A capital loss of $296 (= $1,000 − $1,296)

For this premium bond:

$c = \$60;$
$m = 2;$
$r = .045 \ (= .09/2);$
$n = 50 \ (= 25 \times 2)$

Coupon interest
plus $= \$60 \left[\dfrac{(1.045)^{50} - 1}{.045} \right]$
interest on interest

$\qquad\qquad\qquad = \$60 \left[\dfrac{9.0326 - 1}{.045} \right]$

$\qquad\qquad\qquad = \$60 \ (178.503)$
$\qquad\qquad\qquad = \$10,710.$

The total coupon interest is $50 \times \$60 = \$3,000$.

The interest-on-interest component is then $7,710, as shown below:

Interest on interest $\ = \$60 \left[\dfrac{(1.045)^{50} - 1}{.045} \right] - 50 \ (\$60)$

$\qquad\qquad\qquad\quad = \$10,710 - \$3,000$
$\qquad\qquad\qquad\quad = \$7,710.$

The total dollar return is then

Total coupon interest	$ 3,000
Interest on interest	7,710
Capital loss	(296)
Total	$10,414

The percentage breakdown of the total dollar return is

Total coupon interest	29%
Interest on interest	74%
Capital loss	-3%

For this long-term bond selling at a premium, the interest on interest represents 74% of the total dollar return necessary to produce a 9% yield to maturity.

To see that the total dollar return from investing in this bond agrees with an investment of $1,296 for 50 six-month periods at 4.5%, the future value is

$$\$1,296 \ (1.045)^{50} = \$11,706.$$

Subtracting from the future value the investment of $1,296 gives the total dollar return of $10,410. (The difference between $10,414 and $10,410 is due to rounding.)

Bond Characteristics That Affect the Importance of the Interest-on-Interest Component

There are two characteristics of a bond that determine the importance of the interest-on-interest component: maturity and coupon.

The Effect of Maturity

For a given yield to maturity and a given coupon rate, the longer the maturity of a bond, the greater the interest-on-interest component as a percentage of the total dollar return. The following three illustrations demonstrate this characteristic.

Illustration 7-4.   Consider a 20-year, 9% coupon bond selling at par for a yield to maturity of 9%. Using the formulas presented in the previous section, the total dollar return would be $4,816, broken down as follows:

Total coupon interest	$1,800
Interest on interest	3,016
Total	$4,816

Comparing this bond with the seven-year, 9% coupon bond selling at 9% in Illustration 7-1, we find:

	Total dollar return		% Dollar return	
	7-year	20-year	7-year	20-year
Total coupon interest	$630	$1,800	74%	37%
Interest on interest	222	3,016	26	63
Total	$852	$4,816	100%	100%

The interest-on-interest component is 26% of the total dollar return on the seven-year bond but 63% of the total dollar return for the 20-year bond.

Illustration 7-5.   Consider a five-year, 7% coupon bond selling for $921, thereby offering a yield to maturity of 9%. The breakdown of the total dollar return is:

Total coupon interest	$350
Interest on interest	80
Capital gain	79
Total	$509

A comparison of this bond with the 20-year, 7% bond analyzed in Illustration 7-2 is given below:

	Total dollar return		% Dollar return	
	5-year	20-year	5-year	20-year
Total coupon interest	$350	$1,400	69%	35%
Interest on interest	80	2,346	16	60
Capital gain	79	184	15	5
Total	$509	$3,930	100%	100%

Only 16% of the bond's total dollar return needed to produce a 9% yield to maturity comes from the reinvestment of coupon interest for the five-year bond, compared to 60% for the 20-year bond.

Illustration 7-6.   For a seven-year, 12% coupon bond selling at $1,153 with a yield to maturity of 9%, the total dollar return is as follows:

Total coupon interest	$840
Interest on interest	296
Capital loss	(153)
Total	$983

In Illustration 7-3, the total dollar return breakdown for a 25-year, 12% coupon bond priced to give a yield to maturity of 9% was computed. A comparison of the bond in this illustration with the one in Illustration 7-3 is given below:

	Total dollar return		% Dollar return	
	7-year	*25-year*	*7-year*	*25-year*
Total coupon interest	$840	$ 3,000	85 %	29%
Interest on interest	296	7,710	30	74
Capital loss	(153)	(296)	– 5	– 3
Total	$983	$10,414	100 %	100%

For the longer term bond, the interest-on-interest component is 74% of the potential total dollar return, compared with 30% for the seven-year bond.

The Effect of Coupon Rate

For a given maturity and a given yield to maturity, the higher the coupon rate, the more dependent the bond's total dollar return necessary to produce some yield to maturity will be on the reinvestment of coupon interest. This means that holding maturity and yield to maturity constant, premium bonds will be more dependent on the interest-on-interest component than bonds selling at par. Discount bonds will be less dependent on the interest-on-interest component than bonds selling at par. These statements are verified in the illustrations below.

Illustration 7-7. Let's compare the total dollar return break-down of the 20-year, 9% coupon bond selling at par to offer a yield to maturity of 9% (Illustration 7-4) with a 20-year, 5% coupon bond selling at $632 to offer a yield to maturity of 9%. The breakdown of the total dollar return and the percentage return for each bond, which demonstrates that a lower coupon (discount) bond is less dependent on the interest-on-interest component than the higher coupon (par) bond, is summarized below:

	Total dollar return		% Dollar return	
	5% coupon (discount)	9% coupon (par)	5% coupon (discount)	9% coupon (par)
Total coupon interest	$1,000	$1,800	33%	37%
Interest on interest	1,676	3,016	55	63
Capital gain	368	0	12	0
Total	$3,044	$4,816	100%	100%

Illustration 7-8. A comparison of a seven-year, 9% coupon bond selling at par to offer a yield to maturity of 9% with a seven-year, 14% coupon bond selling at $1,256 to offer a yield to maturity of 9%, summarized below, shows that a bond selling at par is less dependent on the reinvestment of coupon interest than a premium bond:

	Total dollar return		% Dollar return	
	9% coupon (par)	14% coupon (premium)	9% coupon (par)	14% coupon (premium)
Total coupon interest	$630	$980	74%	92%
Interest on interest	222	345	26	32
Capital gain	0	(256)	0	-24
Total	$852	$1,069	100%	100%

Zero-coupon bonds. For zero-coupon bonds, none of the bond's total dollar return is made up of interest on interest. The reason, of course, is that no coupon interest is paid.

Summary and Investment Implications

In this chapter we have explained the three potential sources of dollar return from investing in a bond: (1) coupon interest, (2) interest on interest, and (3) capital gain (or loss). The shortcomings of the three conventional yield measures with respect to each of these sources are explained. The yield to maturity considers all three sources, but this measure assumes that all coupon interest can be reinvested at the yield to maturity. The yield to call assumes that the coupon interest can be reinvested at the yield to call.

The formulas for computing the interest-on-interest component are presented and applied. The formulas are summarized in Exhibit 7-1. For some bonds, particularly high-coupon, long-term bonds, the interest-on-interest component can be well in excess of 50% of the total dollar return in order to generate the promised yield to maturity. The longer the term of a coupon bond, all other factors constant, the greater is the interest-on-interest component needed to realize the promised yield to maturity. Lower coupon bonds, all other factors constant, are less dependent on the reinvestment of coupon interest than higher coupon bonds. For zero-coupon bonds, none of the bond's total dollar return necessary to generate the yield to maturity at the time of purchase is dependent on the reinvestment of coupon interest.

This chapter has focused on bonds that pay interest semiannually. The same principles apply to fixed income instruments with more frequent cash flow payments, such as mortgage pass-through securities.[3] The interest-on-interest component becomes even more important for such securities.

---

[3] See Chapters 15 and 16.

Exhibit 7-1
Summary of Formulas for Computing the Interest-on-Interest Components of a Bond's Total Dollar Return

(1) Coupon interest plus interest on interest:

$$\text{Coupon interest plus interest on interest} = c \left[\frac{(1 + r)^n - 1}{r} \right].$$

where
c = Semiannual coupon interest (\$);
n = Number of periods to maturity;
r = Semiannual reinvestment rate (in decimal).

The reinvestment rate assumed for the yield to maturity is the yield to maturity.

(2) Total coupon interest:

$$\text{Total coupon interest} = n \times c.$$

(3) Interest on interest:

$$\text{Interest on interest} = c \left[\frac{(1 + r)^n - 1}{r} \right] - n \times c.$$

8
Horizon Return

In the previous chapter, we explained the three potential sources of dollar return from investing in a bond. We also demonstrated the importance of the interest-on-interest component as a source of dollar return. In this chapter, we will present a yield measure that is more meaningful than the commonly used yield to maturity and yield to call for assessing the attractiveness of a bond in a portfolio. This yield measure is called the *horizon return*.[1]

Another Look at the Drawbacks of the Yield to Maturity and Yield to Call

Yield to Maturity

In the previous chapter, we explained that the yield to maturity is a *promised* yield. At the time of purchase, an investor is promised a yield, as measured by the yield to maturity, if both of the following conditions are satisfied:

(1) The bond is held to maturity, and
(2) All coupon interest payments are reinvested at the yield to maturity.

---

[1] Other names used for this yield measure by bond market participants are realized compound yield, total return, holding period return, effective yield, holding period yield, and investment horizon return. The term realized compound yield was first used by Sidney Homer and Martin Leibowitz in *Inside the Yield Book* (Prentice-Hall/New York Institute of Finance, 1972).

We focused on the second assumption in the previous chapter, where we showed that the interest-on-interest component for a bond may constitute a substantial portion of the bond's total dollar return. Therefore, failure to reinvest the coupon interest payments at a rate of interest at least equal to the yield to maturity will produce a yield less than the yield to maturity. This risk is called *reinvestment risk*.

Rather than assume that the coupon interest payments are reinvested at a rate of interest equal to the yield to maturity, nothing prevents an investor from making an explicit assumption about the reinvestment rate based on his expectations. The horizon return is a measure of yield that incorporates an explicit assumption about the reinvestment rate.

Let's take a careful look at the first assumption. An investor need not hold a bond until maturity. Suppose, for example, that an investor who has a five-year investment horizon is considering the following four bonds:

Bond	Coupon	Maturity	Yield to Maturity
A	5%	3 years	9.0%
B	6%	20 years	8.6%
C	11%	15 years	9.2%
D	8%	5 years	8.0%

Assuming that all four bonds are of the same credit quality, which one is the most attractive to this investor? An investor who selects Bond C because it offers the highest yield to maturity is failing to recognize that the bond must be sold after five years at a price depending on the yield required in the market for 10-year, 11% coupon bonds at the time. Hence, there could be a capital gain or capital loss that will make the return higher or lower than the yield to maturity promised now. Moreover, the higher coupon on Bond C relative to the other three bonds means that more of this bond's return will be dependent on the reinvestment of coupon interest payments.

Bond A offers the second highest yield to maturity. On the surface, it seems to be particularly attractive because it eliminates the problem posed by purchasing Bond C of realizing a possible capital loss when the bond must be sold prior to the maturity date. In addition, the reinvestment risk seems to be less than for the other three bonds because the coupon rate is the lowest. The investor would not be eliminating the reinvestment risk, however, since after three years he must reinvest the proceeds received at maturity for two more years. The yield that the investor will realize will depend on interest rates three years from now, when the investor must roll over the proceeds.

Which is the best bond? The yield to maturity doesn't seem to be helping us answer this question. The answer depends on the expectations of the investor. Specifically, it depends on the interest rate at which the coupon interest payments can be reinvested until the end of the investor's investment horizon. Also, for bonds with a maturity longer than the investment horizon, it depends on the investor's expectations about interest rates at the end of the investment horizon. Consequently, any of these bonds can be the best investment vehicle on the basis of some reinvestment rate and some future interest rate at the end of the investment horizon. The horizon return measure takes these expectations into account.

Yield to Call

The yield to call is subject to the same problems as the yield to maturity. First, it assumes that the bond will be held until the first call date. Second, it assumes that the coupon interest payments will be reinvested at the yield to call. If an investor's investment horizon is shorter than the time to the first call date, then the potential of having to sell the bond below its acquisition cost exists. If, on the other hand, the investment horizon is longer than the time to the first call date, there is the problem of reinvesting the proceeds when the bond is called until the end of the investment horizon. Consequently, the yield to call doesn't tell us very much. The horizon return, however, can accommodate the analysis of callable bonds.

Computing the Horizon Return for a Bond Held to Maturity

The idea underlying the horizon return is simple. The objective is to compute the total future amount that will result from an investment. The horizon return is the interest rate that will make the initial investment in the bond grow to the computed total future amount. To illustrate the computation, we will first show how the horizon return is computed, assuming a bond is held to the maturity date.

The procedure for computing the horizon return for a bond held to maturity can be summarized as follows. For an assumed reinvestment rate, the dollar return that will be available at maturity can be computed from both the coupon interest payments and the interest-on-interest component. Recall that in the previous chapter we explained how this can be done. In addition, at maturity the investor will receive the par value. The horizon return is then the interest rate that will make the amount invested in the bond (that is, the current market price plus accrued interest) equal to the total future amount available at the maturity date.

More formally, the steps for computing the horizon return for a bond *held to maturity* are as follows:

Step 1.   Compute the total future amount that will be received from the investment. This is the sum of the amount that will be received from the coupon payments, interest on interest based on the coupon payments and the assumed reinvestment rate, and the par value. The coupon payments plus the interest-on-interest can be computed using the formula presented in the previous chapter:

$$\begin{matrix} \text{Coupon interest} \\ \text{plus} \\ \text{interest on interest} \end{matrix} = c \left[\frac{(1 + r)^n - 1}{r} \right]$$

where

   c = *Semiannual* coupon interest (\$);
   n = Number of periods to maturity;
   r = *Semiannual* reinvestment rate.

In the case of the yield to maturity, the reinvestment rate is assumed to be one half the yield to maturity. In computing the horizon return, the reinvestment rate is set equal to one half the simple annual interest that the investor assumes can be earned by reinvesting the coupon interest payments.

Notice that the total future amount is different from the total dollar return that we have used in showing the importance of the interest-on-interest component in the previous chapter. The total dollar return includes only the capital gain (or capital loss if there is one), not the entire par value, which is used to compute the total future amount. That is,

Total dollar return = Total future amount − Price of bond

Step 2. To obtain the semiannual horizon return, use the following formula:

$$\left[\frac{\text{Total future amount}}{\text{Price of bond}}\right]^{1/n} - 1.$$

This formula is an application of the yield discussed in Chapter 4 for an investment that has only one cash flow.

Step 3. Since interest is assumed to be paid semiannually, double the interest rate found in Step 3. The resulting interest rate is the horizon return (on a bond-equivalent basis).

The four illustrations that follow show how to compute the horizon return.

Illustration 8-1. The horizon return for a seven-year, 9% coupon bond selling at par, assuming a reinvestment rate of 5% (simple annual interest rate), is 8.1%, as shown in Exhibit 8-1. Since this bond is selling at par, its yield to maturity is 9%, yet its horizon return is only 8.1%. The horizon return is less than the yield to maturity because the coupon interest payments are assumed to be reinvested at 5% rather than 9%.

Illustration 8-2. The computation of the horizon return for the bond in the previous illustration, assuming a reinvestment rate of 9%, is shown in Exhibit 8-2. The horizon return is 9%. In this case, the horizon return is equal to the yield to maturity because the coupon interest payments are assumed to be reinvested at 9%.

Exhibit 8-1

Computation of the Horizon Return for a Seven-Year, 9% Bond Selling at Par and Held to Maturity: Reinvestment Rate = 5%

Step 1. The total future amount from this bond includes:

(1) Coupon interest of $45 every six months for seven years,
(2) Interest earned from reinvesting the semiannual coupon interest payments at 2.5% (one-half the assumed annual reinvestment rate), and
(3) The par value of $1,000.

The coupon interest plus interest on interest can be found as follows:

$$c = \$45;$$
$$m = 2;$$
$$r = .025 \ (= .05/2);$$
$$n = 14 \ (= 7 \times 2)$$

$$
\begin{aligned}
\text{Coupon interest plus interest on interest} \quad &= \$45 \left[\frac{(1.025)^{14} - 1}{.025} \right] \\[2mm]
&= \$45 \left[\frac{1.4130 - 1}{.025} \right] \\[2mm]
&= \$45 \,(16.5189) \\[1mm]
&= \$743.35.
\end{aligned}
$$

Total future amount:

Coupon interest plus interest on interest	= $ 743.35
Par value	= 1,000.00
Total	$1,743.35

Step 2. Compute the following:

$$\left[\frac{\$1,743.35}{\$1,000.00}\right]^{1/14} - 1$$

$$= (1.74335)^{.07143} - 1$$
$$= 1.0405 - 1$$
$$= .0405 \text{ or } 4.05\%$$

Step 3. Doubling 4.05% gives a horizon return of 8.1%.

Exhibit 8-2
Computation of the Horizon Return for a Seven-Year, 9% Bond Selling at Par and Held to Maturity: Reinvestment Rate = 9%

Step 1. The total future amount for this bond includes:

(1) Coupon interest of $45 every six months for seven years,
(2) Interest earned from reinvesting the semiannual coupon interest payments at 4.5% (one-half the assumed annual reinvestment rate), and
(3) The par value of $1,000.

The coupon interest plus interest on interest can be found as follows:

$$c = \$45;$$
$$m = 2;$$
$$r = .045 \ (= .09/2);$$
$$n = 14 \ (= 7 \times 2)$$

Coupon interest plus interest on interest

$$= \$45 \left[\frac{(1.045)^{14} - 1}{.045}\right]$$

$$= \$45 \left[\frac{1.8519 - 1}{.045}\right]$$

$$= \$45 \ (18.9321)$$
$$= \$851.94.$$

Exhibit 8-2 continued.

Total future amount:

$$
\begin{array}{ll}
\text{Coupon interest plus} & \\
\text{interest on interest} & = \$\ \ 851.94 \\
\text{Par value} & = \ \underline{1,000.00} \\
\text{Total} & \quad \$1,851.94
\end{array}
$$

Step 2.   Compute the following:

$$
\left[\frac{\$1,851.94}{\$1,000.00} \right]^{1/14} - 1
$$

$$
= (1.85194)^{.07143} - 1
$$
$$
= 1.0450 - 1
$$
$$
= .0405 \text{ or } 4.50\%
$$

Step 3.   Doubling 4.50% gives a horizon return of 9.0%.

Illustration 8-3.   The horizon return for a 20-year, 7% coupon bond selling for $816, assuming a reinvestment rate of 6% (simple annual interest rate), is 7.62%, as shown in Exhibit 8-3. The yield to maturity is 9%. The horizon return is less than the yield to maturity because the coupon interest payments are assumed to be reinvested at 6% rather than 9%.

Illustration 8-4.   The horizon return for the bond in the previous illustration is 10.04% if the reinvestment rate is 11%. The computations are shown in Exhibit 8-4. Since the reinvestment rate is greater than the yield to maturity, the horizon return is greater than the yield to maturity of 9%.

Exhibit 8-3
Computation of the Horizon Return for a 20-Year, 7% Bond
Selling for $816 and Held to Maturity:
Reinvestment Rate = 6%

Step 1. The total future amount from this bond includes:

(1) Coupon interest of $35 every six months for 20 years,
(2) Interest earned from reinvesting the semiannual coupon interest payments at 3% (one-half the assumed annual reinvestment rate), and
(3) The par value of $1,000.

The coupon interest plus interest on interest can be found as follows:

$$c = \$35;$$
$$m = 2;$$
$$r = .03 \, (= .06/2);$$
$$n = 40 \, (= 20 \times 2)$$

Coupon interest
plus $= \$35 \left[\dfrac{(1.03)^{40} - 1}{.03} \right]$
interest on interest

$$= \$35 \left[\frac{3.2620 - 1}{.03} \right]$$

$$= \$35 \, (74.4013)$$
$$= \$2,639.04.$$

Total future amount:

Coupon interest plus interest on interest	= $2,639.04
Par value	= 1,000.00
Total	$3,639.04

Step 2. Compute the following:

Exhibit 8-3 continued.

$$\left[\frac{\$3,639.04}{\$816} \right]^{1/40} - 1$$

$$= (4.45961)^{.025} - 1$$
$$= 1.0381 - 1$$
$$= .0381 \text{ or } 3.81\%$$

Step 3.   Doubling 3.81% gives a horizon return of 7.62%.

Exhibit 8-4
Computation of the Horizon Return for a 20-Year, 7% Bond Selling for $816 and Held to Maturity: Reinvestment Rate = 11%

Step 1.   The total future amount from this bond includes:

(1) Coupon interest of $35 every six months for 20 years,
(2) Interest earned from reinvesting the semiannual coupon interest payments at 5.5% (one-half the assumed annual reinvestment rate), and
(3) The par value of $1,000.

The coupon interest plus interest on interest can be found as follows:

$$c = \$35;$$
$$m = 2;$$
$$r = .055 \ (= .11/2);$$
$$n = 40 \ (= 20 \times 2)$$

Coupon interest plus interest on interest
$$= \$35 \left[\frac{(1.055)^{40} - 1}{.055} \right]$$

$$= \$35 \left[\frac{8.5133 - 1}{.055} \right]$$

$$= \$35 \ (136.6056)$$
$$= \$4,781.20.$$

Total future amount:

Coupon interest plus interest on interest	=	$4,781.20
Par value	=	1,000.00
Total		$5,781.20

Step 2. Compute the following:

$$\left[\frac{\$5,781.20}{\$816} \right]^{1/40} - 1$$
$$= (7.08480)^{.025} - 1$$
$$= 1.0502 - 1$$
$$= .0502 \text{ or } 5.02\%$$

Step 3. Doubling 5.02% gives a horizon return of 10.04%.

Computing the Horizon Return for a Bond to Be Sold Prior to Maturity

The horizon return as calculated above suffers from the same problem as the yield to maturity in that it assumes holding the bond until maturity. Fortunately, it is quite simple to modify the calculation of the horizon return to determine the potential yield from holding it until the end of a predetermined investment horizon. We need only make one adjustment to the three steps given above to calculate the horizon return.

In Step 1, the total future amount is calculated on the basis of (1) the coupon interest payments until the end of the investment horizon, (2) the interest on interest from reinvesting the coupon interest payments until the end of the investment horizon, and (3) the expected price of the bond at the end of the investment horizon.

How does one know the expected price? The expected price depends on the investor's expectations about what interest rates will be at the end of the investment horzion. Given the expected future interest rate for the bond and the remaining time to maturity of the bond, the expected price can easily be determined from the formula for the price of a bond given in Chapter 5 (see Exhibit 5-7):

$$p = \frac{c}{(1+i)^1} + \frac{c}{(1+i)^2} + \frac{c}{(1+i)^3} + \cdots + \frac{c}{(1+i)^n} + \frac{M}{(1+i)^n}$$

where

p = Price ($);
c = *Semiannual* coupon payment ($);
M = Maturity value;
n = Number of periods (number of years times 2);
i = *Semiannual* required yield (in decimal).

In applying this formula, it is important to remember that n is the number of periods remaining to maturity *at the end of the investment horizon*. For example, if the investment horizon is five years and the number of years to maturity at the present time is 20, there would remain 15 years to maturity at the end of the investment horizon. In this case, n would be 30.

The present value of the coupon interest payments in the price formula can be computed by using the following formula (see Chapter 5, Exhibit 5-7):

$$c \left[\frac{1 - \left[\frac{1}{(1+i)^n} \right]}{i} \right]$$

Illustration 8-5. Suppose that an investor with a five- year investment horizon is considering purchasing a seven-year, 9% coupon bond selling at par. The investor expects that he can reinvest the coupon interest payments at an annual interest rate of 9.4% and that at the end of the investment horizon two-year bonds will be selling to offer a yield to maturity of 11.2%. As shown in Exhibit 8-5, the horizon return for this bond is 8.54%. The yield to maturity for this bond is 9%.

Exhibit 8-5
Computation of the Horizon Return for a Seven-Year, 9% Bond Selling at Par and Held for Five Years: Reinvestment Rate = 9.4%

Step 1. The total future amount from this bond includes:

(1) Coupon interest of $45 every six months for five years (the investment horizon),

(2) Interest earned from reinvesting the semiannual coupon interest payments at 4.7% (one-half the assumed annual reinvestment rate) until the end of the investment horizon, and

(3) The expected price of the bond at the end of five years.

The coupon interest plus interest on interest can be found as follows:

$$c = \$45;$$
$$m = 2;$$
$$r = .047 \, (= .094/2);$$

$$\text{Coupon interest plus interest on interest} = \$45 \left[\frac{(1.047)^{10} - 1}{.047} \right]$$

$$= \$45 \left[\frac{1.5830 - 1}{.047} \right]$$

$$= \$45 \, (12.4032)$$

$$= \$558.14.$$

$$n = 10 \, (= 5 \times 2)$$

The expected price of the bond five years from now is determined as follows:

(a) Present value of coupon interest payments, assuming the required yield to maturity at the end of the investment horizon is 11.2%:

Exhibit 8-5 continued.

$$c = \$45;$$
$$i = .056 \, (= .112/2);$$
$$n = 4 \, (= \text{remaining years to maturity} \times 2)$$

$$PV = \$45 \left[\frac{1 - \left[\dfrac{1}{(1.056)^4} \right]}{.056} \right]$$

$$= \$45 \left[\frac{1 - .8042}{.056} \right]$$

$$= \$45 \, (3.4964)$$

$$= \$157.34$$

(b) Present value of the maturity value:

$$\frac{\$1,000}{(1.056)^4} = \$804.16$$

$$\text{Expected price} = \$157.34 + \$804.16$$
$$= \$961.50$$

Total future amount:

Coupon interest plus interest on interest	= $ 558.14
Expected price	= 961.50
Total	$1,519.64

Step 2. Compute the following:

$$\left[\frac{\$1,519.64}{\$1,000.00} \right]^{1/10} - 1$$

$$= (1.51964)^{.10} - 1$$
$$= 1.0427 - 1$$
$$= .0427 \text{ or } 4.27\%$$

Step 3. Doubling 4.27% gives a horizon return of 8.54%.

Illustration 8-6. Suppose that an investor with a three-year investment horizon is considering purchasing a 20-year, 8% coupon bond for $828.40. The investor expects that he can reinvest the coupon interest payments at an annual interest rate of 6% and that at the end of the investment horizon 17 year bonds will be selling to offer a yield to maturity of 7%. The horizon return for this bond is 17.16%. (The computations are shown in Exhibit 8-6.) The yield to maturity for this bond is 10%.

Exhibit 8-6

**Computation of the Horizon Return for a 20-Year, 8% Bond
Selling for $828.40 and Held for Three Years:
Reinvestment Rate = 6%**

Step 1. The total future amount from this bond includes:

(1) Coupon interest of $40 every six months for three years (the investment horizon),

(2) Interest earned from reinvesting the semiannual coupon interest payments at 3% (one-half the assumed annual reinvestment rate), and

(3) The expected price of the bond at the end of three years.

The coupon interest plus interest on interest can be found as follows:

$$c = \$40;$$
$$m = 2;$$
$$r = .03 \ (= .06/2);$$
$$n = 6 \ (= 3 \times 2)$$

$$
\begin{aligned}
\text{Coupon interest plus interest on interest} &= \$40 \left[\frac{(1.03)^6 - 1}{.03} \right] \\
&= \$40 \left[\frac{1.1941 - 1}{.03} \right] \\
&= \$40 \ (6.4684) \\
&= \$258.74.
\end{aligned}
$$

The expected price of the bond three years from now is determined as follows:

Exhibit 8-6 continued.

(a) Present value of coupon interest payments, assuming the required yield to maturity at the end of the investment horizon is 7%:

$$c = \$40;$$
$$i = .035 \ (= .07/2);$$
$$n = 34 \ (= \text{Remaining years to maturity} \times 2)$$

$$PV = \$40 \left[\frac{1 - \left[\frac{1}{(1.035)^{34}} \right]}{.035} \right]$$

$$= \$40 \left[\frac{1 - .3105}{.035} \right]$$

$$= \$40 \ (19.7007)$$

$$= \$788.03$$

$$\frac{\$1,000}{(1.035)^{34}} = \$310.48$$

(b) Present value of the maturity value:

$$\text{Expected price} = \$788.03 + \$310.48$$
$$= \$1,098.51$$

Total future amount:

Coupon interest plus interest on interest	= $ 258.74
Expected price	= 1,098.51
Total	$1,357.25

Step 2. Compute the following:

$$\left[\frac{\$1,357.25}{\$828.40} \right]^{1/6} - 1$$

$$= (1.63840)^{.16667} - 1$$
$$= 1.0858 - 1$$
$$= .0858 \text{ or } 8.58\%$$

Step 3. Doubling 8.58% gives a horizon return of 17.16%.

Illustration 8-7. Suppose that an investor has a six-year investment horizon. The investor is considering a 13-year, 9% coupon bond selling at par. The investor's expectations are as follows:

(1) The first four semiannual coupon payments can be reinvested from the time of receipt to the end of the investment horizon at an annual interest rate of 8%.

(2) The last eight semiannual coupon payments can be reinvested from the time of receipt to the end of the investment horizon at a 10% annual interest rate.

(3) The required yield to maturity on seven-year bonds at the end of the investment horizon is 10.6%.

Based on these three assumptions, the horizon return is 8.14%. The calculations are shown in Exhibit 8-7.

Exhibit 8-7
Computation of the Horizon Return for a 13-Year, 9% Bond
Selling at Par and Held for Six Years:
Two Different Reinvestment Rates

Step 1.   The total future amount from this bond includes:

  (1) Coupon interest of $45 every six months for six years (the investment horizon),
  (2) Interest earned from reinvesting the first four semiannual coupon interest payments at 4% (one-half the assumed annual reinvestment rate) until the end of the investment horizon,
  (3) Interest earned from reinvesting the last eight semiannual coupon interest payments at 5% (one-half the assumed annual reinvestment rate) until the end of the investment horizon, and
  (4) The expected price of the bond at the end of six years.

The coupon interest plus interest on interest for the first four coupon payments can be found as follows:

$$c = \$45;$$
$$m = 2;$$
$$r = .04 \ (= .08/2);$$
$$n = 4$$

Coupon interest plus interest on interest

$$= \$45 \left[\frac{(1.04)^4 - 1}{.04} \right]$$

$$= \$45 \left[\frac{1.1699 - 1}{.04} \right]$$

$$= \$45 \ (4.2465)$$

$$= \$191.09.$$

This gives the coupon interest plus interest on interest as of the end of the second year (four periods). Reinvesting at 4% until the end of the investment, four years or eight periods later, $191.09 will grow to

$$\$191.09 \ (1.04)^8 = \$261.52$$

The coupon interest plus interest on interest for the last eight coupon payments can be found as follows:

$$c = \$45;$$
$$m = 2;$$
$$r = .05 \ (= .10/2);$$
$$n = 8$$

Coupon interest plus interest on interest

$$= \$45 \left[\frac{(1.05)^8 - 1}{.05} \right]$$

$$= \$45 \left[\frac{1.47746 - 1}{.05} \right]$$

$$= \$45 \ (9.5491)$$

$$= \$429.71.$$

The coupon interest and interest on interest from all 12 coupon interest payments is $691.23.

The expected price of the bond six years from now is determined as follows:

(a) Present value of coupon interest payments, assuming the required yield to maturity at the end of the investment horizon is 10.6%:

$$c = \$45;$$
$$i = .053 \ (= .106/2);$$
$$n = 14 \ (= \text{Remaining years to maturity} \times 2)$$

$$PV = \$45 \left[\frac{1 - \left[\dfrac{1}{(1.053)^{14}} \right]}{.053} \right]$$

$$= \$45 \left[\frac{1 - .4853}{.053} \right]$$

$$= \$45 \ (9.7115)$$

$$= \$437.02$$

(b) Present value of the maturity value:

Exhibit 8-7 continued.

$$\frac{\$1,000}{(1.053)^{14}} = \$485.29$$

$$\text{Expected price} = \$437.02 + \$485.29$$
$$= \$922.31$$

Total future amount:

Coupon interest plus interest on interest	= $ 691.23
Expected price	= 922.31
Total	$1,613.54

Step 2.   Compute the following:

$$\left[\frac{\$1,613.54}{\$1,000.00} \right]^{1/12} - 1$$

$$= (1.613.54)^{.08333} - 1$$
$$= 1.0407 - 1$$
$$= .0407 \text{ or } 4.07\%$$

Step 3.   Doubling 4.07% gives a horizon return of 8.14%.

Analyzing Callable Bonds with the Horizon Return

The total return can be used to assess the potential return from holding a callable bond. If the first call date falls within the investment horizon, the proceeds from the coupon interest payments plus the interest on interest and the proceeds from calling the issue (the call price) will be available at the first call date. These proceeds are then reinvested until the end of the investment horizon. Given the total future amount at the end of the investment horizon, the horizon return can then be computed. The next illustration shows how this is done.

Illustration 8-8. An investor is considering Bond C, which we presented earlier in this chapter: 11% coupon, 15 years to maturity and 9.2% yield to maturity. The price for this bond is $1,144.88. Suppose that this bond is callable in three years at $1,055. The yield to call for this bond is 7.48%. Since the yield to call is less than the yield to maturity, this investor might use the 7.48% to assess the relative attractiveness of this bond. However, suppose that this investor's investment horizon is five years (a period extending beyond the first call date but shorter than the maturity of the bond). Also assume that this investor believes that any proceeds can be reinvested at a 6% annual interest rate (3% semiannually). Exhibit 8-8 shows the computation of the horizon return on the assumption that the bond is called in three years. The horizon return is 6.66%. Based on this investor's reinvestment assumption and investment horizon, this is the appropriate yield to use in assessing the attractiveness of this bond relative to other bonds that are purchase candidates.

Exhibit 8-8
Computation of the Horizon Return for a 15-Year, 11% Bond Selling for $1,144.88, Callable in Three Years at $1,055 and Held for Three Years: Reinvestment Rate = 6%

Step 1. The total future amount from this bond includes:

(1) Coupon interest of $55 every six months for three years (the first call date),
(2) Interest earned from reinvesting the first six semiannual coupon interest payments at 3% (one-half the assumed annual reinvestment rate) until the first call date, and
(3) Proceeds from reinvesting the call price plus (1) and (2) above for two years at 3% until the end of the investment horizon.

The coupon interest plus interest on interest for the first six coupon payments can be found as follows:

$$c = \$55;$$
$$m = 2;$$
$$r = .03 \ (= .06/2);$$
$$n = 6$$

Exhibit 8-8 continued.

$$\text{Coupon interest plus interest on interest} = \$55 \left[\frac{(1.03)^6 - 1}{.03} \right]$$

$$= \$55 \left[\frac{1.1941 - 1}{.03} \right]$$

$$= \$55 \ (6.4683)$$

$$= \$355.76.$$

This gives the coupon plus interest on interest as of the end of the third year (six periods) when the bond is called. Adding the call price of $1,055 gives the total proceeds that must be reinvested at 3% until the end of the investment horizon, two years or four periods later.

$$\text{Proceeds to be reinvested} = \$355.76 + \$1,055$$
$$= \$1,410.76.$$

Reinvesting $1,410.76 for four periods at 3%:

$$\$1,410.76 \ (1.03)^4 = \$1,587.82$$

Therefore, the total future amount is $1,587.82.

Step 2. Compute the following:

$$\left[\frac{\$1,587.82}{\$1,144.88} \right]^{1/10}$$

$$= (1.38689)^{.10} - 1$$
$$= 1.0304 - 1$$
$$= .0333 \text{ or } 3.33\%$$

Step 3. Doubling 3.33% gives a horizon return of 6.66%.

Comparing Coupon and Zero-Coupon Bonds:
The Break-Even Reinvestment Rate

As we have emphasized throughout this chapter, assessing the relative value of two bonds on the basis of yield to maturity may provide misleading conclusions. For a manager of a tax-exempt portfolio who intends to hold a bond until maturity, there is an analytical framework that can be used to assess the relative value of a zero-coupon bond and a coupon bond. The analytical framework will be presented by means of an illustration.

Suppose that the manager of a tax-exempt portfolio is considering the following two five-year bonds: (1) a 12% bond selling at par ($100) and (2) a zero-coupon bond selling at $57.99 (per $100 par value). Suppose also that the bonds have the same quality rating and that the portfolio manager plans to hold either bond until maturity.

The yield to maturity for the zero-coupon bond is 11.2%, which, since it requires no reinvestment of coupon payments, means that the horizon return will be 11.2%. While the horizon return for the 12% coupon bond is 12%, the horizon return will depend on the rate at which the coupon payments can be reinvested. We can determine the reinvestment rate that will produce the same total future amount from both investments. This rate is called the *break-even reinvestment rate*.

Suppose instead of investing $100 in the 12% coupon bond, an investor invests in the zero-coupon bond. The semiannual yield to maturity is 5.6%; therefore, $100 invested in the zero-coupon bond will grow to $172.44 at the end of 10 periods (five years), as shown below:

$$\$100 \ (1.056)^{10} = \$172.44.$$

If the investor places $100 in the 12% coupon bond, he will be indifferent between the zero-coupon bond and the 12% coupon bond if the latter produces a total future amount of $172.44. The total future amount from holding a bond to maturity will be equal to the sum of (1) the coupon payments, (2) the maturity value, and (3) the interest on interest from reinvesting the coupon payments. For our 12% coupon bond, the investor knows for certain that for each $100 invested, the following future amounts will be received:

$$\text{Coupon payments } (10 \times \$6) = \$ \ 60.00$$
$$\text{Maturity value} = \ \ 100.00$$

That is, $160 will be received with certainty. For the 12% coupon bond to generate $172.44, interest on interest must equal $12.44 ($172.44 – $160). Alternatively, this means that the coupon interest plus the interest on interest must equal $72.44.

Recall that the formula for the coupon plus interest on interest is equal to:

$$c \left[\frac{(1 + r)^n - 1}{r} \right]$$

where

c = Semiannual interest payment;
r = Semiannual reinvestment rate;
n = Number of semiannual coupon payments.

In our illustration, the investor knows the semiannual coupon interest payment is $6 and that the resulting figure should be equal to $72.44. Substituting, we have

$$\$72.44 = \$6 \left[\frac{(1 + r)^{10} - 1}{r} \right]$$

Solving the above equation for r gives a semiannual break-even reinvestment rate of approximately 4%. The break-even reinvestment rate is 8%. Therefore, if the portfolio manager believes he can realize at least an 8% reinvestment rate, the 12% coupon bond will provide more future dollars than the zero coupon bond. If he expects to earn a reinvestment rate less than 8%, the zero coupon bond is a better investment since it will provide a higher total return.

In the analysis, we assumed that the portfolio manager could invest all of the coupon payments at a tax-free rate. When taxes on the coupon payments must be paid, the analysis must take this into consideration.

Summary and Implications

In this chapter we have presented an alternative yield measure, the horizon return, that should be used by investors to assess the relative attractiveness of bonds. The horizon return takes into consideration the investor's (1) investment horizon, (2) expected reinvestment rate over the investment horizon, and (3) expected yield for the bond at the end of the investment horizon. We have also illustrated how multiple reinvestment rates can be incorporated into the analysis (Illustration 8-7) and how callable bonds can be evaluated using the horizon return framework (Illustration 8-8).

The horizon return can also be applied to evaluating mortgage-backed securities and floating-rate securities. The horizon return also can handle the situation where a taxable bond is included in a taxable portfolio so that only a portion of the coupon interest payments can be reinvested. This permits a comparison of taxable and tax-exempt bonds in a taxable portfolio that is more meaningful than the common procedure of multiplying the taxable yield by one minus the marginal tax rate. The evaluation of a bond swap, the sale of a bond in a portfolio for another bond, should be conducted using the horizon return framework.

The objection to the horizon return by some is that it requires the investor to make assumptions about reinvestment rates and future yields, as well as to think in terms of an investment horizon. It is more convenient for some to simply use a meaningless measure such as the yield to maturity or yield to call. If an investor is managing money, expectations are part of the game. It is not difficult to use the horizon return framework to analyze the performance of a bond on the basis of different interest rate scenarios and investment horizons.

III
Bond Price Volatility

9

Price Volatility Characteristics of Option-Free Bonds

To implement effective portfolio trading and hedging strategies, it is necessary to understand the price volatility characteristics of bonds. The three chapters of this section of the book focus on bond price volatility. In this chapter, general price volatility properties of option-free bonds are discussed, as well as bond characteristics that determine price volatility.

A Closer Look at the Price/Yield Relationship for Option-Free Bonds

In Chapter 2 we demonstrated a fundamental principle of all option-free bonds (a bond that does not have an embedded option): *the price of a bond changes in the opposite direction of the change in the required yield for the bond.* This principle follows from the fact that the price of an option-free bond is equal to the present value of its expected cash flows. An increase (decrease) in the required return decreases (increases) the present value of its expected cash flow, and therefore, the bond's price.

Exhibit 9-1 illustrates this property for 12 hypothetical bonds. There are three bonds with the same coupon rate but different maturities (5, 15, and 30 years); there are four bonds with the same maturity but different coupon rates (0%, 8%, 10%, and 14%). These 12 bonds will be used in this and the following two chapters to demonstrate the bond price volatility of option-free bonds and measures of bond price volatility.

For each bond in Exhibit 9-1 the price of the bond (with par equal to 100) is shown for 13 required yields. The top panel shows the price for required yields from 10% to 13%; the bottom panel, the price for required yields from 7% to 10%.

If the price/yield relationship for any of the 12 bonds in Exhibit 9-1 is graphed, the shape of the graph would be as shown in Exhibit 9-2. As the required yield rises, the price of the option-free bond declines. However, the relationship is not linear (that is, it is not a straight line). This nonlinear shape for the price/yield relationship exists for all option-free bonds and is referred to as *convexity*.

While all option-free bonds will have the convex shape shown in Exhibit 9-2, the curvature of every option-free bond will be different. As we will see in this chapter and the following two, it is this convex shape that holds the key to assessing the performance of a bond and thus a portfolio of bonds. Many trading and portfolio strategies are based on buying or selling the convexity of a bond portfolio.

It is important to keep in mind that the price/yield relationship that we have discussed refers to an instantaneous change in the required yield. As we explained in Chapter 2, assuming no change in the perceived credit risk of the issuer as a bond moves toward maturity, there are two factors that influence the price of any option-free bond. First, the bond's price will change as the required yield changes, as we previously discussed. Second, for discount and premium bonds the bond's price will change even if required yields remain the same. In particular, the price of a discount bond will increase as it moves toward maturity, reaching par value at the maturity date; for a premium bond, the bond's price will decrease as it moves closer to maturity, finally declining to the par value at the maturity date.

Exhibit 9-1

Twelve Hypothetical Bonds: Price/Yield Relationship

		Required Yield						
Coupon	Term	10.00%	10.01%	10.10%	10.50%	11.00%	12.00%	13.00%
0.00%	5	$ 61.39	$ 61.36	$ 61.10	$ 59.95	$ 58.54	$ 55.84	$ 53.27
0.00%	15	23.14	23.10	22.81	21.54	20.06	17.41	15.12
0.00%	30	5.35	5.34	5.20	4.64	4.03	3.03	2.29
8.00%	5	92.28	92.24	91.91	90.46	88.69	85.28	82.03
8.00%	15	84.63	84.56	83.95	81.32	78.20	72.47	67.35
8.00%	30	81.07	80.99	80.29	77.30	73.83	67.68	62.42
10.00%	5	100.00	99.96	99.61	98.09	96.23	92.64	89.22
10.00%	15	100.00	99.92	99.24	96.26	92.73	86.24	80.41
10.00%	30	100.00	99.91	99.06	95.46	91.28	83.84	77.45
14.00%	5	115.44	115.40	115.02	113.35	111.31	107.36	103.59
14.00%	15	130.74	130.65	129.81	126.15	121.80	113.76	106.53
14.00%	30	137.86	137.73	136.60	131.79	126.17	116.16	107.52

Exhibit 9-1 continued.

					Required Yield			
Coupon	Term	10.00%	9.99%	9.90%	9.50%	9.00%	8.00%	7.00%
0.00%	5	$ 61.39	$ 61.42	$ 61.68	$ 62.87	$ 64.39	$ 67.56	$ 70.89
0.00%	15	23.14	23.17	23.47	24.85	26.70	30.83	35.63
0.00%	30	5.35	5.37	5.51	6.18	7.13	9.51	12.69
8.00%	5	92.28	92.32	92.65	94.14	96.04	100.00	104.16
8.00%	15	84.63	84.70	85.31	88.13	91.86	100.00	109.20
8.00%	30	81.07	81.15	81.87	85.19	89.68	100.00	112.47
10.00%	5	100.00	100.04	100.39	101.95	103.96	108.11	112.47
10.00%	15	100.00	100.08	100.77	103.96	108.14	117.29	127.57
10.00%	30	100.00	100.09	100.95	104.94	110.32	122.62	137.42
14.00%	5	115.44	115.49	115.87	117.59	119.78	124.33	129.11
14.00%	15	130.74	130.84	131.69	135.60	140.72	151.88	164.37
14.00%	30	137.86	137.99	139.13	144.44	151.60	167.87	187.31

Exhibit 9-2
Shape of Price/Yield Relationship for an Option-Free Bond

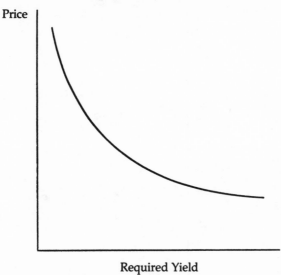

Price

Required Yield

The Price Volatility Characteristics of Option-Free Bonds

To investigate bond price volatility in terms of percentage price change, let's assume that the prevailing yield in the market is 10% for all 12 bonds. The dollar price change per $100 of par value for various changes in the required yield is shown in Exhibit 9-3. Exhibit 9-4 shows the corresponding percentage change in each bond's price. The percentage price change shown in Exhibit 9-4 is found by dividing the dollar price change in Exhibit 9-3 by the price of the bond at a 10% required yield, as shown in Exhibit 9-1.

For example, consider the 8%, 15-year bond. The price for this bond if the required yield is 10% is $84.63. If the required yield increases 100 basis points to 11%, the price of this bond would fall to $78.20. The dollar price change per $100 of par value is – $6.43, as shown in Exhibit 9-3. The percentage price change is then:

Exhibit 9-3

Twelve Hypothetical Bonds: Dollar Price Change per $100 of Par Value as Required Yield Changes

		Change in basis points					
		1	10	50	100	200	300
		Required Yield					
Coupon	Term	10.01%	10.10%	10.50%	11.00%	12.00%	13.00%
0.00%	5	$ – 0.03	$ – 0.26	$ – 1.15	$ – 1.41	$ – 2.70	$ – 2.57
0.00%	15	– 0.03	– 0.33	– 1.59	– 3.07	– 5.73	– 8.02
0.00%	30	– 0.02	– 0.15	– 0.71	– 1.33	– 2.32	– 3.07
8.00%	5	– 0.04	– 0.37	– 1.81	– 3.58	– 7.00	– 10.25
8.00%	15	– 0.07	– 0.68	– 3.31	– 6.43	– 12.16	– 17.27
8.00%	30	– 0.08	– 0.78	– 3.78	– 7.25	– 13.39	– 18.65
10.00%	5	– 0.04	– 0.39	– 1.91	– 3.77	– 7.36	– 10.78
10.00%	15	– 0.08	– 0.76	– 3.74	– 7.27	– 13.76	– 19.59
10.00%	30	– 0.09	– 0.94	– 4.54	– 8.72	– 16.16	– 22.55
14.00%	5	– 0.04	– 0.42	– 2.09	– 4.14	– 8.08	– 11.85
14.00%	15	– 0.09	– 0.94	– 4.59	– 8.94	– 16.98	– 24.22
14.00%	30	– 0.13	– 1.25	– 6.07	– 11.68	– 21.70	– 30.34

		Change in basis points					
		-1	-10	-50	-100	-200	-300
		Required Yield					
Coupon	Term	9.99%	9.90%	9.50%	9.00%	8.00%	7.00%
0.00%	5	$ 0.03	$ 0.29	$ 1.48	$ 3.00	$ 6.17	$ 9.50
0.00%	15	0.03	0.33	1.72	3.56	7.69	12.49
0.00%	30	0.02	0.16	0.82	1.78	4.15	7.34
8.00%	5	0.04	0.37	1.86	3.77	7.72	11.88
8.00%	15	0.07	0.69	3.51	7.23	15.37	24.57
8.00%	30	0.08	0.79	4.12	8.61	18.93	31.40
10.00%	5	0.04	0.39	1.95	3.96	8.11	12.47
10.00%	15	0.08	0.77	3.96	8.14	17.29	27.59
10.00%	30	0.09	0.95	4.94	10.32	22.62	37.42
14.00%	5	0.04	0.42	2.14	4.34	8.89	13.66
14.00%	15	0.09	0.95	4.85	9.98	21.13	33.63
14.00%	30	0.13	1.27	6.58	13.74	30.01	49.45

Exhibit 9-4

Twelve Hypothetical Bonds: Percentage Price Change as Required Yield Changes

		Change in basis points					
		1	10	50	100	200	300
		Required Yield					
Coupon	Term	10.01%	10.10%	10.50%	11.00%	12.00%	13.00%
0.00%	5	−0.05%	−0.47%	−2.35%	−4.64%	−9.04%	−13.22%
0.00%	15	−0.14	−1.42	−6.89	−13.28	−24.75	−34.66
0.00%	30	−0.29	−2.82	−13.30	−24.80	−43.38	−57.30
8.00%	5	−0.04	−0.40	−1.97	−3.88	−7.58	−11.11
8.00%	15	−0.08	−0.80	−3.91	−7.60	−14.37	−20.41
8.00%	30	−0.10	−0.96	−4.66	−8.94	−16.52	−23.01
10.00%	5	−0.04	−0.39	−1.91	−3.77	−7.36	−10.78
10.00%	15	−0.08	−0.76	−3.74	−7.27	−13.76	−19.59
10.00%	30	−0.09	−0.94	−4.54	−8.72	−16.16	−22.55
14.00%	5	−0.04	−0.37	−1.81	−3.58	−7.00	−10.26
14.00%	15	−0.07	−0.72	−3.51	−6.84	−12.99	−18.52
14.00%	30	−0.09	−0.91	−4.40	−8.48	−15.74	−22.01

		Change in basis points					
		−1	−10	−50	−100	−200	−300
		Required Yield					
Coupon	Term	9.99%	9.90%	9.50%	9.00%	8.00%	7.00%
0.00%	5	0.05%	0.48%	2.41%	4.89%	10.04%	15.48%
0.00%	15	0.14	1.44	7.41	15.40	33.25	53.98
0.00%	30	0.29	2.90	15.38	33.16	77.57	137.10
8.00%	5	0.04	0.40	2.02	4.08	8.37	12.87
8.00%	15	0.08	0.81	4.14	8.54	18.16	29.03
8.00%	30	0.10	0.98	5.08	10.62	23.35	38.73
10.00%	5	0.04	0.39	1.95	3.96	8.11	12.47
10.00%	15	0.08	0.77	3.96	8.14	17.29	27.59
10.00%	30	0.09	0.95	4.94	10.32	22.62	37.42
14.00%	5	0.04	0.37	1.86	3.76	7.70	11.84
14.00%	15	0.07	0.73	3.71	7.63	16.16	25.72
14.00%	30	0.09	0.92	4.78	9.96	21.77	35.87

$$\frac{\$78.20 - \$84.63}{\$84.63} = -0.076 \text{ or } -7.60\%.$$

This is shown in Exhibit 9-4.

An examination of Exhibits 9-3 and 9-4 reveals the following four properties about price volatility of an option-free bonds.

Property 1. Price volatility is not the same for all bonds. Although the prices of all option-free bonds move in the opposite direction of the change in required yield, for a given change in the required yield, the price change is not the same for all bonds. A natural question is what characteristics of a bond determine its price volatility. We'll focus on this question in the next section.

Property 2. Price volatility is approximately symmetric for small yield changes. For very small changes in the required yield, the percentage price change for a given bond is roughly the same regardless of whether the required yield increases or decreases. For example, look at the top panel of both Exhibits 9-3 and 9-4. For a 10-basis-point change in the required yield the 10%, 30-year bond's price would decrease by $0.94 per $100 of par value or 0.94% of the initial price. Looking at the bottom panel of the two exhibits, the 10%, 30-year bond price would increase by $0.95 per $100 of par value or 0.95% of the initial price for a 10-basis-point decrease in the required yield.

Property 3. Price volatility is not symmetric for large yield changes. For large changes in the required yield, the percentage price change is not the same for an increase in the required yield as it is for a decrease in the required yield. Once again, looking at the 10%, 30 year coupon bond, if the required yield increases by 300 basis points (from 10% to 13%), the price change per $100 of par value would be a decrease of $22.55 or 22.55% of the initial price, while for a 300-basis-point decrease in the required yield, the price change per $100 of par would be an increase of $37.42 or 37.42% of the initial price.

Property 4. Price increases are greater than price decreases. For a given change in required yield, the price increase is greater than the price decrease. This can be seen in Exhibits 9-3 and 9-4 by comparing the upper panel (which shows price volatility for increases in the required yield) to the lower panel (which shows

Exhibit 9-5

Illustration of Property 4

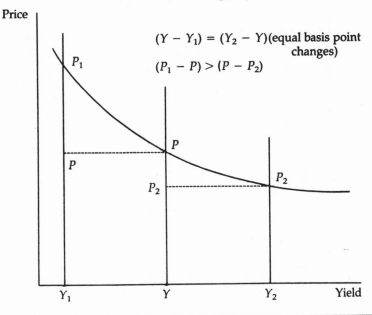

price volatility for decreases in the required yield). For each bond, the price change is larger in the lower panel than in the upper panel for a given change in required yield.

The reason for this property lies in the convex shape of the price/yield relationship. This is illustrated graphically in Exhibit 9-5. Suppose the initial required yield is Y in Exhibit 9-5. The corresponding initial price is P. Consider large equal basis point changes in the initial required yield. Y_1 and Y_2 indicate the higher and lower required yields, respectively; the corresponding prices are denoted P_1 and P_2. The vertical distance from the required yield axis to the price/yield relationship represents the price. The distance between P_1 and P measures the price increase if the required yield decreases; the distance between P and P_2 measures the price decrease if the required yield increases. Notice that the price increase will be greater than the price decrease for an equal change in basis points.

Exhibit 9-6
The Impact of Less Convexity on Property 4

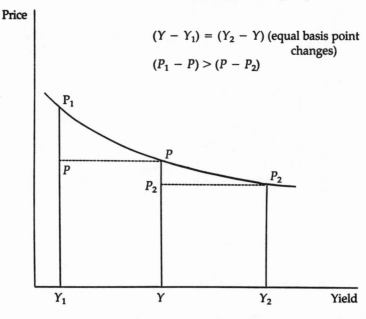

This will always be true when the curve is convex. Since all option-free bonds have a convex price/yield relationship, this property will always hold for option-free bonds. Exhibit 9-6 shows a less convex price/yield relationship than shown in Exhibit 9-5. While the property still holds, the price gain when the required yield falls is not that much greater than the price loss for an equal basis point increase in the required yield.

An implication of Property 4 is that if an investor owns a bond (that is, is long a bond), the price appreciation that will be realized if the required yield decreases is greater than the capital loss that will be realized if the required yield rises by the same number of basis points. For an investor who is short a bond, the reverse is true: the potential capital loss is greater than the potential capital gain if the required yield changes by a given number of basis points.

Characteristics of a Bond
That Affect Its Price Volatility

Property 1 states that price volatility is not the same for each bond. There are two characteristics of an option-free bond that determine its price volatility: coupon and term to maturity.

Characteristic 1. Price volatility is greater, the lower the coupon rate.[1] For a given term to maturity and initial required yield, the price volatility of a bond is greater, the lower the coupon rate. This characteristic can be seen by comparing the 0%,8%, 10%, and 14% coupon bonds with the same maturity. For example, if the required yield for all the 30-year bonds is 10% and the required yield rises to 12% (i.e., a 200 basis point increase), the 0% coupon bond will fall by 43.38% while the 14%, 30-year bond will fall by a smaller percentage, 15.74%.[2]

The investment implication is that bonds selling at a deep discount will have greater price volatility than bonds selling near or above par. Zero-coupon bonds will have the greatest price volatility for a given maturity.

Characteristic 2. Price volatility increases with maturity. For a given coupon rate and initial required yield, the longer the term to maturity, the greater the price volatility. This can be seen in Exhibit 9-4 by comparing the 5-year bonds to the 30-year bonds with the same coupon. For example, if the required yield increases 200 basis points from 10% to 12%, the 10%, 30-year bond's price will fall by 16.16%, while that of the 5-year bond will fall by only 7.36%.

The investment implication is that if an investor wants to increase a portfolio's price volatility because he expects interest rates to fall, all other factors constant, bonds with long maturities should be held in the portfolio. To reduce a portfolio's price volatility in anticipation of a rise in interest rates, bonds with short maturities should be held in the portfolio.

---

[1] This property does not necessarily hold for long-term deep discount *coupon* bonds.

[2] Notice that while the percentage price change is greater the lower the coupon rate, the dollar price change is smaller the lower the coupon rate.

Summary

In this chapter we have discussed the bond price volatility properties of option-free bonds. Four properties of bond price volatility are demonstrated, and two characteristics that affect bond price volatility (coupon rate and maturity) are illustrated.

What market participants would like to have is a measure that can be used to quantify the price volatility of a bond. For example, suppose a portfolio manager expects that interest rates will fall and is considering purchasing one of the following two bonds: (1) Bond A, a 7%, 22-year bond selling to yield 8% and (2) Bond B, a zero coupon, 15-year bond selling to yield 8.40%. Since the portfolio manager expects that interest rates are going to decline, he will want to purchase the bond that offers the greater price volatility. Which has higher price volatility? On the one hand, Bond B has a lower coupon than Bond A, so it would seem that Bond B has greater price volatility. On the other hand, Bond A has a longer maturity than Bond B, so it would seem that Bond A has greater price volatility. The problem with making the comparison is that in the two characteristics of price volatility we illustrated in this chapter—coupon rate and maturity—the required yield and other characteristics were held constant. In the situation faced by the portfolio manager above, none of the three factors (coupon rate, maturity, and yield) is equal for the two bonds. The purpose of the next chapter is to discuss measures of bond price volatility that may be used in a situation such as this.

10
Measuring Bond Price Volatility

Money managers, arbitrageurs, hedgers and traders need to have a way to measure a bond's price volatility in order to implement strategies. The three measures that are commonly employed and that will be explained in this chapter are (1) price value of a basis point, (2) yield value of a price change, and (3) duration. We'll also illustrate the role of price volatility measures in (1) hedging positions and weighting trades and (2) immunization strategies.

Price Value of a Basis Point

The *price value of a basis point*, also referred to as the *dollar value of a basis point*, is the change in the price of the bond if the yield changes by one basis point. Note that this measure of price volatility indicates *dollar* price volatility as opposed to price volatility as a *percentage* of the initial price. The price value of a basis point is expressed as the absolute value of the change in price.

Property 2 of the price/yield relationship explained in the previous chapter states that for small changes in required yield, price volatility is the same, regardless of the direction of a change in yield. Therefore, it does not make any difference if we increase or decrease the required yield by one basis point to compute the price value of a basis point.

We will illustrate the calculation of the price value of a basis point by using the 12 bonds in Exhibit 9-1 of the previous chapter. For each bond, the initial price, the price after increasing the yield by one basis point (from 10.00% to 10.01%) and the price value of a basis point per $100 of par value (the difference between the two prices) are shown in the top panel of Exhibit 10-1. Similarly, if we decrease the required yield by one basis point, from 10.00% to 9.99%, we would find approximately the same price value of a basis point for the 12 bonds, as shown in the bottom panel of Exhibit 10-1.

Exhibits 10-2A and 10-2B graphically show what happens to the price value of a basis point at different yields. Notice that the price value of a basis point is smaller, the higher the initial yield. The investment implication is that at higher yields, dollar price volatility is less. Also notice that the larger the price value of a basis point the greater the convexity. This can be seen by comparing the price value of a basis point in Exhibit 10-2A to that in Exhibit 10-2B, in which the curve is less convex.

The Price Value of More Than One Basis Point

In implementing a strategy some investors will calculate the price value of a change of more than one basis point. The principle of calculating the price value of any number of basis points is the same. For example, the price value of x basis points is found by computing the difference between the initial price and the price if the required yield changed by x basis points. For example, the price value per $100 of par value for several values of x for the 10% coupon, 15-year bond is found as follows if the yield is increased:

Change (x, in basis points)	Initial price (10% yield)	Price at 10%+ x yield	Price value of x basis points
10	100.00	99.2357	0.7643
50	100.00	96.2640	3.7360
100	100.00	92.7331	7.2669

Exhibit 10-1

Computation of the Price Value of a Basis Point

Bond Coupon	Term (years)	Price @10.00%	Price @ 10.01%	Price value of a basis point*
0.00%	5	61.3913	61.3621	0.0292
0.00%	15	23.1377	23.1047	0.0330
0.00%	30	5.3536	5.3383	0.0153
8.00%	5	92.2783	92.2415	0.0367
8.00%	15	84.6275	84.5595	0.0681
8.00%	30	81.0707	80.9920	0.0787
10.00%	5	100.0000	99.9614	0.0386
10.00%	15	100.0000	99.9232	0.0768
10.00%	30	100.0000	99.9054	0.0946
14.00%	5	115.4435	115.4011	0.0423
14.00%	15	130.7449	130.6506	0.0943
14.00%	30	137.8586	137.7323	0.1263

Bond Coupon	Term (years)	Price @10.00%	Price @ 9.99%	Price value of a basis point
0.00%	5	61.3913	61.4206	0.0292
0.00%	15	23.1377	23.1708	0.0331
0.00%	30	5.3536	5.3689	0.0153
8.00%	5	92.2783	92.3150	0.0367
8.00%	15	84.6275	84.6957	0.0681
8.00%	30	81.0707	81.1496	0.0788
10.00%	5	100.0000	100.0386	0.0386
10.00%	15	100.0000	100.0769	0.0769
10.00%	30	100.0000	100.0947	0.0947
14.00%	5	115.4435	115.4858	0.0424
14.00%	15	130.7449	130.8393	0.0944
14.00%	30	137.8586	137.9851	0.1265

*Absolute value per $100 of par value

Exhibit 10-2
Presentation of Price Value of a Basis Point

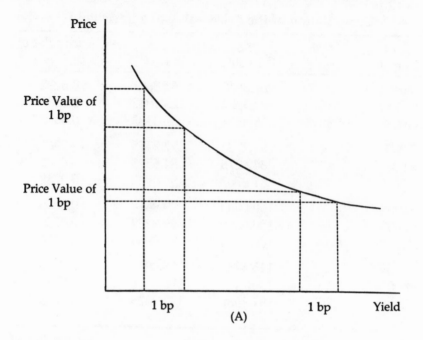

(A)

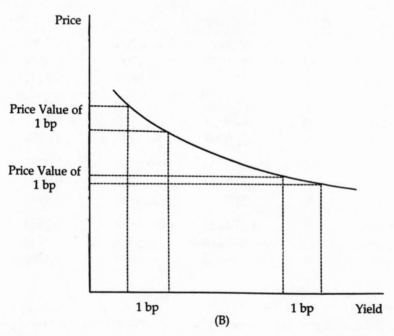

(B)

For small changes in required yield (such as 10 basis points), the price value of x basis points is roughly that found by multiplying the price value of one basis point by x. For example, the price value of 10 basis points computed by multiplying the price value of a basis point, namely, 0.08, by 10 gives 0.80, which is very close to the price value of 10 basis points computed above. In fact, the approximation is much better than indicated here because we computed the price value of a basis point to only two decimals.

For a decrease in the required yield, the price value of an x-basis-point change per \$100 of par value is:

Change (x, in basis points)	Initial price (10% yield)	Price at 10% − x yield	Price value of x basis points
10	100.00	100.7730	0.7730
50	100.00	103.9551	3.9551
100	100.00	108.1444	8.1444

Once again, note the approximate symmetry of the price change for small changes (10 basis points) in the yield (Property 2 of the price/yield relationship). For larger changes in the yield, however, there will be a difference between the price value of an x-basis-point movement, depending on whether the yield is increased or decreased. Many investors who use the price value of a large basis point movement in implementing a strategy will compute the average of the two price values. For example, the price value of 100 basis points would be approximated by averaging 7.2669 and 8.1444 to give 7.7057.

Application of Price Value of a Basis Point to Portfolio and Dealer Position

Suppose that a portfolio manager wants to know the price value of a basis point for a portfolio. Let's assume the following portfolio, comprised of three of our hypothetical bonds, all priced to yield 10%:

Bond	Par amount owned	Price
10%, 5-year	\$4 million	\$4,000,000
8%, 15-year	5 million	4,231,375
14%, 30-year	1 million	1,378,586

The price of a basis point per $100 of par value for each of these bonds, assuming an increase of 1 basis point, is:

		Price value for:	
Bond	Par amount owned	$100 par	Amount owned
10%, 5-year	$4 million	$0.0386	$1,544
8%, 15-year	$5 million	0.0681	3,405
14%, 30-year	$1 million	0.1263	1,263

Thus, the portfolio's exposure to a one-basis-point movement is $6,212, that is, $1,544 + $3,405 + $1,263.

The same analysis can be used to determine the exposure of a bond dealer's inventory.

Price Change Versus Percentage Change

So far we have dealt with the dollar price change. If we want to know the percentage price change, we can find it by dividing the price value of a basis point by the initial price. That is,

$$\text{Percentage price change} = \frac{\text{Price value of a basis point}}{\text{Initial price}}$$

Yield Value of a Price Change

Some investors use another measure of the dollar price volatility of a bond: the change in the yield for a specified price change. This is found by first calculating the bond's yield if the bond's price is increased by, say, X dollars. Then the difference between the initial yield and the new yield is the yield value of the X-dollar price change.

The smaller the yield value of an X-dollar price change, the greater is the *dollar* price volatility. This is because it would take a larger X-dollar price movement to change the yield a specified number of basis points. This is illustrated in Exhibit 10-3.

Yield Value of a 32nd for Treasury Securities

Treasury notes and bonds are quoted in 32nds of a percentage point of par. Consequently, investors in this market compute the yield value of a 32nd. The yield value of a 32nd for the three 10% coupon bonds selling to yield 10% is computed below.

Exhibit 10-3
Presentation of Yield Value of $X Price Change

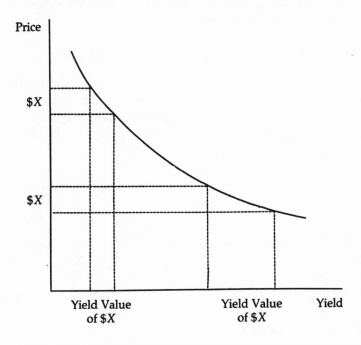

Decreasing the price a 32nd:

Bond	Initial price – one 32nd	Yield at new price	Initial yield	Yield value of a 32nd
10%, 5-year	99.96875	.1000810	.10000	.0000810
10%, 15-year	99.96875	.1000407	.10000	.0000407
10%, 30-year	99.96875	.1000330	.10000	.0000330

Increasing the price by a 32nd:

Bond	Initial price + one 32nd	Yield at new price	Initial yield	Yield value of a 32nd
10%, 5-year	100.03125	.0999190	.10000	.0000809
10%, 15-year	100.03125	.0999593	.10000	.0000407
10%, 30-year	100.03125	.0999670	.10000	.0000330

Notice that the yield value of a 32nd for the 30-year bonds is lower than for the five-year bond. This agrees with our earlier statement that the lower the yield value of an $X price change, the greater the dollar price volatility.

Yield Value of an 8th for Corporate and Municipal Securities

Corporate bonds and municipal bonds are traded in 8ths of a percentage point. Consequently, investors in these markets frequently compute the yield value of an 8th. The calculation of the yield value of an 8th for the three 10% coupon bonds selling to yield 10% is shown below.

Decreasing the price an 8th:

Bond	Initial price – one 8th	Yield at new price	Initial yield	Yield value of an 8th
10%, 5-year	99.875	.10032	.10000	.00032
10%, 15-year	99.875	.10016	.10000	.00016
10%, 30-year	99.875	.10013	.10000	.10013

Increasing the price by an 8th:

Bond	Initial price + one 8th	Yield at new price	Initial yield	Yield value of an 8th
10%, 5-year	100.125	.09968	.10000	.00032
10%, 15-year	100.125	.09984	.10000	.00016
10%, 30-year	100.125	.09987	.10000	.00013

Duration

In 1938, Frederick Macaulay constructed a number that he could use as a proxy for the length of time a bond investment was outstanding.[1] He referred to this number as the *duration* of a bond and defined it as a weighted average term-to-maturity of

---

[1] Frederick Macaulay, *Some Theoretical Problems Suggested by the Movements of Interest Rates, Bond Yields and Stock Prices in the United States Since 1865* (National Bureau of Economic Research, 1938).

the bond's cash flows. The weights in this weighted average are the present values of each cash flow as a percent of the present value of all the bond's cash flows (i.e., the weights are the present value of each cash flow as a percent of the bond's price). As we shall see below, Macaulay's measure is linked to the price volatility of a bond. First, let's look at how this number, referred to as *Macaulay duration*, is computed.

Computing Macaulay Duration

Mathematically, Macaulay duration is computed as follows:

$$\text{Macaulay duration (in periods)} = $$

$$\frac{(1)\ PVCF_1 + (2)\ PVCF_2 + \ldots + (n)\ PVCF_n}{PVTCF}$$

where

$k =$ Number of periods, or payments, per year (i.e. $k =$ 2 for semiannual pay bonds, $k = 12$ for monthly pay bonds);

$n =$ Number of periods until maturity (specifically, number of years to maturity times k, rounded down to the nearest whole number);[2]

$t =$ The period when the cash flow is expected to be received ($t = 1,\ldots,n$);

$PVCF_t =$ The present value of the cash flow in period t discounted at the prevailing period yield (in the case of a semiannual-pay bond, one-half the yield to maturity);

$PVTCF =$ Total present value of the cash flow of the bond, where the present value is determined using the prevailing yield to maturity.

---

[2] For example, if there are 5.2 years to maturity for a semiannual pay bond (i.e., $k = 2$), then:

$$n = 5.2 \times 2$$
$$= 10.4$$

Rounding down to the nearest whole number gives a value of 10 for n.

For an *option-free bond* with semiannual payments, the cash flow for periods 1 to $n - 1$ is one-half the annual coupon interest. The cash flow in period n is the semiannual coupon interest plus the maturity value. Since the bond's price is equal to its cash flow discounted at the prevailing yield to maturity, *PVTCF* is the current market price *plus* accrued interest.

The formula for Macaulay duration gives a value in terms of periods. Dividing by the number of payments made per year converts Macaulay duration to years. That is,

$$\text{Macaulay duration (in years)} = \frac{\text{Macaulay duration (in periods)}}{k},$$

Exhibits 10-4 and 10-5 show the calculation of Macaulay duration for two of our hypothetical bonds (the 10%, five-year bond and the 14%, five-year bond), assuming each bond is selling to yield 10%. The Macaulay durations in years for our 12 hypothetical bonds are given below:

Bond	Macaulay duration (years)
0%, 5-year	5.00
0%, 15-year	15.00
0%, 30-year	30.00
8%, 5-year	4.18
8%, 15-year	8.45
8%, 30-year	10.20
10%, 5-year	4.05
10%, 15-year	8.07
10%, 30-year	9.94
14%, 5-year	3.85
14%, 15-year	7.58
14%, 30-year	9.63

As can be seen from the above summary, the Macaulay duration of a coupon bond is less than its maturity. It should be

Exhibit 10-4
Calculation of Macaulay Duration and Modified Duration
for a 10%, 5-year Bond Selling to Yield 10%

Coupon rate = 10.00%;
Maturity (years) = 5;
Initial yield = 10.00%

Period (t)	Cash flow*	Present value of $1 at 5%	Present value of cash flow (PVCF)	t × PVCF
1	$5.00	0.952380	4.761905	4.761905
2	5.00	0.907029	4.535147	9.070295
3	5.00	0.863837	4.319188	12.957563
4	5.00	0.822702	4.113512	16.454049
5	5.00	0.783526	3.917631	19.588154
6	5.00	0.746215	3.731077	22.386461
7	5.00	0.710681	3.553407	24.873846
8	5.00	0.676839	3.384197	27.073574
9	5.00	0.644608	3.223045	29.007401
10	105.00	0.613913	64.460892	644.608920
Total			100.000000	810.782168

* Cash flow per $100 of par value

$$\text{Macaulay duration (in half years)} = \frac{810.782168}{100.000000} = 8.11$$

$$\text{Macaulay duration (in years)} = \frac{8.11}{2} = 4.05$$

$$\text{Modified duration (in years)} = \frac{4.05}{1.0500} = 3.86$$

Exhibit 10-5
Calculation of Macaulay Duration and Modified Duration
for a 14%, 5-year Bond Selling to Yield 10%

Coupon rate = 14.00%;
Maturity (years) = 5;
Initial yield = 10.00%

Period (t)	Cash flow*	Present value of $1 at 5%	Present value of cash flow (PVCF)	t × PVCF
1	$7.00	0.952380	6.666667	6.666667
2	7.00	0.907029	6.349206	12.698412
3	7.00	0.863837	6.046863	18.140589
4	7.00	0.822702	5.758917	23.035669
5	7.00	0.783526	5.484683	27.423415
6	7.00	0.746215	5.223508	31.341046
7	7.00	0.710681	4.974769	34.823385
8	7.00	0.676839	4.737876	37.903004
9	7.00	0.644608	4.512262	40.610361
10	107.00	0.613913	65.688718	656.887180
Total			115.443470	889.529728

* Cash flow per $100 of par value.

$$\text{Macaulay duration (in half years)} = \frac{889.529728}{115.443470} = 7.71$$

$$\text{Macaulay duration (in years)} = \frac{7.71}{2} = 3.85$$

$$\text{Modified duration (in years)} = \frac{3.85}{1.0500} = 3.67$$

obvious from the formula that the Macaulay duration of a zero-coupon bond is equal to its maturity. The lower the coupon, generally the greater the duration of the bond.[3]

Notice the consistency between the properties of bond price volatility we discussed earlier and the properties of duration. We showed that, all other factors constant, the greater the maturity, the greater the price volatility. A property of duration is that, all other factors constant, the greater the maturity, the greater the duration. We also showed that the lower the coupon rate, all other factors constant, the greater the bond price volatility. As we just noted, generally the lower the coupon rate, the greater the duration. It appears that duration is telling us something about bond price volatility.

Alternative Formulas for Macaulay Duration

Mathematically, Macaulay duration can be shown to be equivalent to:

$$\text{Macaulay duration (in periods)} =$$

$$\left[\frac{1+y}{y}\right] W + \left[\frac{y-c}{y}\right] n(1-W),$$

where

y = One-half the yield;

c = One-half the annual coupon *rate*;

W = Ratio of the present value of the annuity of the coupon payments to the price of the bond.

From Chapter 3, the present value of the coupon payments is:

$$100\, c \left[\frac{1 - \left[\frac{1}{(1+y)^n}\right]}{y}\right].$$

---

[3] This property does not necessarily hold for some long maturity deep discount coupon bonds, as explained below.

Illustration 10-1. From the above formula, the Macaulay duration for the 14% coupon bond with five years to maturity, selling to yield 10%, is found by inserting the following values:

$$y = .05 (.10 /2);$$
$$c = .07 (.14 /2);$$
$$n = 10 (5 \times 2).$$

The price of this bond is 115.44 (see Exhibit 9-1 of Chapter 9). The present value of the coupon payments is:

$$\$100 (.07) \left[\frac{1 - \left[\frac{1}{(1.05)^{10}} \right]}{.05} \right]$$

$$= \$7 \left[\frac{1 - .613913}{.05} \right]$$

$$= \$54.05.$$

Then,

$$W = \frac{\$ 54.05}{\$115.44} = .4682$$

and

Macaulay duration (in periods) =

$$\frac{1.05}{.05} (.4682) + \left[\frac{.05 - .07}{.05} \right] (10) (1 - .4682)$$

$$= 21 (.4682) + (-.40) (10) (.5318)$$
$$= 9.8322 - 2.1272$$
$$= 7.705.$$

Dividing by 2 to give Macaulay duration in years, we have 3.85. Notice that this agrees with the Macaulay duration calculated for this bond in Exhibit 10-5.

When a bond is selling at par, c is equal to y. The formula for Macaulay duration then reduces to

Macaulay duration for a bond selling at par (in periods)

$$= \left[\frac{1+y}{y} \right] W.$$

Illustration 10-2. In the formula for the Macaulay duration for a bond selling at par, the numbers needed to calculate Macaulay duration for the 10% coupon bond with five years to maturity selling to yield 10% are

$$y = .05 \ (.10 \ /2);$$
$$c = .05 \ (.10 \ /2);$$
$$n = 10 \ (5 \times 2).$$

The present value of the coupon payments is:

$$\$100 \ (.05) \left[\frac{1 - \left[\frac{1}{(1.05)^{10}} \right]}{.05} \right]$$

$$= \$5 \left[\frac{1 - .613913}{.05} \right]$$

$$= \$38.61.$$

Then,

$$W = \frac{\$ 38.61}{\$100} = .3861$$

and

Macaulay duration (in periods) =

$$= \frac{1.05}{.05} \ (.3861)$$

$$= 21 \ (.3861)$$
$$= 8.1081.$$

Dividing by 2 gives 4.05, the Macaulay duration in years. This result agrees with the calculation of Macaulay duration in Exhibit 10-4.

For a perpetual bond—a bond that promises to pay the same coupon forever and therefore has no maturity date—the value of W is 1. Then,

Macaulay duration for a perpetual bond (in years) = $\dfrac{1+y}{y}$

For a zero-coupon bond, the present value of the coupon payments is obviously zero, thus W is zero. The Macaulay duration for a zero-coupon bond in periods is

$$\left[\frac{1+y}{y}\right] \; W + \left[\frac{y-c}{y}\right] \; n\,(1-W),$$

$$= \left[\frac{1+y}{y}\right] \; 0 + \left[\frac{y-0}{y}\right] \; n\,(1-0),$$

$$= 0 + \left[\frac{y}{y}\right] n$$

$$= n.$$

Thus we see that the Macaulay duration of a zero-coupon bond in periods is just the number of periods. Dividing by 2 gives the term of the bond in years.

Link Between Duration and Bond Price Volatility

Now that we know how to compute Macaulay duration, how do we interpret it? Some investors continue to think of duration in the context in which it was developed by Macaulay—as a measure of the length of time a bond investment is outstanding. Forget it! The significance and interpretation of Macaulay duration lie in its link to bond price volatility.

The link between bond price volatility and Macaulay duration can be shown to be as follows:[4]

---

[4] Mathematically, this relationship is derived from the first term of a Taylor expansion of the price function. See Appendix A.

approximate percentage change in price =

$$-\left[\frac{1}{(1+y)}\right] \times \text{Macaulay duration} \times \text{Yield change},$$

where y = one-half the yield to maturity.

Generally, the first two terms are combined and the product called *modified duration*; that is,

$$\text{Modified duration} = \frac{\text{Macaulay duration}}{(1+y)}.$$

The relationship can then be expressed as

Approximate percentage change in price =
– Modified duration × Yield change.

Illustration 10-3.   Consider the 8%, 15-year bond selling at 84.63 to yield 10%. The Macaulay duration for this bond is 8.45. Modified duration is 8.05:

$$\text{Modified duration} = \frac{8.45}{(1.05)} = 8.05$$

If the yield increases instantaneously from 10.00% to 10.10%, a yield change of +0.0010, the *approximate* percentage change in price is

$$- 8.05 \times (+.0010) = -.0805 = -.81\%.$$

Exhibit 9-4 of the previous chapter shows that the actual percentage change in price is – 0.80%. Similarly, if the yield decreases instantaneously from 10.00% to 9.90% (a 10 basis point decrease), the approximate percentage change in price would be +0.81%. Exhibit 9-4 of the previous chapter shows that the actual percentage price change would be +0.80%. This example illustrates that for small changes in the required yield, modified duration provides a good approximation of the percentage change in price.

Illustration 10-4.   Instead of a small change in required yield, let's assume that yields increase by 300 basis points, from 10% to 13% (a yield change of +0.03). The approximate percentage change in price estimated from duration would be:

$$- 8.05 \times (+0.03) = - 24.15\%.$$

How good is this approximation? As can be seen from Exhibit 9-4 of the previous chapter, the actual percentage change in price is only –20.41%. Moreover, if the required yield decreased by 300 basis points, from 10% to 7%, the approximate percentage change in price based on duration would be +24.15%, compared to an actual percentage change in price of +29.03%. Thus, not only is the approximation off, but we can see that duration estimates a symmetric percentage change in price, which, as we pointed out in the previous chapter, is not a property of the price/yield relationship for bonds.

Exhibit 10-6 shows the estimated percentage change in price using modified duration for our 12 hypothetical bonds. The difference between the actual percentage price change, as reported in Exhibit 9-4 of the previous chapter, and the estimated percentage change in price using modified duration, as reported in Exhibit 10-6, is shown in Exhibit 10-7. The property that we just illustrated—that duration gives a good estimate of the percentage price change for small changes in yield but a poor estimate for large changes—can be seen in Exhibit 10-7. The percentage price change not explained by modified duration increases, the greater the change in the yield. For some bonds, however, the approximation is in error by less than others. For example, for the 14%, 30-year bond, the unexplained percentage price change for a 300-basis-point increase is 5.5%, while for the zero-coupon bond of the same maturity it is 28.41%.

The reason that duration provides a good approximation for small changes in yield but a poor approximation for large changes in the required yield lies in the convex shape of the price/yield relationship. This point is examined in the next chapter.

Exhibit 10-6   Percentage Change in Price Estimated Using Modified Duration

Coupon	Term (years)	Modified duration (years)	Yield change (in basis points)					
			1	10	50	100	200	300
			Required Yield					
			10.01%	10.10%	10.50%	11.00%	12.00%	13.00%
0.00%	5	4.76	−0.05%	−0.48%	−2.38%	−4.76%	−9.52%	−14.28%
0.00%	15	14.29	−0.14	−1.43	−7.15	−14.29	−28.58	−42.87
0.00%	30	28.57	−0.29	−2.86	−14.29	−28.57	−57.14	−85.71
8.00%	5	3.98	−0.04	−0.40	−1.99	−3.98	−7.96	−11.94
8.00%	15	8.05	−0.08	−0.81	−4.03	−8.05	−16.10	−24.15
8.00%	30	9.72	−0.10	−0.97	−4.86	−9.72	−19.44	−29.16
10.00%	5	3.86	−0.04	−0.39	−1.93	−3.86	−7.72	−11.58
10.00%	15	7.69	−0.08	−0.77	−3.85	−7.69	−15.38	−23.07
10.00%	30	9.46	−0.09	−0.95	−4.73	−9.46	−18.92	−28.38
14.00%	5	3.67	−0.04	−0.37	−1.84	−3.67	−7.34	−11.01
14.00%	15	7.22	−0.07	−0.72	−3.61	−7.22	−14.44	−21.66
14.00%	30	9.17	−0.09	−0.92	−4.59	−9.17	−18.34	−27.51

Exhibit 10-6 continued.

Coupon	Term (years)	Modified duration (years)	Yield change (in basis points)					
			−1	−10	−50	−100	−200	−300
			Required Yield					
			9.99%	9.90%	9.50%	9.00%	8.00%	7.00%
0.00%	5	4.76	0.05%	0.48%	2.38%	4.76%	9.52%	14.28%
0.00%	15	14.29	0.14	1.43	7.15	14.29	28.58	42.87
0.00%	30	28.57	0.29	2.86	14.29	28.57	57.14	85.71
8.00%	5	3.98	0.04	0.40	1.99	3.98	7.96	11.94
8.00%	15	8.05	0.08	0.81	4.03	8.05	16.10	24.15
8.00%	30	9.72	0.10	0.97	4.86	9.72	19.44	29.16
10.00%	5	3.86	0.04	0.39	1.93	3.86	7.72	11.58
10.00%	15	7.69	0.08	0.77	3.85	7.69	15.38	23.07
10.00%	30	9.46	0.09	0.95	4.73	9.46	18.92	28.38
14.00%	5	3.67	0.04	0.37	1.84	3.67	7.34	11.01
14.00%	15	7.22	0.07	0.72	3.61	7.22	14.44	21.66
14.00%	30	9.17	0.09	0.92	4.59	9.17	18.34	27.51

Exhibit 10-7 Percentage Price Change Not Explained by Modified Duration

					Yield change (in basis points)			
			1	10	50	100	200	300
Coupon	Term (years)	Modified duration (years)	10.01%	10.10%	Required Yield 10.50%	11.00%	12.00%	13.00%
0.00%	5	4.76	0.00%	0.00%	0.03%	0.12%	0.48%	1.06%
0.00%	15	14.29	0.00	0.01	0.26	1.01	3.83	8.21
0.00%	30	28.57	0.00	0.04	0.99	3.77	13.76	28.41
8.00%	5	3.98	0.00	0.00	0.02	0.10	0.38	0.83
8.00%	15	8.05	0.00	0.00	0.12	0.45	1.73	3.74
8.00%	30	9.72	0.00	0.01	0.20	0.78	2.92	6.15
10.00%	5	3.86	0.00	0.00	0.02	0.09	0.36	0.80
10.00%	15	7.69	0.00	0.00	0.11	0.42	1.62	3.48
10.00%	30	9.46	0.00	0.01	0.19	0.74	2.76	5.83
14.00%	5	3.67	0.00	0.00	0.02	0.09	0.34	0.75
14.00%	15	7.22	0.00	0.00	0.10	0.38	1.45	3.14
14.00%	30	9.17	0.00	0.01	0.18	0.69	2.60	5.50

Exhibit 10-7 continued.

Coupon	Term (years)	Modified duration (years)	Yield change (in basis points)					
			−1	−10	−50	−100	−200	−300
			Required Yield					
			9.99%	9.90%	9.50%	9.00%	8.00%	7.00%
0.00%	5	4.76	0.00%	0.00%	0.03%	0.13%	0.52%	1.20%
0.00%	15	14.29	0.00	0.01	0.27	1.11	4.67	11.11
0.00%	30	28.57	0.00	0.04	1.09	4.59	20.43	51.39
8.00%	5	3.98	0.00	0.00	0.03	0.10	0.41	0.93
8.00%	15	8.05	0.00	0.00	0.12	0.49	2.06	4.88
8.00%	30	9.72	0.00	0.01	0.22	0.90	3.91	9.57
10.00%	5	3.86	0.00	0.00	0.02	0.10	0.39	0.89
10.00%	15	7.69	0.00	0.00	0.11	0.45	1.91	4.52
10.00%	30	9.46	0.00	0.01	0.21	0.86	3.70	9.04
14.00%	5	3.67	0.00	0.00	0.02	0.09	0.36	0.83
14.00%	15	7.22	0.00	0.00	0.10	0.41	1.72	4.06
14.00%	30	9.17	0.00	0.01	0.19	0.79	3.43	8.36

Modified Duration as a Measure of Percentage Price
Change Per 100 Basis Point Yield Change

For a 100-basis-point change in yield, the percentage change in the bond's price is

Modified duration × (.01).

For example, if the modified duration is 10, the percentage change in the bond's price for a 100-basis-point change is

$$10 \times (.01) = .10 \text{ or } 10\%.$$

Thus, a bond with a modified duration of 10 would change by 10% for a 100-basis-point (1%) change in yield. Similarly, a bond with a modified duration of X would change by X% for a 100- basis-point change in yield. For this reason, some investors refer to modified duration as the percentage price change of a bond. Technically, what they mean is that modified duration represents the percentage price change of a bond for a *100-basis-point* change in yield.

Dollar Duration

The modified duration of a bond can be used to approximate the percentage change in the price of the bond per basis point change. Given the initial price of the bond and the approximate percentage change in price based on modified duration, the dollar price change can be computed. Alternatively, the dollar price change can be computed as follows:

Approximate dollar price change =
− (Modified duration) × (Initial price) × (Yield change).

The product of modified duration and the initial price is called the *dollar duration*; that is,

Dollar duration = Modified duration × Initial price.

Therefore,

$$\text{Approximate dollar price change} =$$
$$-(\text{Dollar duration}) \times (\text{Yield change}).$$

For example, suppose that the required yield for the 8%, 15-year bond selling to yield 10% (price = 84.6275) increased by one basis point; then the approximate dollar price change is found as follows:

$$\text{Dollar duration} = \text{Modified duration} \times \text{Initial price}$$
$$= 8.05 \times 84.6275 = 681.25$$

$$\text{Approximate dollar price change} =$$
$$= -(681.25) \times (.0001) = .0681.$$

Earlier in this chapter, we showed how to compute the price value of a basis point. The dollar duration per basis point change is equal to the price value of a basis point.

How good an estimate of the dollar price change is given by dollar duration? For small changes in yield, it will be good, as we saw in Illustration 10-3, in which modified duration was used to estimate the percentage price change. For large changes in yield, the approximation is not as good. Recall from Illustration 10-4 that when the yield increased by 300 basis points, the estimated percentage decline in price was greater than the actual decline in price. This means that the estimated dollar price decline will be greater than the actual price decline, so that the estimated new price is less than the actual price at the higher yield. Also in Illustration 10-4, the estimated percentage price increase is less than the actual price increase when yield declines by 300 basis points. The actual price increase, therefore, is underestimated using modified duration and the estimated price at the lower yield will be less than the actual price. Thus, whether the yield rises or falls by a large number of basis points, modified duration and dollar duration will underestimate what the new price will be. A graphical explanation for this fact will be given in the next chapter.

Duration and the Yield Curve

The yield curve graphically depicts the relationship between yield to maturity and the term to maturity of bonds. The Macaulay and modified duration formulas presented above to estimate price changes are based on a particular assumption about how the yield curve changes. Specifically, they assume that the yield curve is flat and that when the yield curve shifts, interest rates for all maturities change by the same amount. That is, they assume that there is a parallel shift in the yield curve.[5]

More complicated duration measures have been developed on the assumption that more complex shifts in the yield curve may occur. However, several studies have demonstrated that the Macaulay duration is just as useful as these more complicated duration measures.[6]

Price Volatility Weighting for Hedging

In hedging a portfolio or bond position, a portfolio manager or trader wants to take an opposite position in a cash market security (or securities) or in a derivative instrument (option or futures contract) so that any loss in the position held is offset by a gain in the opposite position. To do so, the *dollar* price volatility of the position used to hedge must equal the *dollar* price volatility of the position to be hedged. That is, the objective in hedging is

Dollar price change in position to be hedged
= Dollar price change of hedging vehicle.

The hedger encounters two problems. First, for a given change in yield, the dollar price volatility of the bond to be

---

[5] See Appendix A.

[6] See G.O. Bierwag, George G. Kaufman, Robert Schweitzer, and Alden Toevs, "The Art of Risk Management in Bond Portfolios," *The Journal of Portfolio Management* (Spring 1981), pp. 27–36.

hedged will not necessarily be equal to the dollar price volatility of the hedging vehicle. For example, if yields change by 50 basis points, the price of the bond to be hedged may change by $X while the price of the hedging vehicle may change by more or less than $X. The second problem is that factors that result in a change in the yield of a given number of basis points for the bond to be hedged may not result in a change of the same number of basis points for the hedging vehicle. That is, if yields change by x basis points for the bond to be hedged, the yield for the hedging vehicle may change by more or less than x basis points.

Consequently, a portfolio manager or trader attempting to hedge a $10 million long position in some bond will not necessarily take a $10 million short position in the vehicle used for hedging because the relative dollar price volatility of the two positions will not necessarily be the same. The hedger would have to consider the relative dollar price volatility of the two positions in constructing the hedge. As a result, the objective in hedging can be restated as follows:

Dollar price change of bond to be hedged =

Dollar price change of hedging vehicle

$\times \dfrac{\text{Dollar price volatility of bond to be hedged}}{\text{Dollar price volatility of hedging vehicle}}$.

The last ratio is commonly referred to as the *hedge ratio*.

The three measures of price volatility discussed in this chapter—price value of a basis point, the yield value of a price change and dollar duration—can be used to compute the hedge ratio. If properly applied they will give the same hedge ratio. Because the dollar price volatility of a bond changes when (1) its yield changes and (2) it moves toward maturity, a hedged position must be monitored and rebalanced periodically.

Using the Price Value of a Basis Point to Compute the Hedge Ratio

The hedge ratio can be computed from the price value of a basis point by the following formula:

$$\frac{\text{Price value of a basis point for bond to be hedged}}{\text{Price value of a basis point for hedging vehicle}}$$
$$\times \frac{\text{Change in yield for bond to be hedged}}{\text{Change in yield for hedging vehicle}}.$$

The first ratio shows the price change for the bond to be hedged relative to the price change for the hedging vehicle, both based on a yield change of one basis point. The second ratio indicates the relative change in the yield of the two instruments. This ratio is commonly referred to as the *yield beta* and is estimated using the statistical technique of regression analysis. Therefore, the hedge ratio can be rewritten as

$$\frac{\text{Price value of a basis point for bond to be hedged}}{\text{Price value of a basis point for hedging vehicle}}$$
$$\times \text{Yield beta}$$

Illustration 10-5. To illustrate the above relationship, we'll look at how to hedge a $10 million long position in a 15-year, 8% coupon bond selling to yield 10% with a 10% coupon bond with the same maturity and selling at the same yield. The following information is known:

Bond to be hedged = 15-year, 8% bond selling to yield 10%;
  Hedging vehicle = 15-year, 10% bond selling to yield 10%;

  For bond to be hedged,
  Price value of a basis point per $100 of par = 0.0681;

  For hedging vehicle,
  Price value of a basis point per $100 of par = 0.0768.

For this illustration, we shall assume that the yield beta is 1. The hedge ratio is then

$$\frac{0.0681}{0.0768} \times 1 = .8867.$$

The hedge ratio of .8867 means that for every $1 of par value of the 15-year, 8% coupon bond to be hedged, the hedger should short $.8867 of $1 par of the hedging vehicle. Since this illustration involves a long position of $10 million of the 15-year, 8% coupon bond, a short position of $8.867 million of the 15-year, 10% bond should be taken.

To demonstrate that this hedge ratio will result in equal dollar price changes for the bond to be hedged and the hedging vehicle, suppose interest rates rise by 10 basis points. The price of the bond to be hedged will decline from 84.6275 per $100 of par to 83.9505, resulting in a loss for the $10 million position of $67,700. The short position, however, will gain. The price of the 15-year, 10% coupon bond will decline from 100 per $100 of par to 99.2357, resulting in a gain of $67,770 for the $8.867 million position. The gain is almost identical to the loss.

Using the Yield Value of a Price Change to Compute the Hedge Ratio

The hedge ratio can be computed using the yield value of a price change from the following formula:

$$\frac{\text{Yield value of a price change for hedging vehicle}}{\text{Yield value of a price change for bond to be hedged}}$$

$\times$ Yield beta.

Using Dollar Duration to Compute the Hedge Ratio

Recall that modified duration is related to the percentage price volatility. In hedging, we are interested in dollar price changes. Consequently, to compute the hedge ratio from duration, dollar duration should be used not modified duration. The hedge ratio is computed from dollar duration as follows:

$$\frac{\text{Dollar duration for bond to be hedged}}{\text{Dollar duration for hedging vehicle}}$$

$\times$ Yield beta.

Recall that the dollar duration per basis point per $100 of par value is the same as the price value of a basis point. Therefore, dollar duration will produce the same hedge ratio as the price value of a basis point.

Weighting Trades

Common trading strategies involve swapping one or more bonds for another bond or bonds so as to capitalize on either (1) changes in yields, (2) changes in spreads between market sectors, or (3) a portfolio's convexity. With the first type of trade, commonly referred to as a *rate anticipation swap*, the objective is to alter the duration so as to capitalize on the forecasted change in interest rates. In contrast, for the last two types of trade, the trader or portfolio manager seeks to hold the dollar price volatility constant.

This can be accomplished by using the same framework we employed in the previous section to construct a hedged portfolio. Thus, if Bond A is to be swapped (exchanged) for Bond B, the portfolio manager or trader will buy enough of Bond B so that it has the same dollar price volatility as Bond A.

Role of Duration in Immunization Strategies: Offsetting Interest Rate Risk and Reinvestment Risk

In Chapter 7, we explained that the return that will be realized by investing in a coupon security will depend on the interest rate earned on the reinvestment of the coupon payments. When interest rates rise, interest on interest from the reinvestment of the coupon payments will be higher, but if the investment horizon is shorter than the maturity of the bond, a loss will be realized upon the sale of the bond. The reverse is true if interest rates fall: price appreciation will be realized when the bond is sold but interest on interest from reinvesting the coupon payments will be lower. Because of these two risks, the investor cannot be assured of locking in the yield at the time of purchase.

Because the interest rate risk and reinvestment risk offset each other, however, is it possible to select a bond or bond portfolio that will lock in the yield at the time of purchase regardless of interest rate changes in the future? That is, is it possible to *immunize* the bond or bond portfolio against interest rate changes?

Fortunately, under certain circumstances, it is. This can be accomplished by constructing a portfolio so that its Macaulay duration is equal to the length of the investment horizon. Thus, if a portfolio manager has an investment horizon of five years and wants to lock in a return over that time period, he should select a portfolio with a Macaulay duration of five years. This is demonstrated in the next illustration.

Illustration 10-6. Suppose a portfolio manager knows that a liability of $17,183,033 must be paid in 5.5 years. Also suppose that interest rates are currently 12.5% on a bond equivalent basis. The present value of the $17,183,033 liability 5.5 years from now assuming interest can be earned at a rate of 6.25% per six-month period is $8,820,262. Thus, if the portfolio manager invested $8,820,262 at the current rate of 6.25% per six-month period for the next 11 six-month periods, the accumulated value would be sufficient to satisfy the liability.

Suppose the portfolio manager buys $8,820,262 par value of a bond selling at par with a 12.5% yield to maturity that matures in 5.5 years. The Macaulay duration for this bond is 4.14 years, which is shorter than the length of the investment horizon. Will the portfolio manager be assured of realizing the target yield of 12.5% or, equivalently, a target accumulated value of $17,183,033? As we explained in Chapter 6, the portfolio manager will realize a 12.5% yield only if the coupon interest payments can be reinvested at 6.25% every six months. That is, the accumulated value will depend on the reinvestment rate.

To illustrate this, suppose that immediately after investing the $8,820,262 in the 12.5% coupon, 5.5-year maturity bond, yields in the market change and stay at the new level for the remainder of the 5.5 years. Exhibit 10-8 illustrates what happens at the end of 5.5 years. The first column shows the new yield. The second column shows the total coupon interest payments. The third column gives the interest on interest over the entire 5.5 years if the coupon interest payments are reinvested at the new yield shown in the first column. The price of the bond at the end of 5.5 years, shown in the fourth column, is the par value. The fifth column is the accumulated value from all three sources: coupon interest, interest on interest, and price of bond. The horizon return is shown in the last column.

Exhibit 10-8

Accumulated Value and Horizon Return:
5.5-year, 12.5% Coupon Bond Selling to Yield 12.5%

Investment horizon (years)	5.5
Coupon rate	12.5000%
Maturity (years)	5.50
Yield to maturity	12.5000%
Price	100.00000
Par value purchased	$8,820,262
Purchase price	$8,820,262
Target accumulated value	$17,183,033

Over 5.5 years

New yield	Coupon	Interest on interest	Price of bond	Accumulated value	Horizon return
16.0%	$6,063,930	$3,112,167	$8,820,262	$17,996,360	13.40%
15.5	6,063,930	2,990,716	8,820,262	17,874,908	13.26
14.5	6,063,930	2,753,177	8,820,262	17,637,369	13.00
14.0	6,063,930	2,637,037	8,820,262	17,521,230	12.88
13.5	6,063,930	2,522,618	8,820,262	17,406,810	12.75

Exhibit 10-8 continued.

			Over 5.5 years		
New yield	Coupon	Interest on interest	Price of bond	Accumulated value	Horizon return
13.0	6,063,930	2,409,894	8,820,262	17,294,086	12.62
12.5	6,063,930	2,298,840	8,820,262	17,183,033	12.50
12.0	6,063,930	2,189,433	8,820,262	17,073,625	12.38
11.5	6,063,930	2,081,648	8,820,262	16,965,840	12.25
11.0	6,063,930	1,975,462	8,820,262	16,859,654	12.13
10.5	6,063,930	1,870,852	8,820,262	16,755,044	12.01
10.0	6,063,930	1,767,794	8,820,262	16,651,986	11.89
9.5	6,063,930	1,666,266	8,820,262	16,550,458	11.78
9.0	6,063,930	1,566,246	8,820,262	16,450,438	11.66
8.5	6,063,930	1,476,712	8,820,262	16,351,904	11.54
8.0	6,063,930	1,370,642	8,820,262	16,254,834	11.43
7.5	6,063,930	1,275,014	8,820,262	16,159,206	11.32
7.0	6,063,930	1,180,808	8,820,262	16,065,000	11.20
6.5	6,063,930	1,088,003	8,820,262	15,972,195	11.09
6.0	6,063,930	996,577	8,820,262	15,880,769	10.98
5.5	6,063,930	906,511	8,820,262	15,790,703	10.87
5.0	6,063,930	817,785	8,820,262	15,701,977	10.77

When yields do not change, so that the coupon payments can be reinvested at 12.5% (6.25% every six months), the target accumulated value will be achieved by the portfolio manager. If market yields rise, an accumulated value (horizon return) higher than the target accumulated value (target yield) will be achieved, because the coupon interest payments can be reinvested at a rate higher than the initial yield to maturity. Contrast this circumstance with what happens when the yield declines. The accumulated value (horizon return) will be less than the target accumulated value (target yield). *Therefore, investing in a coupon bond with a yield to maturity equal to the target yield and a maturity equal to the investment horizon does not assure that the target accumulated value will be achieved.*

Suppose that instead of investing in a bond maturing in 5.5 years, the portfolio manager invests in a 15-year bond with a coupon rate of 12.5% and selling at par to yield 12.5%. The Macaulay duration for this bond is 7.12 years, which is longer than the 5.5-year investment horizon. The accumulated value and horizon return if the market yield changes immediately after the bond is purchased and remains at the new yield are presented in Exhibit 10-9. The fourth column in Exhibit 10-9 is the market price of a 12.5% coupon, 9.5-year bond (since 5.5 years have passed), assuming that the market yield is as shown in the first column. If the market yield increases, the portfolio will fail to achieve the target accumulated value; the opposite is true if the market yield decreases—the accumulated value (horizon return) will exceed the target accumulated value (target yield).

The reason for this result can be seen in Exhibit 10-10, which summarizes the change in interest on interest and the change in price resulting from a change in the market yield. For example, if the market yield rises instantaneously by 200 basis points, from 12.5% to 14.5%, interest on interest will be $454,336 greater; the market price of the bond, however, will decrease by $894,781. The net effect is that the accumulated value will be $440,445 less than the target accumulated value. The reverse is true if the market yield decreases. The change in price of the bond will more than offset the decline in the interest on interest, resulting in an accumulated value that exceeds the target accumulated value. Exhibit 10-10 clearly demonstrates the trade-off between interest-rate (or price) risk and reinvestment risk.

Exhibit 10-9

Accumulated Value and Horizon Return:
15-year, 12.5% Coupon Bond Selling to Yield 12.5%

Investment horizon (years)	5.5
Coupon rate	12.5000%
Maturity (years)	15
Yield to maturity	12.5000%
Price	100.00000
Par value purchased	$8,820,262
Purchase price	$8,820,262
Target accumulated value	$17,183,033

Over 5.5 years

New yield	Coupon	Interest on interest	Price of bond	Accumulated value	Horizon return
16.0%	$6,063,930	$3,112,167	$7,337,902	$16,514,000	11.73%
15.5	6,063,930	2,990,716	7,526,488	16,581,134	11.81
14.5	6,063,930	2,753,177	7,925,481	16,742,587	12.00
14.0	6,063,930	2,637,037	8,136,542	16,837,510	12.11
13.5	6,063,930	2,522,618	8,355,777	16,942,325	12.23

13.0	6,063,930	2,409,894	8,583,555	17,057,379	12.36
12.5	6,063,930	2,298,840	8,820,262	17,183,033	12.50
12.0	6,063,930	2,189,433	9,066,306	17,319,669	12.65
11.5	6,063,930	2,081,648	9,322,113	17,467,691	12.82
11.0	6,063,930	1,975,462	9,588,131	17,627,523	12.99
10.5	6,063,930	1,870,852	9,864,831	17,799,613	13.18
10.0	6,063,930	1,767,794	10,152,708	17,984,432	13.38
9.5	6,063,930	1,666,266	10,452,281	18,182,477	13.59
9.0	6,063,930	1,566,246	10,764,095	18,394,271	13.82
8.5	6,063,930	1,467,712	11,088,723	18,620,366	14.06
8.0	6,063,930	1,370,642	11,426,770	18,861,342	14.31
7.5	6,063,930	1,275,014	11,778,867	19,117,812	14.57
7.0	6,063,930	1,180,808	12,145,682	19,390,420	14.85
6.5	6,063,930	1,088,003	12,527,914	19,679,847	15.14
6.0	6,063,930	996,577	12,926,301	19,986,808	15.44
5.5	6,063,930	906,511	13,341,617	20,312,058	15.76
5.0	6,063,930	817,785	13,774,677	20,656,393	16.09

Exhibit 10-10
Change in Interest on Interest and Price Due
to Interest Rate Change:
15-year, 12.5% Coupon Bond Selling to Yield 12.5%

New yield	Change in interest on interest	Change in price	Total change in accumulated value
16.0%	$813,327	– $1,482,360	– $669,033
15.5	691,875	– 1,293,774	– 601,898
14.5	454,336	– 894,781	– 440,445
14.0	338,197	– 683,720	– 345,523
13.5	223,778	– 464,485	– 240,707
13.0	111,054	– 236,707	– 125,654
12.5	0	0	0
12.0	– 109,407	246,044	136,636
11.5	– 217,192	501,851	284,659
11.0	– 323,378	767,869	444,491
10.5	– 427,989	1,044,569	616,581
10.0	– 531,046	1,332,446	801,400
9.5	– 632,574	1,632,019	999,445
9.0	– 732,594	1,943,833	1,211,239
8.5	– 831,128	2,268,461	1,437,333
8.0	– 928,198	2,606,508	1,678,309
7.5	– 1,023,826	2,958,605	1,934,779
7.0	– 1,118,032	3,325,420	2,207,388
6.5	– 1,210,838	3,707,652	2,496,814
6.0	– 1,302,263	4,106,039	2,803,776
5.5	– 1,392,329	4,521,355	3,129,026
5.0	– 1,481,055	4,954,415	3,473,360

Consider an 8-year, 10.125% coupon bond selling at 88.20262 to yield 12.5%, which has a Macaulay duration of 5.5 years. Suppose $10,000,000 of par value of this bond is purchased for $8,820,262. For this bond, Exhibit 10-11 provides the same information as Exhibits 10-8 and 10-9. Looking at the last two columns, we see that the accumulated value and the horizon return are never less than the target accumulated value and the target yield. Thus, the target accumulated value is assured regardless of what happens to the market yield. Exhibit 10-12 shows why. When the market yield rises, the change in the interest on interest more than offsets the decline in price. On the other hand, when the market yield declines, the increase in price exceeds the decline in interest on interest.

Notice that the last bond, which assures that the target accumulated value will be achieved regardless of what happens to the market yield, has a Macaulay duration equal to the length of the investment horizon. This is the key. To immunize a portfolio's target accumulated value (target yield) against a change in the market yield, a portfolio manager must invest in a bond (or a bond portfolio) such that (1) the Macaulay duration is equal to the investment horizon and (2) the present value of the cash flow from the bond (or bond portfolio) equals the present value of the liability.

In Illustration 10-6, we assumed a one-time instantaneous change in the market yield. In practice, the market yield will fluctuate over the investment horizon. As a result, the Macaulay duration of the portfolio will change as the market yield changes. In addition, the Macaulay duration will change with the passage of time. In the face of changing market yields, a manager can still immunize a portfolio by rebalancing it so that the Macaulay duration of the portfolio is equal to the remainder of the investment horizon. For example, if the investment horizon is initially 5.5 years, the initial portfolio should have a Macaulay duration of 5.5 years. After six months, the remaining investment horizon is five years. The Macaulay duration then will probably be different from five years. Thus the portfolio must be rebalanced so that its Macaulay duration is equal to five years. Six months later, the portfolio must be rebalanced so that its Macaulay duration is equal to 4.5 years, etc.

Exhibit 10-11

Accumulated Value and Horizon Return:
8-year, 10.125% Coupon Bond Selling to Yield 12.5%

Investment horizon (years)	5.5
Coupon rate	10.1250%
Maturity (years)	8
Yield to maturity	12.5000%
Price	88.20262
Par value purchased	$10,000,000
Purchase price	$8,820,262
Target accumulated value	$17,183,033

Over 5.5 years

New yield	Coupon	Interest on interest	Price of bond	Accumulated value	Horizon return
16.0%	$5,568,750	$2,858,028	$8,827,141	$17,253,919	12.58%
15.5	5,568,750	2,746,494	8,919,852	17,235,096	12.56
14.5	5,568,750	2,528,352	9,109,054	17,206,156	12.53
14.0	5,568,750	2,421,697	9,205,587	17,196,034	12.51
13.5	5,568,750	2,316,621	9,303,435	17,188,807	12.51

13.0	5,568,750	2,213,102	9,402,621	17,184,473	12.50
12.5	5,568,750	2,111,117	9,503,166	17,183,033	12.50
12.0	5,568,750	2,010,644	9,605,091	17,184,485	12.50
11.5	5,568,750	1,911,661	9,708,420	17,188,831	12.51
11.0	5,568,750	1,814,146	9,813,175	17,196,071	12.51
10.5	5,568,750	1,718,078	9,919,380	17,206,208	12.53
10.0	5,568,750	1,623,436	10,027,059	17,219,245	12.54
9.5	5,568,750	1,530,199	10,136,236	17,235,185	12.56
9.0	5,568,750	1,438,347	10,246,936	17,254,033	12.58
8.5	5,568,750	1,347,859	10,359,184	17,275,793	12.60
8.0	5,568,750	1,258,715	10,473,006	17,300,472	12.63
7.5	5,568,750	1,170,897	10,588,428	17,328,075	12.66
7.0	5,568,750	1,084,383	10,705,477	17,358,610	12.70
6.5	5,568,750	999,156	10,824,180	17,392,086	12.73
6.0	5,568,750	915,197	10,944,565	17,428,511	12.77
5.5	5,568,750	832,486	11,066,660	17,467,895	12.82
5.0	5,568,750	751,005	11,190,494	17,510,248	12.86

Exhibit 10-12
Change in Interest on Interest and Price Due
to Interest Rate Change:
8-year, 10.125% Coupon Bond Selling to Yield 12.5%

New yield	Change in interest on interest	Change in price	Total change in accumulated value
16.0%	$746,911	− $676,024	$70,887
15.5	635,377	− 583,314	52,063
14.5	417,235	− 394,112	23,123
14.0	310,580	− 297,579	13,001
13.5	205,504	− 199,730	5,774
13.0	101,985	− 100,544	1,441
12.5	0	0	0
12.0	− 100,473	101,925	1,452
11.5	− 199,456	205,254	5,798
11.0	− 296,971	310,010	13,038
10.5	− 393,039	416,215	23,176
10.0	− 487,681	523,894	36,212
9.5	− 580,918	633,071	52,153
9.0	− 672,770	743,771	71,000
8.5	− 763,258	856,019	92,760
8.0	− 852,402	969,841	117,439
7.5	− 940,221	1,085,263	145,042
7.0	− 1,026,734	1,202,311	175,578
6.5	− 1,111,961	1,321,014	209,053
6.0	− 1,195,921	1,441,399	245,478
5.5	− 1,278,632	1,563,494	284,862
5.0	− 1,360,112	1,687,328	327,216

Immunization and the Yield Curve

Constructing a bond portfolio so that its Macaulay duration is equal to the investment horizon will assure that the target yield will be realized only if there is parallel shift in the yield curve. Since the yield curve does not always shift in a parallel fashion, the portfolio is exposed to the risk of not being immunized. There is a measure that can be used to determine this risk.[7] Of all the possible portfolios that can be constructed with a Macaulay duration equal to the investment horizon, the one that minimizes the immunization risk measure should be selected.

Summary

In this chapter we have discussed three measures of bond price volatility. We focused our attention on one measure, duration, and explained the relationship between duration and bond price volatility. There are different measures of duration—Macaulay duration, modified duration, and dollar duration. Modified duration is the percentage price change per 100-basis-point change in yield. It is equal to Macaulay duration divided by the quantity one plus the periodic required yield. Dollar duration indicates the dollar price volatility of a bond and is equal to the product of modified duration and the bond's price. Dollar duration for a one-basis-point change in interest rates is equal to the price value of a basis point. We then showed how all three measures of bond price volatility can be used in weighting swaps and hedges. We also showed the importance of duration in constructing a portfolio so that it will be immunized against interest rate changes over some investment horizon.

One of the properties of duration that we observed was that it provides a good approximation to the change in price for small changes in yield but not for large changes. The reason, as we noted several times throughout the chapter, is the convex shape of the price/yield relationship. We focus on this in the next chapter.

---

[7] See H. Gifford Fong and Oldrich Vasicek, "A Risk Minimizing Strategy for Multiple Liability Immunization," *Journal of Finance* (December 1984), pp. 1541-1546. For a less technical description, see: H. Gifford Fong and Frank J. Fabozzi, *Fixed Income Portfolio Management* (Homewood, Ill.: Dow Jones-Irwin, 1985), pp. 133-136.

11
Convexity of Option-Free Bonds: Measurement and Properties

We're now ready to tie together the price/yield relationship and several of the properties about the bond price volatility that we discussed in the previous chapter. Recall that the shape of the price/yield relationship is convex. It is the convex shape that gives rise to the properties.[1]

Estimating Price with Duration: A Graphical Depiction

In the previous chapter, we explained how duration (modified or dollar) can be used to estimate price change when yield changes. In Exhibit 11-1, a line is drawn tangent to the curve

---

[1] The formulas shown in this chapter are presented without proof. For a mathematical derivation of the formulas, see Appendix A.

Exhibit 11-1

Tangent to Price/Yield Relationship

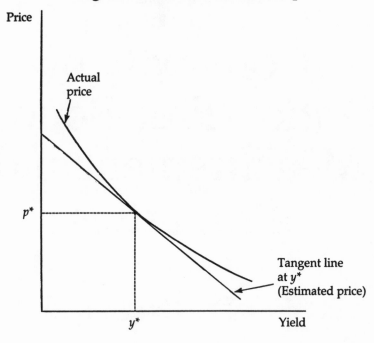

depicting the price/yield relationship at point y^*.[2] The tangent line shows the rate of change of price with respect to a change in interest rates at that point (yield). Consequently, the tangent line is directly related to the dollar duration of the bond.[3]

How can the tangent line be used to approximate the new price if yield changes? If we draw a vertical line.from any yield

[2] In nontechnical terms, a tangent line is defined as a line that touches the price/yield relationship at the point y^* and does not touch the price/yield relationship at any other point.

[3] Technically, the slope of the tangent line is the change in price for a change in yield, sometimes referred to as dP/dy, a term adopted from calculus because the slope is the first derivative of the price function for a bond. The modified duration would be the slope of the tangent line if the price/yield relationship is drawn with the natural logarithm of the bond's price, rather than price, on the vertical axis . To simplify the discussion below, we shall refer to the slope of the tangent line as the dollar duration.

Exhibit 11-2

Estimating Price Using Duration

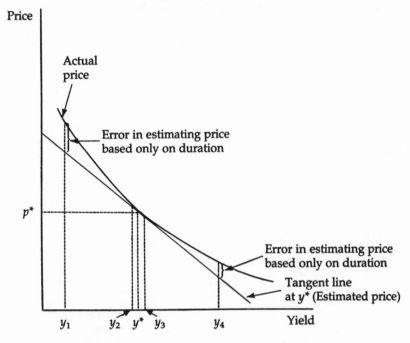

(on the horizontal axis), as we did in Exhibit 11-2, the distance between the horizontal axis and the tangent line represents the price as estimated from duration. Notice that the approximation will always underestimate the actual price at the new yield. This agrees with what we illustrated in the previous chapter: duration leads to an underestimate of the new price.

For small changes in yield, the tangent line gives a satisfactory estimate of the actual price. However, the further away from the initial yield, y^*, the worse the approximation. It should be apparent that the accuracy of the approximation from using duration (the tangent line) depends on the convexity of the price/yield relationship for the bond. Exhibit 11-3 shows the convexity of two hypothetical bonds. Both have the same duration at y^*; but Bond A has less convexity than Bond B. As a result, the duration-based approximation of the price is better for Bond A than Bond B.

Exhibit 11-3
Comparison of Two Bonds with Different Convexities but the Same Duration

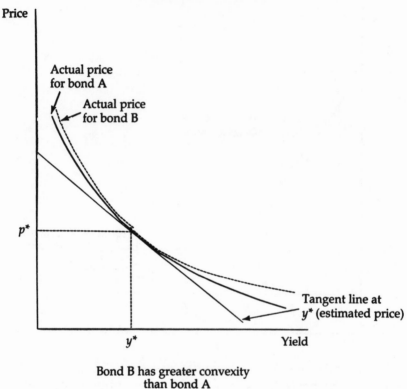

Bond B has greater convexity
than bond A

Measuring Convexity

As shown in Exhibit 11-3, how well we can approximate the new price will depend on the convexity of a bond. In this section, we give a formula for measuring the convexity of a bond. In the next section, we show how the price change due to convexity can be estimated.[4]

---

[4] Sometimes the following formula is used to approximate convexity (in periods):

$$\frac{(1)^2 \, PVCF_1 + (2)^2 \, PVCF_2 + (3)^2 \, PVCF_3 + \dots + (t)^2 \, PVCF_n}{(1+y)^2 \times PVTCF}.$$

The convexity of an option-free bond is measured as follows:

$$\text{convexity (in periods)} =$$

$$\frac{1(2)\ PVCF_1 + 2(3)\ PVCF_2 + 3(4)\ PVCF_3 + \ldots + n(n+1)\ PVCF_n}{(1+y)^2 \times PVTCF},$$

where

n = Number of periods until maturity;

t = The period when the cash flow is expected to be received ($t = 1,..,n$);

$PVCF_t$ = The present value of the cash flow in period t discounted at the prevailing period yield (in the case of a semiannual pay bond, one-half the yield to maturity)

$PVTCF$ = Total present value of the cash flow of the bond where the present value is determined by using the prevailing yield to maturity.

For a zero-coupon bond, the convexity in periods reduces to

$$\text{Convexity for a zero-coupon bond (in periods)} = \frac{n\,(n+1)}{(1+y)^2}.$$

To convert a bond's convexity from periods to years, the following formula is used:

$$\text{Convexity (in years)} = \frac{\text{Convexity (in periods)}}{k^2},$$

where

k = Number of payments per year (i.e., $k = 2$ for semiannual-pay bonds, $k = 12$ for monthly pay bonds).

For an option-free bond, the convexity measure will always be positive.

Exhibits 11-4 and 11-5 summarize the calculation of convexity for two of our hypothetical bonds (the 10%, five-year bond and the 14%, five-year bond, whose Macaulay durations are calculated in Exhibits 10-4 and 10-5 of Chapter 10, respectively), assuming each bond is selling to yield 10%. For the five-year, zero-coupon bond, the convexity is

Exhibit 11-4

Worksheet for Computation of Convexity for Five-Year, 8% Coupon Bond Selling to Yield 10%

Coupon rate =	8 %	
Term (years) =	5	
Initial yield =	10 %	
Price	= 92.27826	

Period (t)	Cash flow	PVCF	t(t+1)	PVCF × t(t+1)
1	$4.00	$ 3.8095	2	$ 7.6190
2	4.00	3.6281	6	22.7687
3	4.00	3.4554	12	41.4642
4	4.00	3.2908	20	65.8162
5	4.00	3.1341	30	94.0231
6	4.00	2.9849	42	125.3642
7	4.00	2.8427	56	159.1926
8	4.00	2.7074	72	194.9297
9	4.00	2.5784	90	232.0592
10	104.00	63.8470	110	7,023.1676
			Total	$7,965.4046

$$\text{Convexity (in half years)} = \frac{7{,}965.4046}{(1.05)^2 \, 92.27826} = 78.2942$$

$$\text{Convexity (in years)} = \frac{78.2942}{2^2} = 19.58$$

Exhibit 11-5

Worksheet for Computation of Convexity for Five-Year,
14% Coupon Bond Selling to Yield 10%

	Coupon rate	=	14 %
	Term (years)	=	5
	Initial yield	=	10 %
	Price	=	115.4434

Period (t)	Cash flow	PVCF	t(t+1)	PVCF × t(t+1)
1	$7.00	$ 6.6667	2	$ 13.3333
2	7.00	6.3492	6	38.0952
3	7.00	6.0469	12	72.5624
4	7.00	5.7589	20	115.1783
5	7.00	5.4847	30	164.5405
6	7.00	5.2235	42	219.3873
7	7.00	4.9748	56	278.5871
8	7.00	4.7379	72	341.1270
9	7.00	4.5123	90	406.1036
10	107.00	65.6887	110	7,225.7590
			Total	$8,874.6738

$$\text{Convexity (in half years)} = \frac{8,874.6738}{(1.05)^2\ 115.4434} = 69.7276$$

$$\text{Convexity (in years)} = \frac{69.7276}{2^2} = 17.44$$

$$\text{Convexity for a zero coupon bond (in periods)} = \frac{n\,(n+1)}{(1+y)^2};$$

since $n = 10$ (number of periods) and y is .05;

$$\text{Convexity} = \frac{10\,(10+1)}{(1.05)^2} = 24.94.$$

The convexities in years for the 12 hypothetical bonds we examined in the previous chapter are given below:

Coupon	Maturity	Convexity
0.00%	5	24.94
0.00	15	210.88
0.00	30	829.94
8.00	5	19.58
8.00	15	94.36
8.00	30	167.56
10.00%	5	18.74
10.00	15	87.62
10.00	30	158.70
14.00%	5	17.44
14.00	15	78.90
14.00	30	148.28

What do these convexity numbers mean? How can they be used? We will answer these question in the sections that follow.

Percentage Price Change Due to Convexity

Modified duration provides a first approximation to the percentage change in price. Convexity provides a second approximation, based on the following relationship:

Approximate percentage change in price due to convexity =
(0.5) × convexity × (yield change)^2.

Since the convexity measure is always positive, the approximate percentage change in price due to convexity is positive for either an increase or a decrease in yield.

Illustration 11-1. Consider the 8%, 15-year bond selling to yield 10%. If the yield increases from 10% to 13% (a 300 basis point or 0.03 yield change), then the percentage price change due to convexity is

$$(0.5) \times 94.36 \times (.03)^2 = .0425 = 4.25\%.$$

If the yield decreases by 300 basis points, from 10% to 7%, the percentage price change due to convexity is 4.25%.

Exhibit 11-6 shows the percentage price change due to convexity for various changes in yield for each of the 12 hypothetical bonds.

Percentage Price Change Due to Duration and Convexity

The approximate percentage change in price resulting from both duration and convexity is found by simply adding the two estimates.

Illustration 11-2. If yields change from 10% to 13%, we have:

Source of price change	*Approx. % price change*
Duration	− 24.15
Convexity	+ 4.25
Total	− 19.90

The actual percentage change in price would be –20.41%.
For a decrease of 300 basis points, from 10% to 7%:

Source of price change	*Approx. % price change*
Duration	+24.15
Convexity	+ 4.25
Total	28.40

Exhibit 11-6

Percentage Price Change Due to Convexity

Coupon	Term (years)	Convexity	Change (in basis points)					
			1	10	50	100	200	300
0%	5	24.94	0.00%	0.00%	0.03%	0.12%	0.50%	1.12%
0	15	210.88	0.00	0.01	0.26	1.05	4.22	9.49
0	30	829.94	0.00	0.04	1.04	4.15	16.60	37.35
8%	5	19.58	0.00%	0.00%	0.02%	0.10%	0.39%	0.88%
8	15	94.36	0.00	0.00	0.12	0.47	1.89	4.25
8	30	167.56	0.00	0.01	0.21	0.84	3.35	7.54
10%	5	18.74	0.00%	0.00%	0.02%	0.09%	0.37%	0.84%
10	15	87.62	0.00	0.00	0.11	0.44	1.75	3.94
10	30	158.70	0.00	0.01	0.20	0.79	3.17	7.14
14%	5	17.44	0.00%	0.00%	0.02%	0.09%	0.35%	0.78%
14	15	78.90	0.00	0.00	0.10	0.39	1.58	3.55
14	30	148.28	0.00	0.01	0.19	0.74	2.97	6.67

The actual percentage price change would be +29.03%.

Consequently, for large yield movements, a better approximation for bond price volatility is obtained by combining duration and convexity.

Exhibit 11-7 shows the percentage price changes due to both duration and convexity for our 12 hypothetical bonds. The percentage price change not explained by duration and convexity is shown in Exhibit 11-8 (see the column labeled "residual"). As can be seen from this exhibit, most of the change in price is explained by the combined effects of duration and convexity.

Dollar Convexity

In the previous chapter, we explained that dollar duration can be obtained by multiplying modified duration by the initial price. Dollar convexity can be obtained by multiplying convexity by the initial price:

$$\text{Dollar convexity} = \text{Convexity} \times \text{Initial price.}$$

To determine the dollar price change, the following formula is used:

$$\text{Dollar price change due to convexity} =$$
$$(0.5) \times \text{Dollar convexity} \times (\text{Yield change})^2.$$

Illustration 11-3. For the 8%, 15-year bond selling to yield 10%, the dollar convexity per $100 of par value is

$$94.36 \times \$84.63 = \$7,985.69.$$

The dollar price change per $100 of par value for a 100- basis-point change is

$$(0.5) \times \$7,985.69 \times (.01)^2 = \$0.399.$$

Thus, for a 100-basis-point change, the price of the bond will change by approximately $0.40 per $100 par value.

Exhibit 11–7   **Percentage Price Change Explained by Duration and Convexity**

		Yield change (in basis points)					
		1	10	50	100	200	300
		Required yield					
Coupon	Term (years)	10.01%	10.10%	10.50%	11.00%	12.00%	13.00%
0%	5	-0.05%	-0.47%	-2.35%	-4.64%	-9.02%	-13.16%
0	15	-0.14	-1.42	-6.88	-13.24	-24.36	-33.38
0	30	-0.29	-2.82	-13.25	-24.42	-40.54	-48.36
8%	5	-0.04%	-0.40%	-1.97%	-3.88%	-7.57%	-11.06%
8	15	-0.08	-0.80	-3.91	-7.58	-14.21	-19.90
8	30	-0.10	-0.96	-4.65	-8.88	-16.09	-21.62
10%	5	-0.04%	-0.39%	-1.91%	-3.77%	-7.35%	-10.74%
10	15	-0.08	-0.76	-3.74	-7.25	-13.63	-19.13
10	30	-0.09	-0.94	-4.53	-8.67	-15.75	-21.24
14%	5	-0.04%	-0.37%	-1.81%	-3.58%	-6.99%	-10.23%
14	15	-0.07	-0.72	-3.51	-6.83	-12.86	-18.11
14	30	-0.09	-0.91	-4.40	-8.43	-15.37	-20.84

		Yield change (in basis points)					
		−1	−10	−50	−100	−200	−300
Coupon	Term	Required yield					
		9.99%	9.90%	9.50%	9.00%	8.00%	7.00%
0%	5	0.05%	0.48%	2.41%	4.88%	10.02%	15.40%
0	15	0.14	1.44	7.41	15.34	32.80	52.36
0	30	0.29	2.90	15.32	32.72	73.74	123.06
8%	5	0.04%	0.40%	2.01%	4.08%	8.35%	12.82%
8	15	0.08	0.81	4.14	8.52	17.99	28.40
8	30	0.10	0.98	5.07	10.56	22.79	36.70
10%	5	0.04%	0.39%	1.95%	3.95%	8.09%	12.42%
10	15	0.08	0.77	3.95	8.13	17.13	27.01
10	30	0.09	0.95	4.93	10.25	22.09	35.52
14%	5	0.04%	0.37%	1.86%	3.76%	7.69%	11.79%
14	15	0.07	0.73	3.71	7.61	16.02	25.21
14	30	0.09	0.92	4.77	9.91	21.31	34.18

Exhibit 11-8

Percentage Price Change Not Explained by Using Both Duration and Convexity

Coupon	Term (years)	Yield change (in basis points)					
		1	10	50	100	200	300
		Required yield					
		10.01%	10.10%	10.50%	11.00%	12.00%	13.00%
0%	5	0.00%	0.00%	0.00%	0.00%	-0.02%	-0.07%
0	15	0.00	0.00	0.00	-0.05	-0.39	-1.28
0	30	0.00	0.00	-0.05	-0.38	-2.83	-8.94
8%	5	0.00%	0.00%	0.00%	0.00%	-0.02%	-0.05%
8	15	0.00	0.00	0.00	-0.02	-0.15	-0.51
8	30	0.00	0.00	-0.01	-0.06	-0.43	-1.39
10%	5	0.00%	0.00%	0.00%	0.00%	-0.01%	-0.05%
10	15	0.00	0.00	0.00	-0.01	-0.14	-0.46
10	30	0.00	0.00	-0.01	-0.06	-0.42	-1.31
14%	5	0.00%	0.00%	0.00%	0.00%	-0.01%	-0.04%
14	15	0.00	0.00	0.00	-0.02	-0.13	-0.41
14	30	0.00	0.00	-0.01	-0.05	-0.36	-1.17

Yield change (in basis points)

Coupon	Term	-1	-10	-50	-100	-200	-300
		9.99%	9.90%	9.50%	9.00%	8.00%	7.00%
				Required yield			
0%	5	0.00%	0.00%	0.00%	0.00%	0.02%	0.07%
0	15	0.00	0.00	0.00	0.05	0.46	1.62
0	30	0.00	0.00	0.05	0.44	3.83	14.05
8%	5	0.00%	0.00%	0.00%	0.00%	0.02%	0.05%
8	15	0.00	0.00	0.00	0.02	0.18	0.64
8	30	0.00	0.00	0.01	0.06	0.56	2.03
10%	5	0.00%	0.00%	0.00%	0.00%	0.02%	0.05%
10	15	0.00	0.00	0.00	0.02	0.16	0.58
10	30	0.00	0.00	0.01	0.07	0.53	1.90
14%	5	0.00%	0.00%	0.00%	0.00%	0.01	0.04%
14	15	0.00	0.00	0.00	0.02	0.14	0.51
14	30	0.00	0.00	0.01	0.05	0.46	1.69

For a 200-basis-point change, the dollar price change per $100 of par value is

$$(0.5) \times \$7,985.69 \times (.02)^2 = \$1.597.$$

For a 200-basis-point change, the dollar price change is approximately $1.60 per $100 of par value — more than double the $0.40 for a 100-basis-point change. Consequently, unlike dollar duration in which the dollar price change due to duration is proportionate to the change in yield—doubling the yield change from 100 basis points to 200 basis points, for example, doubles the dollar price change due to duration—the dollar price change due to convexity changes more than proportionately.

Convexity as a Measure of the Change in Dollar Duration

The tangent line in Exhibit 11-1 is a measure of the dollar duration of the price/yield relationship at point y^*. The steeper the tangent line, the greater the dollar duration; the flatter the line, the lower the duration.

Exhibit 11-9 graphically depicts what happens to the dollar duration as the yield changes. Notice that for an option-free bond, as the yield declines below y^*, the dollar duration increases; as the yield increases above y^*, the dollar duration decreases. This is true for all option-free bonds: *the dollar duration increases as the yield decreases and decreases as the yield increases.* Exhibit 11-10 shows the dollar durations for our 12 hypothetical bonds for various yields and confirms our graphical illustration.

Why is this property of an option-free bond attractive? As the yield declines, an investor who is long a bond would want its price to increase as much as possible — hence, an investor wants dollar duration to increase. The opposite is true if the yield increases. An investor wants the dollar duration to decline when the yield increases. For this reason, investors commonly refer to the shape of the price/yield relationship for an option-free bond as having "positive" convexity, "positive" indicating that it is a good attribute of a bond. In Chapter 13, we'll discuss bonds that have "negative" convexity which means that dollar duration does not change in the desired direction.

Exhibit 11-9

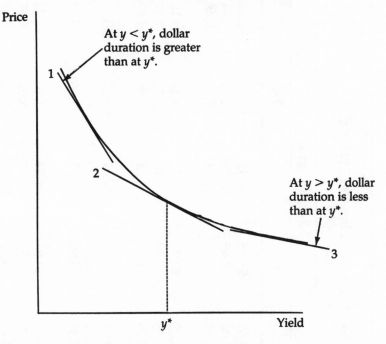

Dollar Duration at Different Yields

Price

At $y < y^*$, dollar duration is greater than at y^*.

1

2

At $y > y^*$, dollar duration is less than at y^*.

3

y^*

Yield

Exhibit 11-11 is the same as Exhibit 11-3, which shows the price/yield relationship of two bonds, A and B, with different convexities. Bond B has greater convexity than Bond A, while both have the same duration. Bond B is preferred to Bond A because it provides a higher bond price regardless of how yield changes — greater price appreciation if yield declines and smaller price loss if yield increases. Notice that the steepness of Bond B is greater than that of Bond A at yields below y^*. This means that the dollar duration of Bond B is greater than Bond A if the yield decreases. Thus, the investor realizes greater price appreciation from Bond B than from Bond A. Look at what happens if the yield increases above y^*. The tangent line is flatter for Bond B than for Bond A, indicating a lower dollar duration for Bond B than for Bond A. The investor in Bond B realizes a smaller price decline than the investor in Bond A.

Exhibit 11-10 Dollar Duration Per 100 Basis Points Per $100 Par

Coupon	Term	Required yield						
		4%	6%	8%	10%	12%	14%	16%
0%	5	$4.02	$3.61	$3.25	$2.92	$2.63	$2.38	$2.14
0	15	8.12	6.00	4.45	3.31	2.46	1.84	1.38
0	30	8.96	4.94	2.74	1.53	0.86	0.48	0.27
8%	5	$5.14	$4.65	$4.21	$3.82	$3.47	$3.16	$2.87
8	15	14.72	11.45	8.98	7.10	5.67	4.57	3.71
8	30	26.48	17.34	11.75	8.24	5.98	4.48	3.46
10%	5	$5.42	$4.91	$4.45	$4.04	$3.68	$3.35	$3.06
10	15	16.37	12.81	10.11	8.05	6.47	5.25	4.30
10	30	30.86	20.44	14.00	9.92	7.26	5.48	4.26
14%	5	$5.97	$5.43	$4.93	$4.49	$4.10	$3.74	$3.42
14	15	19.67	15.53	12.38	9.95	8.07	6.61	5.46
14	30	39.61	26.64	18.50	13.27	9.82	7.48	5.85

Exhibit 11-11
Dollar Duration for Different Convexities

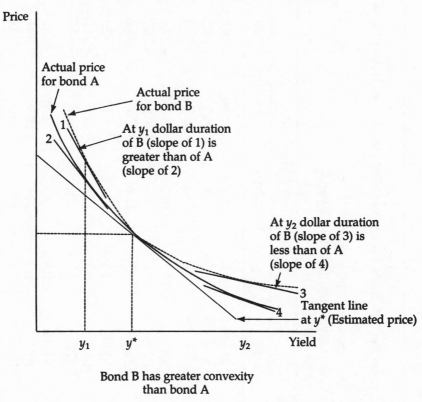

Bond B has greater convexity
than bond A

Exhibit 11-12 shows for each of our 12 hypothetical bonds the percentage change in dollar duration per 100 basis points per $100 par value, assuming an initial yield of 10%. This exhibit is constructed from the dollar durations in Exhibit 11-10. Also shown is the convexity for each bond at a 10% yield. Notice that the change in dollar duration is greater, the higher the convexity. Convexity measures the rate of change of dollar duration for a bond.

Exhibit 11–12
Percentage Change in Dollar Duration Per 100 Basis Points Per $100 Par Value (Initial Yield is 10%)

Assumption: Initial yield = 10%
Convexity computed at 10% yield

Coupon	Term (years)	Convexity	Required yield					
			4%	6	8%	12%	14%	16%
0%	5	24.94	37.6%	23.6%	11.1%	-9.9%	-18.7%	-26.6%
0	15	210.88	145.6	81.5	34.5	-25.5	-44.3	-58.2
0	30	829.94	486.1	223.2	79.3	-43.9	-68.4	-82.1
8%	5	19.58	34.5%	21.7%	10.2%	-9.2%	-17.4%	-24.8%
8	15	94.36	107.2	61.2	26.4	-20.2	-35.7	-47.7
8	30	167.56	221.4	110.5	42.6	-27.4	-45.6	-58.0
10%	5	18.74	33.9%	21.3%	10.1%	-9.0%	-17.1%	-24.4%
10	15	87.62	103.3	59.1	25.6	-19.6	-34.8	-46.6
10	30	158.70	211.2	106.1	41.2	-26.8	-44.7	-57.1
14%	5	17.44	33.0%	20.8%	9.8%	-8.8%	-16.7%	-23.9%
14	15	78.90	97.6	56.1	24.4	-18.9	-33.6	-45.1
14	30	148.28	198.5	100.7	39.4	-26.0	-43.6	-55.9

Summary of Properties of Convexity

The convexity properties of all option-free bonds are summarized below.

Property 1. As the yield increases (decreases) the dollar duration of a bond decreases (increases). We demonstrated this in the previous section.

Property 2. For a given yield and maturity, the lower the coupon, the greater the convexity of a bond. This can be seen from the computed convexity for our 12 hypothetical bonds.

Property 3. For a given yield and modified duration, the lower the coupon the smaller the convexity. The investment implication of this property is that zero coupon bonds have the lowest convexity for a given modified duration.

To see this, consider the following three bonds:

Coupon	Maturity (years)	Yield to maturity	Modified duration (years)	Convexity
11.625%	10.00	10%	6.05	50.48
5.500	8.00	10	6.02	44.87
zero	6.33	10	6.03	39.24

Notice that all three bonds are selling to yield 10% and have a modified duration of approximately six years.[5] The convexity of the bonds decreases as the coupon rate decreases.

Property 4. The convexity of a bond increases at an increasing rate as duration increases. This is depicted in Exhibit 11-13. Doubling duration, for example, will more than double convexity.

---

[5] A six-year, zero-coupon bond has a Macaulay duration equal to the maturity. It has a modified duration that is less than six years.

Exhibit 11-13
Comparison of Two Bonds with Different Convexities but the Same Duration

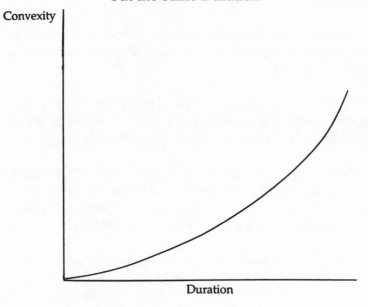

Value of Convexity

Look again at Exhibit 11-3, in which Bonds A and B have the same duration but different convexities. We stated that Bond B would be preferred to Bond A because both have the same price (same yield) and the same duration but Bond B has greater convexity than Bond A. Thus, it offers better price performance if yield changes.

Generally, the market will take the greater convexity of Bond B compared to Bond A into account in pricing the two bonds. That is, the market will price convexity. Consequently, while there may be times when a situation such as depicted in Exhibit 11-3 may exist, generally the market will require investors to "pay up" (accept a lower yield) for the greater convexity offered by Bond B.

How much should the market want investors to pay up for convexity? Look again at Exhibit 11-3. Notice that if investors expect that yields will change by very little—that is, they expect low interest rate volatility—the advantage of owning Bond B over Bond A is insignificant because the two bonds will offer approximately the same price for small changes in yields. Thus, investors should not be willing to pay much for convexity. In fact, if the market is pricing convexity high, which means that Bond A will be offering a higher yield than Bond B, then investors with expectations of low interest rate volatility would probably be willing to "sell convexity"— sell Bond B if they own it and buy Bond A. In contrast, if investors expect substantial interest rate volatility, Bond B would probably sell at a much lower yield than Bond A.

Illustration 11-4. A Treasury security held in a portfolio can be synthetically created from two Treasury securities, one with a maturity less than the bond held in the portfolio and another with a maturity greater than the bond held in the portfolio. The single security currently held is called the *bullet* security. The portfolio of two securities created to replace the bullet security is called a *barbell*.

Consider an actual market situation.[6] On November 20, 1987, the 7-year, 10-year and 30-year on-the-run Treasuries had the following yield to maturity, modified duration and convexity:

Issue	Yield to maturity	Modified duration	Convexity
7-year	8.66%	5.00	0.321
10-year	8.84	6.54	0.586
30-year	8.93	10.15	1.809

Suppose that a money manager held $1 million of the 10-year Treasury. A Treasury security with a modified duration of the 10-year Treasury (6.54) can be synthetically created by buy-

---

[6] This illustration is adapted from N.R. Vijayaraghavan and Monte H. Shapiro, "Duration-Equivalent Butterfly Swaps," in *Fixed Income Portfolio Strategies*, Frank J. Fabozzi, ed. (Chicago: Probus Publishing, 1989)

ing $0.7 million of the 7-year Treasury and $0.3 million of the 30-year Treasury security.[7] The convexity of the barbell would be greater than the bullet security by 0.199 per 1-basis-point change in price. Thus, there is a convexity gain. There would be a yield-to-maturity give-up of 5.7 basis points.[8]

The horizon return for a one-month investment horizon can be computed for a range of yield changes. Assuming a parallel shift in the yield curve, the difference between the one-month horizon return of the barbell and the bullet (10-year Treasury) would be as follows:

Yield change (basis points)	Difference in horizon return Barbell - Bullet (in basis points)
+ 100	13.4
+ 50	3.3
0	- 1.5
- 50	7.1
- 100	43.2

As can be seen, the barbell will outperform the bullet under each interest rate scenario except when the yield is unchanged. This result is due to the greater convexity of the barbell and the cost of acquiring the better convexity.

However, there are risks associated with this strategy in addition to the probability that yields will remain stable. As we discussed at the end of the previous chapter, modified duration provides a good approximation to the change in price if the yield curve changes in a parallel fashion. If the yield curve shift is not parallel, the outcome may or may not be favorable, even if interest rates move substantially. For example, consider a steepening of the yield curve as follows:

---

[7] The modified duration of the barbell is the market value weighted modified duration of the two securities.

[8] The yield to maturity of the barbell is the internal rate of return for the cash flows of the two securities. See Illustration 6-11 in Chapter 6 for an explanation of how the yield for a portfolio is calculated.

Maturity (years)	Yield change (basis points)
7	− 100
10	− 75
30	− 50

The barbell will outperform the bullet by 16 basis points. In contrast, suppose the yield curve flattens as follows:

Maturity (years)	Yield change (basis points)
7	100
10	75
30	50

The barbell will underperform the bullet by nine basis points.

Thus, for the proper analysis of a duration-equivalent swap, it is important to investigate what will happen if the yield curve does not change in a parallel fashion.

Summary

In this chapter, we have presented a graphical explanation of how duration is used to approximate the change in price when yield changes. We showed why duration will underestimate the new price and why the error in estimating price becomes greater for large yield changes. The explanation lies in the convex shape of the price/yield relationship for an option-free bond. We then introduced a convexity measure for an option-free bond and provide a formula that links the convexity measure to price change. Properties of convexity were then summarized.

The convexity of a bond will determine its price performance when yield changes. For two bonds with the same duration and the same yield to maturity, the bond with the greater convexity will be the more attractive. Typically, convexity does not come without a cost, however. The cost is the yield give-up necessary to improve convexity. Just how much investors should be willing to pay for better convexity depends on their expectations about the volatility of future interest rates. The greater the expected volatility, the more investors should be willing to pay for convexity. Trades that hold duration constant and improve convexity may enhance return over some specified holding period if the movement in yield is sufficient to offset the cost of obtaining the better convexity. When a synthetic security is created to replace a bullet security so as to improve convexity, the effect of a change in the shape of the yield curve on performance should be analyzed.

IV
Applications to Bonds with Embedded Call Options

12
Call Options: Investment and Price Characteristics

In previous chapters, we described the investment characteristics of option-free bonds. Most of the bonds that we encounter in the market, however, are not option free. Instead, they have embedded options. To understand the price/yield relationship and price volatility characteristics of bonds with embedded options, we will review the investment and price characteristics of options in this chapter. Our focus is on *call* options since most corporate bonds and municipal bonds and all mortgage pass-through securities have embedded call options.

What is an Option?

An option is an agreement in which the writer of the option grants the buyer of the option the right to purchase from or sell to the writer a designated instrument at a specified price within a specified period of time. The writer, also referred to as the seller, grants this right to the buyer in exchange for a certain sum of money called the *option price* or *option premium*. The price at which the instrument may be bought or sold is called the *exercise price* or *strike price*. The date after which an option is void is called the *expiration date* or *maturity date*. An option is said to be an *American option* if the buyer may exercise the option at any time up to and including the expiration date. An option is said to be a *European option* if the buyer may exercise the option on only the expiration date.

When an option grants the buyer the right to purchase the designated instrument from the writer, it is called a *call option*. When the option buyer has the right to sell the designated instrument to the writer (seller), the option is called a *put option*. The buyer of an option is said to be *long the option;* the writer (seller) is said to be *short the option*.

The most popular exchange-traded interest-rate options are options in which the designated instrument is an interest-rate futures contract. In this chapter we focus on options on cash market bonds because we will be applying the principles and concepts in this chapter to bonds with embedded options in which the cash market bond is the underlying instrument.

Payoffs from Buying and Selling Options

The maximum amount that an option buyer can lose is the option price. The maximum profit that the option writer (seller) can realize is the option price. The option buyer has substantial upside return potential while the option writer has substantial downside risk. This is illustrated below.

The profit/loss or payoff profile for the following four basic option positions are presented below: (1) long call (buying a call option), (2) short call (selling or writing a call option), (3) long put (buying a put option), and (4) short put (selling or writing a put option). It is assumed that a position in only one option is taken. That is, no position is taken in another option or bond. *The profit/loss profiles presented assume that each option position is held to the expiration date and not exercised early.* Also, to simplify the illustrations we assume that there are no transaction costs in implementing the position.

Long Call Position (Buying a Call Option)

An investor who purchases a call option is said to be in a *long call position*. This is the most straightforward option position for participating in an anticipated decrease in interest rates (increase in the price of bonds).

To illustrate this strategy, assume that there is a call option on a particular 10% coupon bond with a par value of $100 and 15 years and 2 months to maturity. The call option expires in two months and the strike price is $100. Suppose the option price is $5.

Suppose that the current price of the bond is $100 (i.e., the bond is selling at par), which means that the yield on this bond is currently 10%. The payoff from this position will depend on the price of the bond at the expiration date. The price, in turn, will depend on the yield on 15-year bonds with a 10% coupon, since in two months the bond will have only 15 years to maturity.

If the price of the bond at the expiration date is less than or equal to $100 (which means that the market yield is greater than or equal to 10%), then the investor would not exercise the option. The option buyer will lose the entire option price of $5. Notice, however, that this is the maximum loss that the option buyer will realize, regardless of how far the price of the bond declines.

If the price of the bond is greater than $100 (that is, the market yield at expiration is less than 10%), the option buyer will exercise the option. By exercising, the option buyer purchases the bond for $100 (the strike price) and can then sell it in the market for a higher price. The option buyer will realize a loss at expiration if the price of the bond is greater than $100 but less than $105 (which correspond to a market yield at expiration of 10% and approximately 9.35%, respectively). The option buyer will break even if the price of the bond at expiration is $105. It is the break-even price because it cost the option buyer $5 to acquire the call option and $100 to exercise the option to purchase the bond. A profit will be realized if the price of the bond at expiration is greater than $105 (that is, the market yield declines to at least 9.35%).

Exhibit 12-1 shows the profit/loss profile. While the break-even point and the loss will depend on the option price, the

Exhibit 12-1

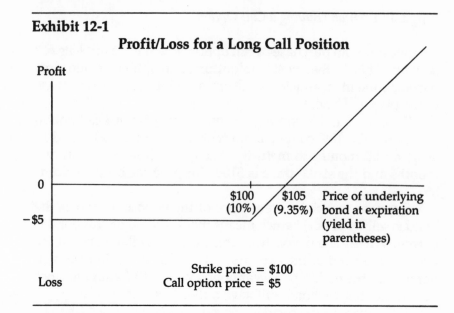

Profit/Loss for a Long Call Position

shape of the curve shown in the exhibit will hold for all buyers of call options. The shape indicates that the maximum loss is the option price and that there is substantial upside potential.

Short Call Position (Selling or Writing a Call Option)

An investor who sells or writes a call option is said to be in a *short call position*. An investor who believes that interest rates will rise or change very little can, if his expectations are correct, realize income by writing (selling) a call option.

To illustrate this option position we shall use the call option used to illustrate the long call position. The profit/loss profile of the short call position is the mirror image of the payoff of the long call strategy. That is, the profit (loss) of the short call position for any given price of the bond at the expiration date is the same as the loss (profit) of the long call position. Consequently, the maximum profit that the short call position can produce is the option price; the maximum loss is limited only by how much the price of the bond can increase (i.e., how far the market yield can fall) by the expiration date, less the option price. This can be

Exhibit 12-2

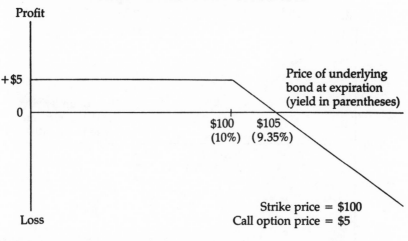

Profit/Loss for a Short Call Position

seen in Exhibit 12-2, which shows the profit/loss profile for this short call position.

Long Put Position (Buying a Put Option)
The most straightforward option position an investor can take to benefit from an expected increase in interest rates is to buy a put option. This investment position is called a *long put position.*

To illustrate the payoff profile for this position, we'll assume a hypothetical put option for a 10% coupon bond with a par value of $100, 15 years and 2 months to maturity, and a strike price of $100, selling for $5.50. The current price of the bond is $100 (yield of 10%). The payoff for this strategy at the expiration date depends on the market yield at the time.

If the price of the bond is equal to $100 or greater than $100 because the market yield has fallen below 10%, the buyer of the put option will not exercise it, and will incur a loss of $5.50 (the option price). The investor will exercise the option when the price of the bond at expiration is less than $100 (the market yield

Exhibit 12-3

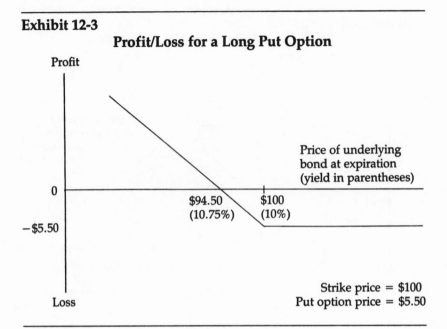

Profit/Loss for a Long Put Option

Profit

Price of underlying
bond at expiration
(yield in parentheses)

0

$94.50
(10.75%) $100
(10%)

−$5.50

Strike price = $100
Put option price = $5.50

Loss

at expiration is above 10%). If the market yield is higher than approximately 10.75%, the price of the bond will be less than $94.50, resulting in a profit from the position. For market yields between 10% and about 10.75%, the investor will realize a loss but the loss is less than $5.50. The break-even market yield is approximately 10.75%, since this will result in a bond price of $94.50.

Exhibit 12-3 shows the profit/loss profile for this position. As with all long option positions, the loss is limited to the option price. The profit potential, however, is substantial, the theoretical maximum profit being generated if the bond price falls to zero.

Short Put Position (Selling or Writing a Put Option)

The *short put position* involves the selling (writing) of a put option. This position is taken if the investor expects interest rates to fall or stay flat so that the price of the bond will increase or stay the same. The profit/loss profile for a short put position is

Exhibit 12-4

Profit/Loss for a Short Put Position

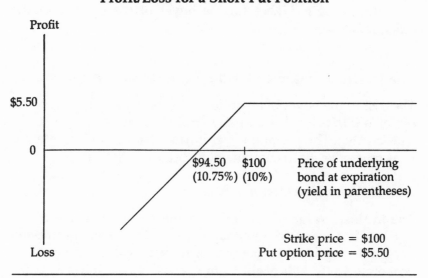

the mirror image of the long put option. The maximum profit from this strategy is the option price. The maximum loss is limited only by how low the price of the bond can fall by the expiration date less the option price received for writing the option. Exhibit 12-4 graphically depicts the profit/loss profile.

Considering the Time Value of Money

In our illustration of the four basic option positions, we neglected the time value of money. Specifically, the buyer of an option must pay the seller the option price at the time the option is purchased. Thus, the buyer must finance the purchase of the option or, if the funds do not have to be borrowed, the buyer loses the interest that can be earned by investing the option price. In contrast, assuming that the seller does not have to use the option price as margin for the short position, the seller has the opportunity to invest the option price.

Because of the time value of money, the profit profile of the option positions will change. The break-even price for the buyer and the seller of an option will not be the same as in our illustrations. The break-even price for the underlying instrument at the expiration date is higher for the buyer of the option; for the seller, it is lower.

The Intrinsic Value and Time Value of an Option

The cost to the buyer of an option is primarily a reflection of the option's *intrinsic* value and any additional amount over its intrinsic value. The premium over intrinsic value is often referred to as *time value*. Each component is discussed below.

Intrinsic Value of an Option

The intrinsic value of an option is the economic value of the option if it is exercised immediately. Since the buyer of an option need not exercise the option and, in fact, will not do so if no economic value will result from exercising, the intrinsic value cannot be less than zero.

The intrinsic value of a call option on a bond is the difference between the current bond price and the strike price. For example, if the *strike price* for a call option is $100 and the *current bond price* is $107, the intrinsic value is $7. That is, if the option buyer exercised the option and simultaneously sold the bond, the option buyer would realize $107 from the sale of the bond, which would be covered by acquiring the bond from the option writer for $100, thereby netting $7.

When a call option has intrinsic value, it is said to be "in the money." Our call option with a strike price of $100 is in the money when the price of the underlying bond is greater than $100. When the strike price of a call option exceeds the current bond price, the call option is said to be "out of the money" and has no intrinsic value. A call option for which the strike price is equal to the current bond price is said to be "at the money."

These relationships are summarized below for a call option:

If the current bond price is greater than the strike price, then

(1)   The intrinsic value is the difference between the current bond price and strike price;

(2)   The option is said to be "in the money."

If the current bond price equals the strike price, then
    (1) The intrinsic value is zero;
    (2) The option is said to be "at the money."
If the current bond price is less than the strike price, then
    (1) The intrinsic value is zero;
    (2) The option is said to be "out of the money."

For a put option, the intrinsic value is equal to the amount by which the current bond price is below the strike price. For example, if the strike price of a put option is $100 and the current bond price is $88, the intrinsic value is $12. That is, if the buyer of the put option exercises it and simultaneously buys the bond, he will net $12. The bond will be sold to the writer for $100 and purchased in the market for $88.

When the put option has intrinsic value, the option is said to be *in the money*. For our put option with a strike price of $100, the option will be in the money when the bond price is less than $100. A put option is *out of the money* when the current bond price exceeds the strike price. A put option is *at the money* when the strike price is equal to the current bond price.

These relationships are summarized below for a put option:

If the current bond price is less than the strike price, then
    (1) The intrinsic value is the difference between the strike price and current bond price;
    (2) The option is said to be "in the money."
If the current bond price equals the strike price, then
    (1) The intrinsic value is zero;
    (2) The option is said to be "at the money."
If the current bond price is greater than the strike price, then
    (1) The intrinsic value is zero;
    (2) The option is said to be "out of the money."

Time Value of an Option

The time value of an option is the amount by which the option price exceeds the intrinsic value. That is,

Time value of an option = Option price – Intrinsic value.

For example, if the price of a call option with a strike price of

$100 is $18 when the current bond price is $107, then for this option:

$$\text{Intrinsic value} = \$107 - \$100 = \$7;$$
$$\text{Time value of option} = \$18 - \$7 = \$11.$$

If the current bond price is $88 instead of $107, then the time value of this option is $18 since the option has no intrinsic value. Notice that for an at-the-money or out-of-the-money option, the time value of the option is equal to the option price since the intrinsic value is zero.

At the expiration date, the time value of the option will be zero. The option price at the expiration date will be equal to its intrinsic value.

Why would an option buyer be willing to pay a premium over the intrinsic value for an option? The reason is that the option buyer believes that at some time prior to expiration, changes in the market yield will increase the value of the rights conveyed by the option.

The Option Price

In the next two chapters we shall see that the price of a bond with an embedded option will be determined by the price of the underlying bond and the price of the option. While we can easily determine the value of an option at the expiration date and the intrinsic value of an option at any time prior to the expiration date, the fair value or price of the option at any time prior to the expiration date must be estimated. In this section, we will discuss the factors that influence the fair or "theoretical" value of an option.[1]

Factors that Influence the Option Price

The following six factors will influence the option price:

    (1) Current price of the underlying bond,

---

[1] For a more detailed discussion of the impact of these factors on the price of an option, see Mark Pitts and Frank J. Fabozzi, *Interest Rate Options and Futures* (Chicago: Probus Publishing, 1989).

(2) Strike price,
(3) Time to expiration,
(4) Short-term risk-free interest rate over the life of the option,
(5) Coupon rate, and
(6) Expected interest rate volatility over the life of the option.

The effect of each of these factors will depend on whether (1) the option is a call or a put and (2) the option is an American option (an option that may be exercised up to and including the expiration date) or a European option (an option that may be exercised only at the expiration date).[2]

CURRENT PRICE OF THE UNDERLYING INSTRUMENT. For a call option, as the current price of the underlying bond increases (decreases), the option price increases (decreases). For a put option, as the current price of the bond decreases (increases), the option price increases (decreases).

STRIKE PRICE. All other factors constant, the higher the strike price, the lower the price of a call option. For a put option, the opposite is true: the higher the strike price, the higher the price of a put option.

TIME TO EXPIRATION. For American options, all other factors constant, the longer the time to expiration, the higher the option price. No general statement can be made for European options.

SHORT-TERM RISK-FREE INTEREST RATE OVER THE LIFE OF THE OPTION. Holding all other factors constant, the price of a call option on a bond will increase as the short-term risk-free interest rate rises. For a put option, the opposite is true: an increase in the short-term risk-free interest rate will decrease the price of a put option.

---

[2] The option price also will depend on whether the underlying instrument is a cash market bond or an interest rate futures contract. As stated earlier in this chapter, we are focusing in this chapter on options on cash market bonds.

COUPON RATE. Coupons for options on bonds tend to decrease the price of a call option because the coupons make it more attractive to hold the bond than the option. Thus, call options on coupon-bearing bonds will tend to be priced lower than other similar call options on non–coupon-bearing bonds. For put options, coupons tend to increase their price.

EXPECTED INTEREST RATE VOLATILITY OVER THE LIFE OF THE OPTION. As the expected interest rate volatility over the life of the option increases, the price of an option increases. The reason is that the greater the expected volatility, as measured by the standard deviation or variance of interest rates, the greater the probability that the price of the underlying bond will move in the direction that will benefit the option buyer.

Option Pricing Model

Several models have been developed to estimate the theoretical or fair price of an option. These models are based on an arbitrage or riskless hedge valuation model. Our purpose here is not to describe option pricing models but, instead, to bring to the reader's attention some of the models that are commercially available from software vendors. Most of the dealer firms have developed their own option pricing models that are typically not available to clients.

The most popular option pricing model for American call options on common stocks is the Black-Scholes option pricing model.[3] The key insight of the Black-Scholes option pricing model is that a synthetic option can be created by taking an appropriate position in the underlying common stock and borrowing or lending funds at the riskless interest rate.[4]

The Black-Scholes option pricing model involves several assumptions that are necessary to create the synthetic option.

---

[3] Fischer Black and Myron Scholes, "The Pricing of Corporate Liabilities," *Journal of Political Economy* (May–June 1973), pp. 637–659.

[4] The appropriate position in the underlying common stock depends on how the price of the option will change when the price of the stock changes. This relationship between the change in price of the option and the change in price of the underlying common stock is called the *delta* of the option and is discussed later in this chapter.

While some of these assumptions have been relaxed in modified versions of the model, one critical assumption is that the variance (volatility) of the price of the underlying instrument is constant over the life of the option. In the case of options on bonds, we know that this is not true. As a bond approaches its maturity date, we know from Chapter 9 that its price volatility will decline.

An alternative option pricing model that is more adaptable to options on bonds and interest rate futures is the *binomial option pricing model*.[5] Specifically, different assumptions about the process driving interest rates, and therefore bond prices, can be incorporated into a binomial option pricing model.[6]

Implied Interest Rate Volatility

Option pricing models provide a theoretical option price based on the six factors that we discussed earlier. Of the six factors, the only one that is not known and must be estimated is the expected interest rate volatility over the life of the option. A popular methodology for assessing whether an option is fairly priced is to assume that the option is priced correctly and to estimate the interest rate volatility that is implied by an option pricing model. Exhibit 12-5 describes the process for computing implied interest rate volatility.

For example, suppose that a money manager—using some option, pricing model, the current price of the option, and the five factors that determine the price of an option—computes an implied interest rate volatility of 12%. If the money manager expects that the interest rate volatility over the life of the option will be greater than the implied interest rate volatility of 12%, the

---

[5] The following are credited with the development of the binomial option pricing model: John Cox, Stephen Ross, and Mark Rubinstein, "Option Pricing: A Simplified Approach," *Journal of Financial Economics* (September 1979), pp. 229–63; Richard Rendleman and Brit Bartter, "Two-State Option Pricing," *Journal of Finance* (December 1979), pp. 1093–110, and William Sharpe, *Investments* (Englewood Cliffs, N.J.: Prentice-Hall, 1981), Chapter 16.

[6] For a more technical discussion of these models, see Peter Ritchken, *Options: Theory, Strategy, and Applications*, (Glenview, Ill: Scott, Foresman, 1987), Chapter 13.

Exhibit 12-5
The Process of Obtaining Implied Interest Rate Volatility

A. To obtain theoretical option price

estimated →
input

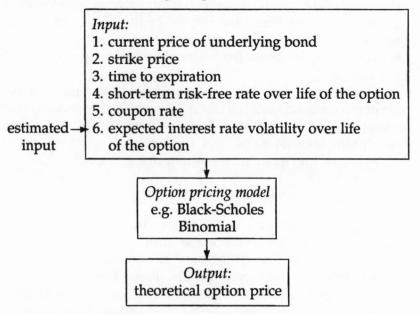

Input:
1. current price of underlying bond
2. strike price
3. time to expiration
4. short-term risk-free rate over life of the option
5. coupon rate
6. expected interest rate volatility over life of the option

Option pricing model
e.g. Black-Scholes
Binomial

Output:
theoretical option price

B. To obtain implied interest rate volatility

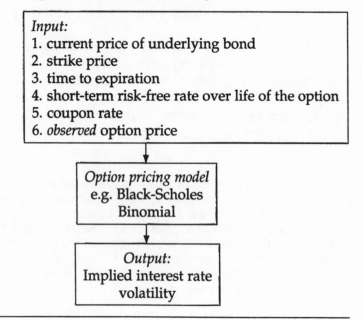

Input:
1. current price of underlying bond
2. strike price
3. time to expiration
4. short-term risk-free rate over life of the option
5. coupon rate
6. *observed* option price

Option pricing model
e.g. Black-Scholes
Binomial

Output:
Implied interest rate
volatility

option is undervalued. In contrast, if the money manager's expected interest rate volatility over the life of the option is less than the implied interest rate volatility, the option is overvalued.

While we have focused on the option price, the key to understanding the options market is that trading and investment strategies in this market involve buying and selling interest rate volatility. Looking at the implied interest rate volatility and comparing it to the trader's or money manger's expectations of future interest rate volatility is just another way of evaluating options.

Sensitivity of the Theoretical Call Option Price to Changes in Factors

When any of the six factors that affect the price of an option changes, the option price will change. Since the price of a bond with an embedded option will be affected by how the price of the embedded option changes, we will look at the sensitivity of the option price to three of the factors—the price of the underlying bond, time to expiration, and expected interest rate volatility. We focus our attention on call options.[7]

The Call Option Price and the Price of the Underlying Bond

Exhibit 12-6 shows the theoretical price of a call option based on the price of the underlying bond. The horizontal axis is the price of the underlying bond at any point in time. The vertical axis is the option price. The shape of the curve representing the theoretical price of a call option, given the price of the underlying bond, would be the same regardless of the actual option pricing model used. In particular, the relationship between the price of the underlying bond and the theoretical call option price is convex. Thus, option prices also exhibit convexity.

---

[7] For a detailed discussion of the role of these measures in option strategies, see Pitts and Fabozzi, *Interest Rate Options and Futures;* Richard M. Bookstaber, *Option Pricing and Investment Strategies* (Chicago: Probus Publishing, 1987), Chapter 4; and James F. Meisner and John A. Richards, "Option Premium Dynamics: With Applications to Fixed Income Portfolio Analysis," in *Advances in Bond Analysis and Portfolio Strategies* Frank J. Fabozzi and T. Dessa Garlicki, eds. (Chicago: Probus Publishing, 1987).

Exhibit 12-6

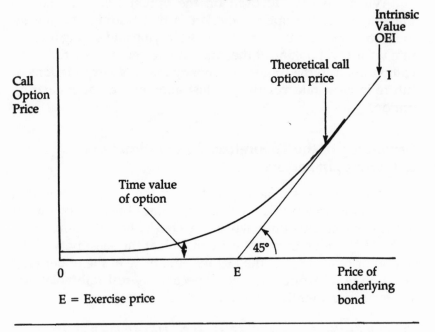

Theoretical Call Price and the Price
of the Underlying Bond

The line from the origin to the strike price on the horizontal axis in Exhibit 12-6 is the intrinsic value of the call option when the price of the underlying bond is less than the strike price, since the intrinsic value is zero. The 45-degree line extending from the horizontal axis is the intrinsic value of the call option once the price of the underlying bond exceeds the strike price. The reason is that the intrinsic value of the call option will increase by the same dollar amount as the increase in the price of the underlying bond. For example, if the exercise price is $100 and the price of the underlying bond increases from $100 to $101, the intrinsic value will increase by $1. If the price of the bond increases from $101 to $110, the intrinsic value of the option will increase from $1 to $10. Thus, the slope of the line representing the intrinsic value after the strike price is reached is 1.

Exhibit 12-7

Delta of a Call Option

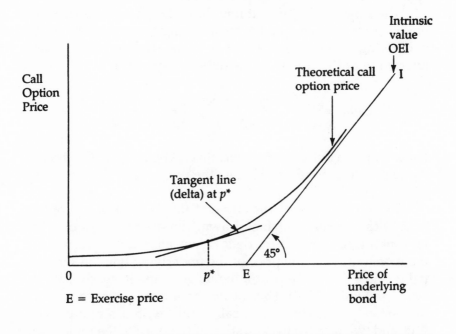

E = Exercise price

Since the theoretical call option price is shown by the convex line, the difference between the theoretical call option price and the intrinsic value at any given price for the underlying bond is the time value of the option.

Exhibit 12-7 shows the theoretical call option price, but with a tangent line drawn at the price of p^*. Recall from the previous chapter that the tangent line was used to estimate the new price of a bond at a new yield level. Here we have an analogous situation. The tangent line in Exhibit 12-7 can be used to estimate what the new option price will be (and therefore what the change in the option price will be) if the price of the underlying bond changes. Once again, because of the convexity of the relationship between the option price and the price of the underlying bond, the tangent line closely approximates the new option price for a small change in the price of the underlying bond. For large changes, however, the tangent line does not provide as good an approximation of the new option price.

The slope of the tangent line shows how the theoretical call option price will change for small changes in the price of the underlying bond. The slope of the tangent line is commonly referred to as the "delta" of the option.[8] Specifically,

$$\text{Delta} = \frac{\text{Change in price of call option}}{\text{Change in price of underlying bond}}.$$

For example, a delta of 0.5 means that a $1 change in the price of the underlying bond will change the price of the call option by $0.50.

Exhibit 12-8 shows the curve of the theoretical call option price with three tangent lines drawn. The steeper the slope of the tangent line, the greater the delta. When an option is deep out of the money (that is, the price of the underlying bond is substantially below the strike price), the tangent line is nearly flat (see Line 1 in Exhibit 12-8). This means that delta is close to zero. To understand why, consider a call option with a strike price of $100 and two months to expiration. If the price of the underlying bond is $20, the option price would not increase by much if the price of the underlying bond increased by $1, from $20 to $21.

For a call option that is deep in the money, the delta will be close to one. That is, the call option price will increase almost dollar for dollar with an increase in the price of the underlying bond. In terms of the graph in Exhibit 12-8, the slope of the tangent line approaches the slope of the intrinsic value line after the strike price. As we stated earlier, the slope of that line is 1.

Thus, the delta for a call option varies from zero (for call options deep out of the money) to one (for call options deep in the money). The delta for a call option at the money is approximately 0.5.

Related to the delta is the *lambda* of an option, which measures the percentage change in the price of the option for a 1% change in the price of the underlying bond. That is,

---

[8] The delta is also referred to as the *hedge ratio*.

Exhibit 12-8
Delta of a Call Option at Three Prices
for the Underlying Bond

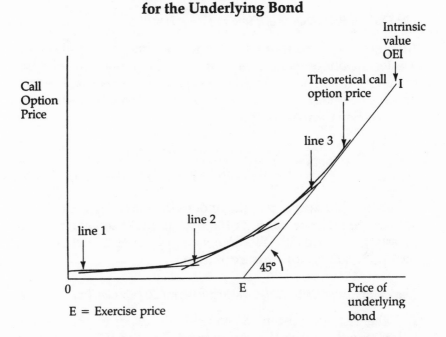

E = Exercise price

$$\text{Lambda} = \frac{\text{Percentage change in the price of the call option}}{\text{Percentage change in the price of the underlying bond}}.$$

For example, a lambda of 1.5 indicates that if the price of the call option changes by 1%, the call option's price will change by 1.5%. The lambda of a call option will be greater than one because of the leverage offered by an option. As the price of the underlying bond increases, the option's lambda decreases.

In the previous chapter, we measured the convexity of an option-free bond. We also can measure the convexity of a call option. Recall from the previous chapter that the convexity of a bond measures the rate of change in dollar duration. For call options, convexity measures the rate of change in delta. The measure of convexity for options is commonly referred to as *gamma* and is defined as follows:

$$\text{Gamma} = \frac{\text{Change in delta}}{\text{Change in price of underlying bond}}$$

The Call Option Price and Time to Expiration

All other factors constant, the longer the time to expiration, the greater the option price. Since each day the option moves closer to the expiration date, the time to expiration decreases. The *theta* of an option measures the change in the option price as the time to expiration decreases. That is,

$$\text{Theta} = \frac{\text{Change in price of option}}{\text{Decrease in time to expiration}}$$

Assuming that the price of the underlying bond does not change so that the intrinsic value of the option does not change, theta measures how quickly the time value of the option changes as the option moves towards expiration.

The Call Option Price and Expected Interest Rate Volatility

All other factors constant, a change in the expected interest rate volatility will change the option price. The *kappa* (or *vega*) of an option measures the dollar price change in the price of the option for a 1% change in the expected interest rate volatility. That is,

$$\frac{\text{Kappa}}{\text{(Vega)}} = \frac{\text{Change in option price}}{\text{1\% change in expected interest rate volatility}}$$

Put-Call Parity Realtionship

There is a relationship between the price of a call option and the price of a put option on the same underlying bond, with the same strike price and the same expiration date. This relationship is commonly referred to as the *put-call parity relationship* and, for coupon bearing bonds, is

Put price = Call price + Present value of strike price
+ Present value of coupon − Price of underlying bond

The above relationship is one form of the put-call parity relationship for European options. It is approximately true for American options. The relationship is based on arbitrage arguments.[9]

Summary

In this chapter the investment and price characteristics of options have been explained, focusing on call options since they are the most common type of option embedded in bonds. The key concepts that should be understood are as follows. First, the maximum profit that an option writer (seller) can realize is the option price; the option writer, however, is exposed to substantial downside risk. For an option buyer, the maximum loss is the option price. The option buyer retains all the upside potential (reduced by the option price).

Second, there are six factors that influence an option's price: current price of the underlying bond, strike price, time to expiration, short-term risk-free interest rate over the life of the option, coupon rate, and expected interest rate volatility over the life of the option. Option pricing models such as the Black-Scholes model and the binomial model attempt to estimate the theoretical price of an option. Modifications of the binomial option pricing model are more commonly used to price options on bonds.

Third, buying and selling of options involves buying and selling expected interest rate volatility. Notice that we said the same thing in the previous chapter when we said that the value of convexity depends on expected interest rate volatility over some investment horizon. Rather than looking at the value of an option in terms of price, it is common for investors to compute the implied interest rate volatility of an option and compare it to expected interest rate volatility.

Fourth, there are measures that are used to assess the sensitivity of the option price to a change in factors such as the price of

---

[9] See Ritchken, *Options: Theory, Strategy, and Applications*, Chapter 4, or Robert Jarrow and Andrew Rudd, *Option Pricing* (Homewood, Ill: Dow Jones-Irwin, 1983), Chapters 4 and 6.

the underlying bond (delta and lambda), time (theta) and expected interest rate volatility (kappa or vega). A graph of the relationship between the theoretical call price and the price of the underlying bond is convex. Gamma measures the convexity (that is, how the delta changes).

Finally, the put-call parity relationship defines the relationship between the prices of a put option, a call option, and the underlying bond.

13

Price and Performance Characteristics of Callable Corporate Bonds

Most corporate bonds are callable prior to maturity.[1] As explained in Chapter 6, the traditional yield-to-call measure does not permit an investor to assess the relative performance of callable bonds over a predetermined investment horizon. In this chapter, a framework for evaluating callable corporate bonds is presented.

Price/Yield Relationship for a Callable Corporate Bond

As we demonstrated in previous chapters, the price/yield relationship for an option-free (i.e., noncallable) bond is convex.

---

[1] For a complete explanation of the various terms and conditions for the early redemption of a corporate bond, see Richard W. Wilson, *Senior Corporate Securities* (Chicago: Probus Publishing, 1987), Chapter 4.

Exhibit 13-1

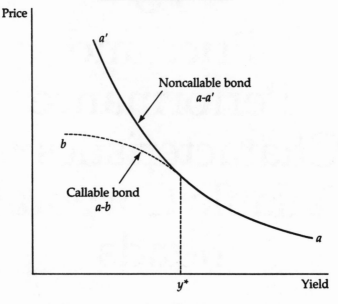

Price/Yield Relationship for a Noncallable and a Callable Bond

Exhibit 13-1 shows the price/yield relationship for a noncallable bond and for the same bond if it is callable. The convex curve a–a' is the price/yield relationship for the noncallable (option-free) bond. The unusually shaped curve a–b is the price/yield relationship for the callable bond.

The reason for the shape of the price/yield relationship for the callable bond is as follows. When the prevailing market yield for comparable bonds is higher than the coupon rate on the bond, it is unlikely that the corporate issuer will call the bond. For example, if the coupon rate on a bond is 8% and the prevailing yield on comparable bonds is 16%, it is highly improbable that the corporate issuer will call in an 8% bond so that it can issue a 16% bond. In option terminology, the call option is deep out of the money. Since the bond is unlikely to be called when it is deep out of the money, a callable bond will have the same price/yield relationship as a noncallable bond. However, even when the option is near the money (the coupon rate is just below the market yield), investors may not pay the same price for the bond had it been not callable because there is still the chance the market yield may drop further so that it would become beneficial for the issuer to call the bond.

As yields in the market decline, the likelihood that yields will decline further—so that the issuer will benefit from calling the bond—increases. We may not know the exact yield at which investors begin to view the issue as likely to be called, but we do know that there is some level. In Exhibit 13-1, at yields below y^*, the price/yield relationship for the callable bond departs from the price/yield relationship for the noncallable bond. If, for example, the market yield is such that a noncallable bond would be selling for 109 but, since it is callable would be called at 104, investors would not pay 109. If they did and the bond is called, investors would receive 104 (the call price) for a bond they purchased for 109. Notice that for a range of yields below y^*, there is price compression—that is, there is limited price appreciation as yields decline.

Illustration 13-1. To illustrate the difference between the price/yield relationship for a noncallable and that for a callable corporate bond, consider the the General Motors Acceptance Corporation 12% coupon bond maturing June 2005.[2] This issue is callable at 102 in June 1990. Exhibit 13-2 shows the price/yield relationship, assuming a June 1, 1988, settlement date for this bond and assuming it is noncallable. Also shown in Exhibit 13-2 is the theoretical price for the callable bond. The computation of the *theoretical* price requires that certain assumptions be made. We will discuss these assumptions in later illustrations. The price/yield relationship is graphed in Exhibit 13-3.

Notice the following from Exhibits 13-2 and 13-3. As the (noncallable) yield rises above approximately 14.5%, the price of the noncallable bond approaches the price of the callable bond. This is consistent with what we observe in Exhibit 13-1. In con-

---

[2] The numerical values for this illustration and the others in this chapter involving the GMAC callable bond were provided by Mark Dunetz and James Mahoney of Kidder Peabody's Fixed Income Research Group.

Exhibit 13-2
Price/Yield Relationship for GMAC 12% of June 2005
Callable at 102 in June 1990 (Settlement 6/1/88)

Yield	Noncallable bond price	Theoretical callable bond price
20.51	60	60.000
20.18	61	61.000
19.86	62	62.000
19.55	63	63.000
19.24	64	64.000
18.95	65	65.000
18.66	66	66.000
18.39	67	67.000
18.11	68	68.000
17.85	69	68.999
17.59	70	69.999
17.34	71	70.999
17.10	72	71.998
16.86	73	72.998
16.63	74	73.997
16.40	75	74.995
16.18	76	75.994
15.96	77	76.992
15.75	78	77.988
15.54	79	78.984
15.33	80	79.980
15.13	81	80.973
14.94	82	81.964
14.75	83	82.954
14.56	84	83.943
14.38	85	84.925
14.20	86	85.905
14.02	87	86.884
13.85	88	87.854
13.68	89	88.817
13.51	90	89.777
13.35	91	90.735

Yield	Noncallable bond price	Theoretical callable bond price
13.19	92	91.670
13.03	93	92.602
12.87	94	93.531
12.72	95	94.443
12.57	96	95.333
12.42	97	96.217
12.28	98	97.096
12.00	100	98.765
11.73	102	100.384
11.46	104	101.888
11.33	105	102.620
11.20	106	103.339
11.07	107	103.988
10.95	108	104.627
10.83	109	105.258
10.71	110	105.866
10.59	111	106.404
10.47	112	106.933
10.35	113	107.452
10.24	114	107.944
10.13	115	108.369
10.02	116	108.785
9.91	117	109.192
9.80	118	109.571
9.69	119	109.889
9.59	120	110.199
9.48	121	110.501
9.38	122	110.780
9.28	123	111.004
9.18	124	111.222
9.08	125	111.433
8.98	126	111.628
8.89	127	111.776
8.79	128	111.920
8.60	130	112.187
8.42	132	112.368

Exhibit 13-2 continued.

Yield	Noncallable bond price	Theoretical callable bond price
8.24	134	112.534
8.07	136	112.638
7.90	138	112.733
7.73	140	112.790
7.24	146	112.894
6.79	152	112.925
6.36	158	112.934
5.96	164	112.936
5.57	170	112.936

trast, when the yield falls below 14.5%, the difference between the price of the noncallable bond and that of the callable bond increases. Once again, this is consistent with Exhibit 13-1. The price/yield relationship flattens as the yield moves deep in the money.

Breaking a Callable Corporate Bond into Its Component Parts

To develop an analytical framework for assessing relative value and evaluating the potential performance of callable bonds over some investment horizon, it is necessary to understand what the components of the bond are. A callable corporate bond is a bond in which the bondholder has sold the issuing corporation a call option that allows the issuer to repurchase the contractual cash flow of the bond from the time the bond is first callable until the maturity date.

Illustration 13-2.   Consider a callable corporate bond—with an 8% coupon, 20 years to maturity—that is and callable in five years at 104. The bondholder then owns a five-year noncallable bond and has sold a call option granting the issuer the right to call away from the bondholder 15 years of cash flow five years from now. The exercise price is 104.

Exhibit 13-3
Price/Yield Relationship for GMAC 12%,
June 2005, Callable at 102 on June 1990
(June 1, 1988, Settlement)

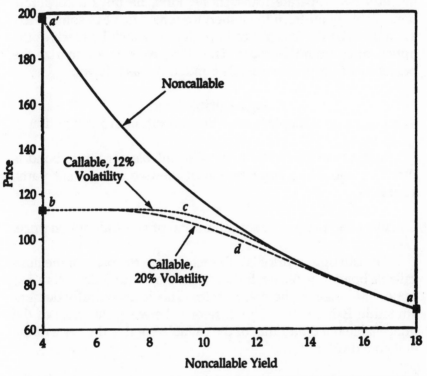

Illustration 13-3.   Consider an investor who owns a 10-year, 9% corporate bond that is immediately callable at 100 (par). The investor owns a 10-year noncallable bond and has sold a call option granting the issuer the right immediately to call the entire 10-year contractual cash, flow or any cash flow remaining at the time the issue is called, for 100.

Illustration 13-4. Consider the General Motors Acceptance Corporation 12% coupon bond of June 2005 that is callable in June 1990 at 102. A bondholder who owns this bond on June 1, 1988, effectively owns a noncallable bond with two years to maturity (the first call date is June 1, 1990) and has sold a call option granting the issuer the right to call away from the bondholder 15 years of cash flows beginning June 1, 1990. The exercise price for this call option is 102.

Effectively, the owner of a corporate callable bond is entering into two separate transactions. First, he buys a corporate noncallable bond from the issuer, for which he pays some price. Then, he sells the issuer a call option, for which he receives the option price from the issuer. Therefore, we can summarize the position of a corporate callable bondholder as follows:[3]

Long a callable bond
= Long a noncallable bond + Short position in a call option

In terms of price, the price of a callable corporate bond is therefore equal to a combination of the two component parts. That is,

Callable bond price = Noncallable bond price – Call option price.

The call option price is subtracted from the price of the noncallable bond. The reason is that when the bondholder sells a call option, he receives the option price. This is graphically demonstrated in Exhibit 13-1. The difference between the price of the noncallable bond and that of the callable bond is the price of the embedded call option.

Illustration 13-5. Returning to the GMAC callable bond, the price of the noncallable bond and the theoretical price of the embedded call option are shown in Exhibit 13-4. The theoretical

---

[3] Actually, the position is more complicated. The issuer may be entitled to call the bond at the first call date or any time thereafter, or at the first call date and any subsequent coupon anniversary. Thus the investor has effectively sold a strip of call options to the issuer. The exercise price is the call price, which may vary with the date the issue may be called. The cash flows of the underlying bond for the call option are the remaining coupon payments that would have been made by the issuer had the bond not been called. For exposition purposes, it is easier to understand the principles associated with the investment characteristics of callable corporate bonds by describing the investor's position as long a noncallable bond and short a call option.

Exhibit 13-4
Price/Yield Relationship and Theoretical Option Price for
GMAC 12% of June 2005 Callable at 102 in June 1990
(Settlement 6/1/88, 12% Interest Rate Volatility Assumption)

Assumptions to compute theoretical call option price:
Binomial option pricing model
Interest rate volatility: 12%
Short-term interest rate: 6%

Yield	Noncallable bond price	Theoretical option price	Theoretical callable bond price
20.51	60	0.000	60.000
20.18	61	0.000	61.000
19.86	62	0.000	62.000
19.55	63	0.000	63.000
19.24	64	0.000	64.000
18.95	65	0.000	65.000
18.66	66	0.000	66.000
18.39	67	0.000	67.000
18.11	68	0.000	68.000
17.85	69	0.001	68.999
17.59	70	0.001	69.999
17.34	71	0.001	70.999
17.10	72	0.002	71.998
16.86	73	0.002	72.998
16.63	74	0.003	73.997
16.40	75	0.005	74.995
16.18	76	0.006	75.994
15.96	77	0.008	76.992
15.75	78	0.012	77.988
15.54	79	0.016	78.984
15.33	80	0.020	79.980
15.13	81	0.027	80.973
14.94	82	0.036	81.964
14.75	83	0.046	82.954
14.56	84	0.057	83.943
14.38	85	0.075	84.925

Exhibit 13-4 continued.

Yield	Noncallable bond price	Theoretical option price	Theoretical callable bond price
14.20	86	0.095	85.905
14.02	87	0.116	86.884
13.85	88	0.146	87.854
13.68	89	0.183	88.817
13.51	90	0.223	89.777
13.35	91	0.265	90.735
13.19	92	0.330	91.670
13.03	93	0.398	92.602
12.87	94	0.469	93.531
12.72	95	0.557	94.443
12.57	96	0.667	95.333
12.42	97	0.783	96.217
12.28	98	0.904	97.096
12.00	100	1.235	98.765
11.73	102	1.606	100.394
11.46	104	2.112	101.888
11.33	105	2.380	102.620
11.20	106	2.661	103.339
11.07	107	3.012	103.988
10.95	108	3.373	104.627
10.83	109	3.742	105.258
10.71	110	4.134	105.866
10.59	111	4.596	106.404
10.47	112	5.067	106.933
10.35	113	5.548	107.452
10.24	114	6.056	107.944
10.13	115	6.631	108.369
10.02	116	7.215	108.785
9.91	117	7.808	109.192
9.80	118	8.429	109.571
9.69	119	9.111	109.889
9.59	120	9.801	110.199
9.48	121	10.499	110.501
9.38	122	11.220	110.780
9.28	123	11.996	111.004

Yield	Noncallable bond price	Theoretical option price	Theoretical callable bond price
9.18	124	12.778	111.222
9.08	125	13.567	111.433
8.98	126	14.372	111.628
8.89	127	15.224	111.776
8.79	128	16.080	111.920
8.60	130	17.813	112.187
8.42	132	19.632	112.368
8.24	134	21.466	112.534
8.07	136	23.362	112.638
7.90	138	25.267	112.733
7.73	140	27.210	112.790
7.24	146	33.106	112.894
6.79	152	39.075	112.925
6.36	158	45.066	112.934
5.96	164	51.064	112.936
5.57	170	57.064	112.936

price of the call option is based on a binomial option pricing model.[4] Recall from the previous chapter that an assumption about future interest rate volatility is required as an input into the option pricing model to obtain the the theoretical option price. The volatility assumption made to compute the theoretical call option price in Exhibit 13-4 is that it will be 12% per year. The difference between the price of the noncallable bond and the theoretical price of the call option is the price of the callable bond. Notice that the price of the callable bond is the same as that shown in Exhibit 13-2.

From the previous chapter we know that the price of a call option increases when the expected interest rate volatility increases. Exhibit 13-5 shows the theoretical price of the call option when interest rate volatility is assumed to be 20% per year. The

---

[4] The theoretical option price for this illustration was provided by Andrew Ho of Kidder Peabody.

Exhibit 13-5
**Price/Yield Relationship and Theoretical Option Price for
GMAC 12% of June 2005 Callable at 102 in June 1990
(Settlement 6/1/88, 20% Interest Rate Volatility Assumption)**

Assumptions to compute theoretical call option price:
Binomial option pricing model
Interest rate volatility: 20%
Short-term interest rate: 6%

Yield	Noncallable bond price	Theoretical option price	Theoretical callable bond price
20.51	60	0.019	59.981
20.18	61	0.024	60.976
19.86	62	0.029	61.971
19.55	63	0.035	62.965
19.24	64	0.044	63.956
18.95	65	0.055	64.945
18.66	66	0.066	65.934
18.39	67	0.078	66.922
18.11	68	0.092	67.908
17.85	69	0.112	68.888
17.59	70	0.134	69.866
17.34	71	0.158	70.842
17.10	72	0.182	71.818
16.86	73	0.208	72.792
16.63	74	0.248	73.752
16.40	75	0.290	74.710
16.18	76	0.334	75.666
15.96	77	0.379	76.621
15.75	78	0.427	77.573
15.54	79	0.491	78.509
15.33	80	0.564	79.436
15.13	81	0.640	80.360
14.94	82	0.718	81.282
14.75	83	0.800	82.200
14.56	84	0.887	83.113
14.38	85	1.006	83.994

Yield	Noncallable bond price	Theoretical option price	Theoretical callable bond price
14.20	86	1.128	84.872
14.02	87	1.254	85.746
13.85	88	1.384	86.616
13.68	89	1.518	87.482
13.51	90	1.665	88.335
13.35	91	1.851	89.149
13.19	92	2.041	89.959
13.03	93	2.235	90.765
12.87	94	2.434	91.566
12.72	95	2.637	92.363
12.57	96	2.855	93.145
12.42	97	3.125	93.875
12.28	98	3.399	94.601
12.00	100	3.964	96.036
11.73	102	4.550	97.450
11.46	104	5.285	98.715
11.33	105	5.664	99.336
11.20	106	6.049	99.951
11.07	107	6.439	100.561
10.95	108	6.835	101.165
10.83	109	7.272	101.728
10.71	110	7.752	102.248
10.59	111	8.238	102.762
10.47	112	8.730	103.270
10.35	113	9.228	103.772
10.24	114	9.731	104.269
10.13	115	10.240	104.760
10.02	116	10.821	105.179
9.91	117	11.414	105.586
9.80	118	12.013	105.987
9.69	119	12.618	106.382
9.59	120	13.227	106.773
9.48	121	13.842	107.158
9.38	122	14.479	107.521
9.28	123	15.172	107.828
9.18	124	15.871	108.129

Exhibit 13-5 continued.

Yield	Noncallable bond price	Theoretical option price	Theoretical callable bond price
9.08	125	16.575	108.425
8.98	126	17.283	108.717
8.89	127	17.996	109.004
8.79	128	18.713	109.287
8.60	130	20.250	109.750
8.42	132	21.832	110.168
8.24	134	23.431	110.569
8.07	136	25.076	110.924
7.90	138	26.797	111.203
7.73	140	28.529	111.471
7.24	146	33.925	112.075
6.79	152	39.541	112.459
6.36	158	45.311	112.689
5.96	164	51.183	112.817
5.57	170	57.117	112.883

theoretical price of the call option is greater in Exhibit 13-5 than in Exhibit 13-4 because of the higher interest rate volatility assumed. Since the theoretical price of the call option is higher, the price of the callable bond is lower in Exhibit 13-5 than in Exhibit 13-4.

This also can be seen in Exhibit 13-6, which shows the price/yield relationship assuming (1) the issue is not callable, (2) the issue is callable and interest rate volatility is assumed to be 12% per year, and (3) the issue is callable and interest rate volatility is assumed to be 20% per year. Notice that the price/yield relationship for the callable bond assuming a 20% interest rate volatility begins to depart from the price/yield relationship for the noncallable bond at a higher yield than the price/yield relationship for the callable bond with a 12% interest rate volatility. When the market yield is deep in the money, the price/yield relationship for the callable bond is the same regardless of the interest rate volatility assumption.

Exhibit 13-6

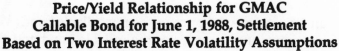

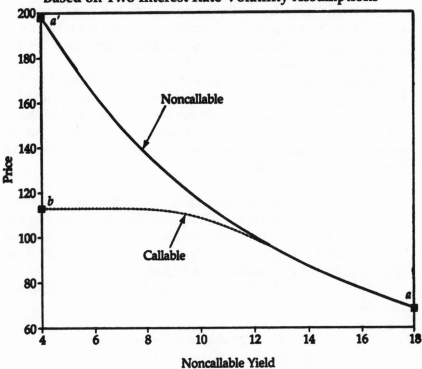

Call-Adjusted Yield for a Callable Corporate Bond

Given the above relationship for the callable bond, an investor wants to know if the noncallable bond is correctly priced, in the sense that he is being rewarded adequately for the credit risk associated with owning the bond. Although in our previous illustrations we have started with the price of the noncallable bond and computed the theoretical price of the callable bond by subtracting the theoretical price of the call option, the price that the noncallable bond will sell at in the market is not directly observable. It can be estimated by rewriting the relationship as

Noncallable bond price = Callable bond price + Call option price.

Can we estimate the price of the noncallable bond? We can, if we can determine the price of the callable bond and the call option price. The price of the callable bond can be observed in the market. The price of the call option can be estimated by using an option pricing model. Adding the two prices gives the implied price of the noncallable bond.

Given the implied price of the noncallable bond, it is then simple to compute the yield on this bond if it is not called but held to maturity. Recall from Chapter 6 that yield is the interest rate that will make the present value of the cash flows for the bond if held to maturity equal to the price. The yield computed is referred to as the *call-adjusted yield*.

Illustration 13-6. Suppose an investor is considering an 8% coupon callable corporate bond selling at 102 with 20 years to maturity and callable at 104. Suppose also that by using an option pricing model, the call option price is estimated to be 4.21. Then the call-adjusted yield is found as follows.

First the implied price for the noncallable bond is computed as follows:

Observed callable bond price = 102;
Theoretical call option price = 4.21;
Noncallable bond price = 102 + 4.21 = 106.21.

The call-adjusted yield is computed by finding the interest rate that will make the present value of 40 coupon payments of $4 every six months plus $100 at the end of 40 six-month periods equal to $106.21. The calculated six-month interest rate that satisfies this is 3.7%. Doubling this interest rate gives the call-adjusted yield of 7.4% on a bond equivalent yield basis.

Illustration 13-7. Consider once again the GMAC callable bond. Suppose that for June 1, 1988 settlement the *observed* price for the bond is 106.933. Also suppose that, based on an option pricing model and a volatility assumption of 12% per year, the theoretical option price for the call option is 5.067. The implied noncallable bond price is found as follows:

Observed callable bond price = 106.933;
Theoretical call option price = 5.067;
Noncallable bond price = 106.933 + 5.067 = 112.

The call-adjusted yield is found by determining the interest rate that will make the present value of the cash flows if this bond is not called but held to maturity, equal to the implied price of the noncallable bond (112) plus the accrued interest. There is no accrued interest on this bond, since we assumed the settlement date falls on a coupon date (June 1). The semiannual interest rate that will make the present value of the cash flows equal to 112 is 5.237%. Doubling this interest rate gives the call-adjusted yield, computed on a bond equivalent basis. The call-adjusted yield is therefore 10.474%.

The call-adjusted yield is the implied yield on the noncallable bond. A noncallable bond is priced fairly if the call-adjusted yield for a callable bond is the proper yield for a noncallable bond with the same features and of the same issuer. A bond is rich or overvalued if the call-adjusted yield is less; and cheap or undervalued if the call-adjusted yield is more.

Call-Adjusted Duration

As we have stressed throughout this book, yield is only one side of the valuation equation and, in fact, has limited value if a bond is not held to maturity. The other side of the equation is price volatility, since it will determine the performance of a bond over an investment horizon less than the maturity. The two parameters of a bond that determine price volatility are duration and convexity. In Chapters 10 and 11 we illustrated how to compute the duration and convexity of an option-free bond, respectively. In this section we shall explain how to compute the duration of a callable bond and in the next section we explain how to compute the convexity of a callable bond.[5]

---

[5] The mathematical derivations are given in Appendix A.

The duration of a callable bond after adjusting for the call option, commonly referred to as the *call-adjusted (modified) duration*, is:[6]

Call-adjusted duration =

$$\frac{\text{Price}_{NCB}}{\text{Price}_{CB}} \times \text{Dur}_{NCB} \times (1 - \text{Delta}),$$

where

Price_{NCB} = Price of noncallable bond;

Price_{CB} = Price of callable bond;

Dur_{NCB} = Modified duration of the noncallable bond;

Delta = Delta of the call option.

As can be seen, the call-adjusted duration depends on the following three elements:

(1) The ratio of the price of the noncallable bond to the price of the callable bond. Recall that the difference between the prices of a noncallable bond and a callable bond is equal to the price of the call option. The greater (smaller) the price of the call option, the higher (lower) the ratio. Thus we see that the call-adjusted duration will depend on the price of the call option.

(2) The duration of the corresponding noncallable (option-free) bond.

(3) The delta of the call option. In the previous chapter we discussed this delta, which measures the change in the price of the call option when the price of the underlying bond changes.

Let's apply the call-adjusted duration to the following two extreme cases—a deep-discount callable bond and a premium

---

[6] A *synthetic maturity date* for a callable bond is the maturity of a noncallable bond with the same coupon rate that would give the same duration as the call-adjusted duration for the callable bond. The probability that the call will be exercised at each interest rate can be calculated. Based on the probability of exercise, an expected maturity can be estimated. See Ravi Dattatreya and Frank J. Fabozzi, *Active Total Return Management of Fixed Income Portfolios* (Chicago: Probus Publishing, forthcoming 1989).

callable bond with a coupon rate substantially above the prevailing market yield. First consider the deep discount bond.

For a deep-discount bond, the coupon rate is substantially below the current market yield. For example, a 20-year bond with a coupon rate of 5% will trade at a deep discount when the current market yield on comparable bonds is 15%. Since it would not be economic for the corporate issuer to call the 5% coupon bond and replace it with a 15% coupon bond, the call option is deep out of the money. The option price would be small for this bond, and therefore the ratio of the noncallable bond price to the callable bond price would be close to one. From the previous chapter, recall our discussion of the delta of a call option. When the option is deep out of the money, the delta is close to zero. Therefore,

$$\frac{Price_{NCB}}{Price_{CB}} = 1;$$
$$Delta = 0$$

Substituting into the formula for the call-adjusted duration, we have

$$Call\text{-}adjusted\ duration = 1 \times Dur_{NCB} \times (1 - 0)$$
$$= Dur_{NCB}$$

Thus, the call-adjusted duration of a deep-discount callable bond will be the same as its duration, assuming it is noncallable.

Now let's consider the duration of a premium callable bond with a coupon rate substantially greater than the current market yield. As an example, consider a 20 year bond with a coupon rate of 16% when the current market yield is 6% (the bond would sell at a premium). The call option would be deep in the money since it would be highly beneficial for the corporate issuer to call the issue and issue new bonds with a coupon rate of 6%. Once again, recall from the previous chapter that the delta of a deep in the money call option is 1. Substituting 1 for delta into the formula for the call-adjusted duration, we have

$$\text{Call-adjusted duration} = \frac{\text{Price}_{NCB}}{\text{Price}_{CB}} \times \text{Dur}_{NCB} \times (1 - 1)$$

Call-adjusted duration = 0

Thus, the call-adjusted duration for a premium callable bond for which the coupon rate is substantially greater than the current market yield would be zero.

Anywhere in between a deep-discount bond and a premium bond with a high coupon rate relative to the prevailing market yield, the call-adjusted duration of a callable bond will be less than the duration of a noncallable bond.

Illustration 13-8. As in Illustration 13-7, suppose that for the GMAC callable bond the observed price is 106.933 and the theoretical call option price is 5.067. The implied price of the noncallable bond is 112, and the call-adjusted yield is 10.474%. The modified duration of the noncallable bond selling for 112 and with a yield of 10.474% would be 7.67. On the basis of the same option pricing model that generated the theoretical call option price of 5.067, the delta for the call option would be 0.486. The call-adjusted duration for the GMAC callable bond, based on the above information would be

P_{NCB} = Implied price of noncallable bond = 112;
P_{CB} = Observed price of callable bond = 106.933;
Dur_{NCB} = Duration of noncallable bond = 7.67;
Delta = Delta of call option = 0.486;

$$\text{Call-adjusted duration} = \frac{112}{106.933} \times 7.67 \times (1 - 0.486)$$
$$= 4.13.$$

Call-Adjusted Convexity

Convexity measures how the duration of a bond changes as yield changes. Let's look at the convexity of a callable corporate bond.

Exhibit 13-7 blows up the portion of the price/yield relationship in Exhibit 13-1 below y^*. Two tangent lines are shown.

Exhibit 13-7
Blow-up of Negative Convexity Portion of
Price/Yield Relationship for a Callable Bond

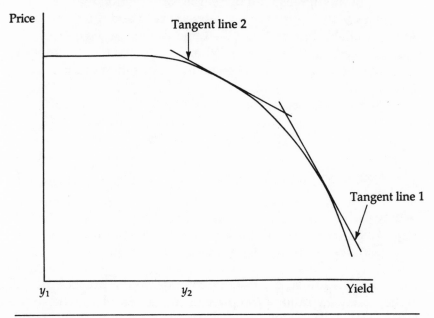

Recall from Chapter 11 that the duration of a bond is related to the slope of the tangent line—the steeper the tangent line, the greater the duration. A property of an option- free bond is that the duration changes in the desired direction as interest rates change: that is, the duration increases (decreases) as the interest rate decreases (increases).

This is not true for the portion of the callable bond's price/ yield relationship shown in Exhibit 13-7. As the yield declines, the tangent line flattens. That is, the duration gets smaller as the yield declines. This is exactly what an investor who is long a bond does not want to happen. In fact, there is a range of yields at which the duration is zero (between y_1 and y_2). For this range, a decline in yield will not change the price of the bond. In contrast, as yields increase, the duration gets larger—the tangent line becomes steeper. Once again, this is not what an investor wants. Because of this feature—duration changing in the wrong direction—the shape of the price/yield relationship shown in Exhibit 13-7 is referred to as *negative convexity*.[7]

All of this agrees with our earlier observation that the duration of a callable bond ranges between zero and the duration of the noncallable bond. When the bond is deep in the money, the call-adjusted duration is zero. When it is deep out of the money, the call-adjusted duration is equal to the duration of the noncallable bond.

The call-adjusted convexity can be found as follows:

$$\text{Call-adjusted convexity} =$$

$$\frac{\text{Price}_{NCB}}{\text{Price}_{CB}} \quad [\text{Con} \times (1 - \text{Delta}) - \text{Price}_{NCB} \times \text{Gamma} \times (\text{Dur}_{NCB})^2]$$

where

$\quad$ $\text{Con}_{NCB} = $ Convexity of the noncallable bond;
$\quad$ Gamma = Gamma of the call option.

The call-adjusted duration depends on the price of the call option (i.e., the ratio of the price of the noncallable bond to the price of the callable bond), the duration of the noncallable bond, and the delta. The call-adjusted convexity depends on the same three factors plus the convexity of the noncallable bond and the gamma of the call option. As we explained at the end of the previous chapter, the gamma of the call option measures the convexity of the call option.

Since the gamma of a call option is positive and the delta is between 0 and 1, call-adjusted convexity will be less than the convexity of the noncallable bond. Unlike the convexity for an option-free bond, which is always positive, the call-adjusted convexity may be negative. This occurs when the term in the square bracket is negative. That is, when

$$\text{Con}_{NCB} \times (1 - \text{Delta}) < \text{Price}_{NCB} \times \text{Gamma} \times (\text{Dur}_{NCB})^2.$$

---

[7]Mathematicians refer to the shape in Exhibit 13-7 as *concave*. The term negative convexity is used to stress the negative feature with respect to changes in duration.

When will this condition result? When the yield falls such that the call option moves deep in the money, the delta will approach 1. The term on the left hand side will approach zero and the term on the right hand side will be positive, resulting in a negative value for the term in the square brackets in the formula for the call-adjusted convexity.

Illustration 13-9. Continuing with our examination of the GMAC callable bond, assume the same information as in Illustration 13-8. The convexity of the noncallable bond is 91.82. The gamma for the call option (based on the option pricing model used to calculate the theoretical call option price) is 0.02878. The call-adjusted convexity is then:

P_{NCB} = Implied price of noncallable bond = 112;
P_{CB} = Observed price of callable bond = 106.933;
Dur_{NCB} = Duration of noncallable bond = 7.67;
Con_{NCB} = Convexity of noncallable bond = 91.82;
Delta = Delta of call option = 0.486;
Gamma = 0.02878;

Call-adjusted convexity =

$$\frac{112}{106.933} \left[91.82 \times (1 - 0.486) - 112 \times 0.02878 \times (7.67)^2 \right]$$

$$= -149.$$

The call-adjusted convexity is negative in this example because the call-adjusted yield is 10.474%, which is less than the coupon rate of 12%. The call option is therefore in the money.

Exhibits 13-8 and 13-9 show the price/yield relationship for the GMAC callable bond, the duration for the noncallable bond, the call-adjusted duration, the convexity of the noncallable bond, the delta of the call option, the gamma of the call option, and the call-adjusted convexity. Exhibits 13-8 and 13-9 assume that interest rate volatility will be 12% and 20%, respectively. (It is from Exhibits 13-8 and 13-9 that we constructed Exhibits 13-2 and 13-3.) Notice in both Exhibits 13-8 and 13-9 that

Exhibit 13-8

Call-Adjusted Duration and Call-Adjusted Convexity for GMA 12% of June 2005
Callable at 102 in June 1990 (Settlement 6/1/88, 12% Interest Rate Volatility Assumption)

Assumptions to compute theoretical call option price:
Binomial option pricing model
Interest rate volatility: 12%
Short-term interest rate: 6%

Yield	Noncallable bond			Call option			Callable bond		
	Price	Dur.	Con.	Price	Delta	Gamma	Price	Dur.	Con.
20.51	60	4.96	45.4	0.000	0.00	.000001	60.000	4.9	45.4
20.18	61	5.03	46.5	0.000	0.00	.000003	61.000	5.0	46.5
19.86	62	5.10	47.6	0.000	0.00	.000004	62.000	5.1	47.6
19.55	63	5.17	48.7	0.000	0.00	.000007	63.000	5.1	48.7
19.24	64	5.24	49.7	0.000	0.00	.000011	64.000	5.2	49.7
18.95	65	5.30	50.8	0.000	0.00	.000016	65.000	5.3	50.8
18.66	66	5.37	51.8	0.000	0.00	.000026	66.000	5.3	51.8
18.39	67	5.43	52.9	0.000	0.00	.000037	67.000	5.4	52.8
18.11	68	5.49	53.9	0.000	0.00	.000051	68.000	5.4	53.8
17.85	69	5.56	54.9	0.001	0.00	.000077	68.999	5.5	54.8
17.59	70	5.62	55.9	0.001	0.00	.000105	69.999	5.6	55.7

17.34	71	5.68	57.0	0.001	0.00	.000139	70.999	5.6	56.6
17.10	72	5.74	58.0	0.002	0.00	.000198	71.998	5.7	57.5
16.86	73	5.80	59.0	0.002	0.00	.000262	72.998	5.8	58.3
16.63	74	5.86	59.9	0.003	0.00	.000331	73.997	5.8	59.0
16.40	75	5.92	60.9	0.005	0.00	.000455	74.995	5.9	59.6
16.18	76	5.98	61.9	0.006	0.00	.000587	75.994	5.9	60.2
15.96	77	6.04	62.8	0.008	0.00	.000725	76.992	6.0	60.7
15.75	78	6.09	63.8	0.012	0.00	.000942	77.988	6.0	60.9
15.54	79	6.15	64.7	0.016	0.00	.001187	78.984	6.1	60.9
15.33	80	6.20	65.7	0.020	0.00	.001441	79.980	6.1	60.9
15.13	81	6.26	66.6	0.027	0.00	.001775	80.973	6.2	60.5
14.94	82	6.31	67.5	0.036	0.01	.002191	81.964	6.2	59.7
14.75	83	6.36	68.4	0.046	0.01	.002620	82.954	6.2	58.9
14.56	84	6.42	69.4	0.057	0.01	.003079	83.943	6.3	57.7
14.38	85	6.47	70.3	0.075	0.01	.003725	84.925	6.3	55.8
14.20	86	6.52	71.1	0.095	0.02	.004383	85.905	6.3	53.6
14.02	87	6.57	72.0	0.116	0.02	.005054	86.884	6.4	51.2
13.85	88	6.62	72.9	0.146	0.03	.005875	87.854	6.4	48.0
13.68	89	6.67	73.8	0.183	0.03	.006795	88.817	6.4	44.1
13.51	90	6.72	74.6	0.223	0.04	.007724	89.777	6.4	39.9
13.35	91	6.77	75.5	0.265	0.05	.008673	90.735	6.4	35.4
13.19	92	6.82	76.3	0.330	0.06	.009839	91.670	6.4	29.5
13.03	93	6.86	77.2	0.398	0.07	.01006	92.602	6.3	23.3

Exhibit 13-8 continued.

	Nomcallable bond			Call option			Callable bond		
Yield	Price	Dur.	Con.	Price	Delta	Gamma	Price	Dur.	Con.
12.87	94	6.91	78.0	0.469	0.08	.012174	93.531	6.3	16.8
12.72	95	6.96	78.8	0.557	0.09	.013406	94.443	6.3	9.5
12.57	96	7.00	79.6	0.667	0.11	.014725	95.333	6.2	1.4
12.42	97	7.05	80.4	0.783	0.12	.016032	96.217	6.2	−7.0
12.28	98	7.09	81.2	0.904	0.14	.017327	97.096	6.1	−15.8
12.00	100	7.18	82.8	1.235	0.18	.019921	98.765	5.9	−35.2
11.73	102	7.27	84.4	1.606	0.22	.022422	100.394	5.8	−55.9
11.46	104	7.35	85.9	2.112	0.26	.024551	101.888	5.4	−76.7
11.33	105	7.39	86.7	2.380	0.29	.025551	102.620	5.3	−87.4
11.20	106	7.43	87.4	2.661	0.31	.026493	103.339	5.2	−98.1
11.07	107	7.47	88.2	3.012	0.34	.027128	103.988	5.0	−107.5
10.95	108	7.51	88.9	3.373	0.37	.027716	104.627	4.8	−117.0
10.83	109	7.55	89.6	3.742	0.40	.028259	105.258	4.6	−126.4
10.71	110	7.59	90.3	4.134	0.42	.028689	105.866	4.5	−135.5
10.59	111	7.63	91.1	4.596	0.45	.028756	106.404	4.3	−142.5
10.47	112	7.67	91.8	5.067	0.48	.028778	106.933	4.1	−149.3
10.35	113	7.71	92.5	5.548	0.51	.028757	107.452	3.9	−155.9
10.24	114	7.75	93.2	6.056	0.54	.028601	107.944	3.7	−161.7
10.13	115	7.78	93.9	6.631	0.57	.028099	108.369	3.5	−165.1
10.02	116	7.82	94.6	7.215	0.59	.027564	108.785	3.3	−168.2

9.91	117	7.86	95.2	7.808	0.62	.026997	109.192	3.1	−170.9
9.80	118	7.89	95.9	8.429	0.65	.026317	109.571	2.9	−172.7
9.69	119	7.93	96.6	9.111	0.67	.025370	109.889	2.7	−172.0
9.59	120	7.96	97.2	9.801	0.70	.024405	110.199	2.5	−171.0
9.48	121	8.00	97.9	10.499	0.72	.023425	110.501	2.3	−169.6
9.38	122	8.03	98.6	11.220	0.75	.022384	110.780	2.2	−167.3
9.28	123	8.07	99.2	11.996	0.77	.021192	111.004	2.0	−163.1
9.18	124	8.10	99.9	12.778	0.79	.020000	111.222	1.8	−158.6
9.08	125	8.14	100.5	13.567	0.81	.018809	111.433	1.7	−153.6
8.98	126	8.17	101.1	14.372	0.83	.017610	111.628	1.5	−148.1
8.89	127	8.20	101.8	15.224	0.84	.016387	111.776	1.4	−141.7
8.79	128	8.24	102.4	16.080	0.86	.015178	111.920	1.2	−134.9
8.60	130	8.30	103.6	17.813	0.89	.012809	112.187	1.0	−120.3
8.42	132	8.36	104.8	19.632	0.91	.010663	112.368	0.8	−105.4
8.24	134	8.43	106.0	21.466	0.93	.008606	112.534	0.6	−89.6
8.07	136	8.49	107.2	23.362	0.95	.006928	112.638	0.4	−75.7
7.90	138	8.55	108.4	25.267	0.96	.005337	112.733	0.3	−61.3
7.73	140	8.61	109.5	27.210	0.97	.004155	112.790	0.2	−50.0
7.24	146	8.78	112.8	33.106	0.99	.001608	112.894	0.0	−22.1
6.79	152	8.94	116.0	39.075	0.99	.000538	112.925	0.0	−8.4
6.36	158	9.10	119.1	45.066	0.99	.000135	112.934	0.0	−2.3
5.96	164	9.25	122.0	51.064	1.00	.000029	112.936	0.0	−0.5
5.57	170	9.39	124.8	57.064	1.00	.000004	112.936	0.0	−0.0

Exhibit 13-9

Call-Adjusted Duration and Call-Adjusted Convexity for GMAC 20% of June 2005
Callable at 102 in June 1990 (Settlement 6/1/88, 20% Interest Rate Volatility Assumption)

Assumptions to compute theoretical call option price:
Binomial option pricing model
Interest rate volatility: 20%
Short-term interest rate: 6%

Yield	Noncallable bond Price	Dur.	Con.	Call option Price	Delta	Gamma	Callable bond Price	Dur.	Con.
20.51	60	4.96	45.4	0.019	0.00	.000845	59.981	4.9	44.0
20.18	61	5.03	46.5	0.024	0.00	.000987	60.976	5.0	44.8
19.86	62	5.10	47.6	0.029	0.00	.001130	61.971	5.0	45.5
19.55	63	5.17	48.7	0.035	0.00	.001274	62.965	5.1	46.2
19.24	64	5.24	49.7	0.044	0.00	.001493	63.956	5.1	46.7
18.95	65	5.30	50.8	0.055	0.01	.001716	64.945	5.2	47.1
18.66	66	5.37	51.8	0.066	0.01	.001939	65.934	5.3	47.5
18.39	67	5.43	52.9	0.078	0.01	.002161	66.922	5.3	47.9
18.11	68	5.49	53.9	0.092	0.01	.002397	67.908	5.4	48.2
17.85	69	5.56	54.9	0.112	0.01	.002718	68.888	5.4	48.1

17.59	70	5.62	55.9	0.134	0.02	.003036	69.866	5.5	48.1
17.34	71	5.68	57.0	0.158	0.02	.003352	70.842	5.5	47.9
17.10	72	5.74	58.0	0.182	0.02	.003665	71.818	5.5	47.7
16.86	73	5.80	59.0	0.208	0.03	.003982	72.792	5.6	47.4
16.63	74	5.86	59.9	0.248	0.03	.004400	73.752	5.6	46.7
16.40	75	5.92	60.9	0.290	0.04	.004812	74.710	5.7	45.9
16.18	76	5.98	61.9	0.334	0.04	.005218	75.666	5.7	45.0
15.96	77	6.04	62.8	0.379	0.05	.005621	76.621	5.7	44.0
15.75	78	6.09	63.8	0.427	0.05	.006018	77.573	5.7	43.0
15.54	79	6.15	64.7	0.491	0.06	.006480	78.509	5.7	41.5
15.33	80	6.20	65.7	0.564	0.07	.006963	79.436	5.8	39.8
15.13	81	6.26	66.6	0.640	0.07	.007438	80.360	5.8	38.1
14.94	82	6.31	67.5	0.718	0.08	.007906	81.282	5.8	36.2
14.75	83	6.36	68.4	0.800	0.09	.008367	82.200	5.8	34.2
14.56	84	6.42	69.4	0.887	0.10	.008828	83.113	5.8	32.1
14.38	85	6.47	70.3	1.006	0.11	.009336	83.994	5.8	29.6
14.20	86	6.52	71.1	1.128	0.12	.009835	84.872	5.8	26.9
14.02	87	6.57	72.0	1.254	0.13	.010323	85.746	5.7	24.1
13.85	88	6.62	72.9	1.384	0.14	.010803	86.616	5.7	21.2
13.68	89	6.67	73.8	1.518	0.15	.011274	87.482	5.7	18.2
13.51	90	6.72	74.6	1.665	0.16	.011739	88.335	5.7	15.0
13.35	91	6.77	75.5	1.851	0.17	.012198	89.149	5.7	11.6
13.19	92	6.82	76.3	2.041	0.18	.012646	89.959	5.6	8.0

Exhibit 13-9 continued.

Yield	Noncallable bond			Call option			Callable bond		
	Price	Dur.	Con.	Price	Delta	Gamma	Price	Dur.	Con.
13.03	93	6.86	77.2	2.235	0.20	.013084	90.765	5.6	4.4
12.87	94	6.91	78.0	2.434	0.21	.013511	91.566	5.5	0.6
12.72	95	6.96	78.8	2.637	0.22	.013929	92.363	5.5	−3.2
12.57	96	7.00	79.6	2.855	0.24	.014328	93.145	5.4	−7.2
12.42	97	7.05	80.4	3.125	0.25	.014669	93.875	5.4	−11.1
12.28	98	7.09	81.2	3.399	0.27	.015000	94.601	5.3	−15.2
12.00	100	7.18	82.8	3.964	0.30	.015630	96.036	5.2	−23.7
11.72	102	7.27	84.4	4.550	0.33	.016222	97.450	5.1	−32.5
11.46	104	7.35	85.9	5.285	0.36	.016563	98.715	4.9	−40.6
11.33	105	7.39	86.7	5.664	0.38	.016714	99.336	4.8	−44.8
11.20	106	7.43	87.4	6.049	0.39	.016857	99.951	4.7	−49.0
11.07	107	7.47	88.2	6.439	0.41	.016991	100.561	4.6	−53.2
10.95	108	7.51	88.9	6.835	0.43	.017117	101.165	4.5	−57.5
10.83	109	7.55	89.6	7.272	0.44	.017167	101.728	4.4	−61.5
10.71	110	7.59	90.3	7.752	0.46	.017135	102.248	4.3	−65.1
10.59	111	7.63	91.1	8.238	0.48	.017097	102.762	4.2	−68.6
10.47	112	7.67	91.8	8.730	0.50	.017051	103.270	4.1	−72.2
10.35	113	7.71	92.5	9.228	0.51	.017000	103.772	4.0	−75.7
10.24	114	7.75	93.2	9.731	0.53	.016942	104.269	3.9	−79.3
10.13	115	7.78	93.9	10.240	0.55	.016879	104.760	3.8	−82.9

10.02	116	7.82	94.6	10.821	0.56	.016680	105.179	3.7	−85.5
9.91	117	7.86	95.2	11.414	0.58	.016465	105.586	3.6	−87.9
9.80	118	7.89	95.9	12.013	0.60	.016246	105.987	3.5	−90.3
9.69	119	7.93	96.6	12.618	0.61	.016023	106.382	3.4	−92.7
9.59	120	7.96	97.2	13.227	0.63	.015797	106.773	3.2	−95.0
9.48	121	8.00	97.9	13.842	0.64	.015568	107.158	3.1	−97.3
9.38	122	8.03	98.6	14.479	0.66	.015308	107.521	3.0	−99.3
9.28	123	8.07	99.2	15.172	0.67	.014961	107.828	2.9	−100.4
9.18	124	8.10	99.9	15.871	0.69	.014613	108.129	2.8	−101.4
9.08	125	8.14	100.5	16.575	0.70	.014265	108.425	2.7	−102.3
8.98	126	8.17	101.1	17.283	0.72	.013915	108.717	2.6	−103.1
8.89	127	8.20	101.8	17.996	0.73	.013564	109.004	2.5	−103.8
8.79	128	8.24	102.4	18.713	0.75	.013212	109.287	2.4	−104.4
8.60	130	8.30	103.6	20.250	0.77	.012414	109.750	2.2	−104.1
8.42	132	8.36	104.8	21.832	0.79	.011589	110.168	2.0	−103.0
8.24	134	8.43	106.0	23.431	0.82	.010769	110.569	1.8	−101.3
8.07	136	8.49	107.2	25.076	0.84	.009946	110.924	1.6	−98.9
7.90	138	8.55	108.4	26.797	0.86	.009118	111.203	1.4	−95.4
7.73	140	8.61	109.5	28.529	0.87	.008301	111.471	1.3	−91.5
7.24	146	8.78	112.8	33.925	0.92	.006038	112.075	0.8	−77.0
6.79	152	8.94	116.0	39.541	0.95	.004126	112.459	0.5	−60.3
6.36	158	9.10	119.1	45.311	0.97	.002635	112.689	0.3	−43.8
5.96	164	9.25	122.0	51.183	0.98	.001563	112.817	0.1	−29.3
5.57	170	9.39	124.8	57.117	0.99	.000854	112.883	0.1	−17.9

the duration for the callable bond approaches the duration of the noncallable bond as the yield rises above the coupon rate of 12%. As yields decline below 12%, the difference between the duration of the callable bond and that of the noncallable bond increases.

Horizon Return

The call-adjusted yield suffers from the same drawbacks as the yield to maturity: it assumes that the bond will be held to the maturity date and the coupon payments can be reinvested at an interest rate equal to the call-adjusted yield. In Chapter 8, we explained how the horizon analysis framework should be used to determine the horizon return so that the relative value of a bond can be analyzed. To compute the horizon return for a bond over some investment horizon, the following must be determined:

(1) The coupon interest;
(2) Interest on interest from reinvesting the coupon payments;
(3) Any capital gain or loss from the disposal of the bond at the end of the investment horizon.

The last element depends on the duration and convexity of the bond. For an option-free bond, horizon return analysis is simple to conduct because the price of the bond at some specified investment horizon can be easily computed, given the projected yield to maturity offered on comparable bonds. For a callable bond, horizon return analysis requires that more assumptions be made. Specifically, because the price of the callable bond at the horizon date will depend on the option price, factors that determine the option price must be considered. The factor that will influence the option price that is difficult to assess in horizon return analysis is the expected interest rate volatility at the end of the investment horizon. Thus, horizon return analysis requires not only assumptions about the yield at the investment horizon date and the reinvestment rate but also the expected interest rate volatility at the end of the investment horizon.

Summary

The owner of a callable corporate bond is effectively long a noncallable bond and short a call option on that noncallable bond. The price and price performance of the callable corporate bond will therefore depend on the price characteristics of both the noncallable bond and the call option. In this chapter we have presented formulas to determine the call-adjusted yield, the call-adjusted duration, and the call-adjusted convexity of a callable bond.

Unlike that of an option-free bond, the duration of a callable bond may not increase as interest rates decline. At some yield level, the duration of a callable bond may exhibit negative convexity. The convexity of the callable bond will depend on the price of the call option, the delta of the call option, and the gamma of the call option.

While call-adjusted yield measures the yield after adjusting for the call option, the portfolio manager should use the horizon return analysis framework to determine the potential return over some investment horizon. The horizon return will depend on how the price of the embedded call option changes. To determine how the price of the call option changes, assumptions must be made about expected interest rate volatility at the end of the investment horizon.

14
Cash Flow Characteristics of Mortgages

A mortgage is a pledge of real estate to secure the payment of the loan originated for the purchase of that real property. The mortgage gives the lender (*mortgagee*) the right to foreclose on the loan and seize the property in order to ensure that the loan is paid off if the borrower (*mortgagor*) fails to make the contracted payments.

A mortgage loan specifies the interest rate of the loan, the frequency of payment, and the number of years to maturity. In this chapter we show how to compute the cash flow of mortgages or, as they are more popularly referred to, *whole loans*. While there are many types of mortgages, we focus in this chapter on level-payment fixed-rate mortgages. A level-payment, fixed-rate mortgage has the following features: (1) the term of the loan is fixed, (2) the interest rate is fixed, and (3) the amount of the monthly mortgage payment is fixed for the entire term of the loan (i.e., the mortgage is "level-pay").

A characteristic shared by mortgages and callable corporate bonds is that the cash flow is not known with certainty. For callable corporate bonds, this situation arises because the bondholder has effectively granted the corporate issuer the option to call the issue. For mortgages, the lender has effectively granted the homeowner the right to repay *all* or *any part* of the mortgage balance at any time.

Mortgages are the underlying collateral for mortgage pass-through securities. The level-payment fixed-rate mortgage is the most common type of collateral for pass-through securities.[1] In the next chapter we shall describe the cash flow characteristics of these securities, taking into consideration the effect of prepayments.

Determining the Monthly Mortgage Payment

In Chapter 3 we explained the calculation of the present value of an ordinary annuity. To compute the monthly mortgage payment for a level-payment fixed-rate mortgage requires the application of the formula for the present value of an ordinary annuity formula which is

$$PV = A \left[\frac{1 - \left[\frac{1}{(1 + i)^n} \right]}{i} \right],$$

where
  A = Amount of the annuity (\$);
  n = Number of periods;
  PV = Present value of an annuity (\$);
  i = Periodic interest rate.

We can redefine the terms in the above formula for a level-payment fixed-rate mortgage as follows:

$$MB_0 = MP \left[\frac{1 - \left[\frac{1}{(1 + i)^n} \right]}{i} \right],$$

---

[1] Other types of mortgages can serve as the underlying collateral for mortgage pass-through securities. These include adjustable-rate mortgages and graduated payment mortgages. For a discussion of the characteristics of these mortgages, see Frank J. Fabozzi and T. Dessa Fabozzi, *Bond Markets, Analysis and Strategies* (Englewood Cliffs, N.J.: Prentice-Hall, 1989), Chapters 9 and 10.

where

MP = Monthly mortgage payment ($);
n = Number of months;
MB_0 = Original mortgage balance ($);
i = Simple monthly interest rate (annual interest rate/ 12).

Solving for the monthly mortgage payment (MP) gives

$$MP = \frac{MB_0}{\left[\dfrac{1 - \left[\dfrac{1}{(1+i)^n}\right]}{i}\right]}$$

Alternatively, this can be expressed in a simplified form as follows:

$$MP = MB_0 \left[\frac{[i(1+i)^n]}{[(1+i)^n - 1]}\right].$$

Illustration 14-1. Suppose a loan for $100,000 is obtained by a homeowner for 360 months (30 years), and the mortgage rate is 9.5%. The monthly mortgage payment is determined as follows:

n = 360;
MB_0 = $100,000;
i = .0079167 (= .095/12).

The monthly mortgage payment is then

$$MP = \$100,000 \ \frac{[.0079167\,(1.0079167)^{360}]}{[(1.0079167)^{360} - 1]}$$

$$= \$100,000 \ \frac{[.0079167\,(17.095)]}{[17.095 - 1]}$$

$$= \$840.85.$$

Cash Flow of a Level-Payment Fixed-Rate Mortgage

Each monthly mortgage payment for a level-payment fixed rate-mortgage is due on the first of each month and consists of:

(1) Interest of 1/12th of the fixed annual interest rate times the amount of the outstanding mortgage balance at the beginning of the previous month (interest "in arrears"), and

(2) Repayment of a portion of the outstanding mortgage balance (principal).

The difference between the monthly mortgage payment and the portion of the payment that represents interest equals the amount that is applied to reduce the outstanding mortgage balance. The monthly mortgage payment is designed so that after the last scheduled monthly payment of the loan is made, the amount of the outstanding mortgage balance is zero (i.e., the mortgage is fully repaid).

Illustration 14-2. Consider the mortgage in Illustration 14-1. Exhibit 14-1 shows how each monthly mortgage payment is divided between interest and repayment of principal. At the beginning of month 1, the mortgage balance is $100,000, the amount of the original loan. The mortgage payment for month 1 includes interest for the month on the $100,000 borrowed. Since the interest rate is 9.5%, the monthly interest rate is 0.0079167 (.095 divided by 12). Interest for month 1 is therefore $791.67 ($100,000 times 0.0079167). The portion of the monthly mortgage payment that represents repayment of principal is the difference between the monthly mortgage payment of $840.85 and the interest of $791.67. Thus, the scheduled principal repayment is $49.18, and the mortgage balance is reduced by this amount.

The mortgage balance at the end of month 1 (beginning of month 2) is then $99,950.81 ($100,000 minus $49.19). The interest for the second month is $791.28, the monthly interest rate (0.0079167) times the mortgage balance at the end of month 1 ($99,950.81). The difference between the $840.85 monthly mortgage payment and the $791.28 interest is $49.57, representing the amount of the mortgage balance paid off with that monthly mortgage payment.[2]

---

[2] Because Exhibit 14-1 was computer-generated, rounding resulted in the value of $49.48 shown in the exhibit.

Exhibit 14-1

Amortization Schedule for a Level-Payment Fixed-Rate Mortgage

Mortgage loan: $100,000
Mortgage rate: 9.5%
Monthly payment: $840.85
Term of loan: 30 years (360 months)

Month	Beginning mortgage balance	Monthly mortgage payment	Interest for month	Principal repayment	Ending mortgage balance
1	$100,000.00	$840.85	$791.67	$ 49.19	$99,950.81
2	99,950.81	840.85	791.28	49.58	99,901.24
3	99,901.24	840.85	790.88	49.97	99,851.27
4	99,851.27	840.85	790.49	50.37	99,800.90
5	99,800.90	840.85	790.09	50.76	99,750.14
6	99,750.14	840.85	789.69	51.1	99,698.97
7	99,698.97	840.85	789.28	51.57	99,647.40
8	99,647.40	840.85	788.88	51.9	99,595.42
9	99,595.42	840.85	788.46	52.39	99,543.03
10	99,543.03	840.85	788.05	52.81	99,490.23
11	99,490.23	840.85	787.63	53.22	99,437.00

Exhibit 14-1 continued.

Month	Beginning mortgage balance	Monthly mortgage payment	Interest for month	Principal repayment	Ending mortgage balance
12	99,437.00	840.85	787.21	53.64	99,383.36
13	99,383.36	840.85	786.78	54.07	99,329.29
14	99,329.29	840.85	786.36	54.50	99,274.79
15	99,274.79	840.85	785.93	54.93	99,219.86
16	99,219.86	840.85	785.49	55.36	99,164.50
17	99,164.50	840.85	785.05	55.80	99,108.70
18	99,108.70	840.85	784.61	56.24	99,052.45
19	99,052.45	840.85	784.17	56.69	98,995.77
20	98,995.77	840.85	783.72	57.14	98,938.63
21	98,938.63	840.85	783.26	57.59	98,881.04
22	98,881.04	840.85	782.81	58.05	98,822.99
23	98,822.99	840.85	782.35	58.51	98,764.49
24	98,764.49	840.85	781.89	58.97	98,705.52
25	98,705.52	840.85	781.42	59.44	98,646.08
26	98,646.08	840.85	780.95	59.91	98,586.18
27	98,586.18	840.85	780.47	60.38	98,525.80
28	98,525.80	840.85	780.00	60.86	98,464.94
29	98,464.94	840.85	779.51	61.34	98,403.60
30	98,403.60	840.85	779.03	61.83	98,341.77

31	98,341.77	840.85	778.54	62.32	98,279.46
32	98,279.46	840.85	778.05	62.81	98,216.65
33	98,216.65	840.85	777.55	63.31	98,153.34
34	98,153.34	840.85	777.05	63.81	98,089.53
35	98,089.53	840.85	776.54	64.31	98,025.22
36	98,025.22	840.85	776.03	64.82	97,960.40
:	......	......	......	......	......
:	......	......	......	......	......
:	......	......	......	......	......
98	92,862.54	840.85	735.16	105.69	92,756.85
99	92,756.85	840.85	734.33	106.53	92,650.32
100	92,650.32	840.85	733.48	107.37	92,542.95
101	92,542.95	840.85	732.63	108.22	92,434.72
102	92,434.72	840.85	731.77	109.08	92,325.64
103	92,325.64	840.85	730.91	109.94	92,215.70
104	92,215.70	840.85	730.04	110.81	92,104.89
105	92,104.89	840.85	729.16	111.69	91,993.20
106	91,993.20	840.85	728.28	112.57	91,880.62
107	91,880.62	840.85	727.39	113.47	91,767.16
108	91,767.16	840.85	726.49	114.36	91,652.79
109	91,652.79	840.85	725.58	115.27	91,537.52
110	91,537.52	840.85	724.67	116.18	91,421.34
111	91,421.34	840.85	723.75	117.10	91,304.24

Exhibit 14-1 continued.

Month	Beginning mortgage balance	Monthly mortgage payment	Interest for month	Principal repayment	Ending mortgage balance
112	91,304.24	840.85	722.83	118.03	91,186.21
113	91,186.21	840.85	721.89	118.96	91,067.25
114	91,067.25	840.85	720.95	119.91	90,947.34
115	90,947.34	840.85	720.00	120.85	90,826.49
:	......	......	......	......	......
:	......	......	......	......	......
:	......				
201	76,135.92	840.85	602.74	238.11	75,897.80
202	75,897.80	840.85	600.86	240.00	75,657.81
203	75,657.81	840.85	598.96	241.90	75,415.91
204	75,415.91	840.85	597.04	243.81	75,172.10
205	75,172.10	840.85	595.11	245.74	74,926.36
206	74,926.36	840.85	593.17	247.69	74,678.67
207	74,678.67	840.85	591.21	249.65	74,429.02
208	74,429.02	840.85	589.23	251.62	74,177.40
209	74,177.40	840.85	587.24	253.62	73,923.78
210	73,923.78	840.85	585.23	255.62	73,668.16
211	73,668.16	840.85	583.21	257.65	73,410.51
212	73,410.51	840.85	581.17	259.69	73,150.82

No.				
213	72,889.08	261.74	579.11	840.85	73,150.82
214	72,625.26	263.82	577.04	840.85	72,889.08
215	72,359.36	265.90	574.95	840.85	72,625.26
216	72,091.35	268.01	572.84	840.85	72,359.36
217	71,821.22	270.13	570.72	840.85	72,091.35
218	71,548.95	272.27	568.58	840.85	71,821.22
219	71,274.52	274.43	566.43	840.85	71,548.95
220	70,997.93	276.60	564.26	840.85	71,274.52
:	……	……	……	……	……
:	……	……	……	……	……
342	14,054.73	723.86	117.00	840.85	14,778.59
343	13,325.15	729.59	111.27	840.85	14,054.73
344	12,589.78	735.36	105.49	840.85	13,325.15
345	11,848.60	741.19	99.67	840.85	12,589.78
346	11,101.55	747.05	93.80	840.85	11,848.60
347	10,348.58	752.97	87.89	840.85	11,101.55
348	9,589.65	758.93	81.93	840.85	10,348.58
349	8,824.71	764.94	75.92	840.85	9,589.65
350	8,053.72	770.99	69.86	840.85	8,824.71
351	7,276.63	777.10	63.76	840.85	8,053.72
352	6,493.38	783.25	57.61	840.85	7,276.63
353	5,703.93	789.45	51.41	840.85	6,493.38

Exhibit 14-1 continued.

Month	Beginning mortgage balance	Monthly mortgage payment	Interest for month	Principal repayment	Ending mortgage balance
354	5,703.93	840.85	45.16	795.70	4,908.23
355	4,908.23	840.85	38.86	802.00	4,106.24
356	4,106.24	840.85	32.51	808.35	3,297.89
357	3,297.89	840.85	26.11	814.75	2,483.14
358	2,483.14	840.85	19.66	821.20	1,661.95
359	1,661.95	840.85	13.16	827.70	834.25
360	834.25	840.85	6.60	834.25	0.00

Looking at the last row of Exhibit 14-1, we see that the last monthly mortgage payment is sufficient to pay off the remaining mortgage balance. When a loan repayment schedule is structured so that the payments made by the borrower will completely pay off the interest and principal, the loan is said to be *self-amortizing*. Exhibit 14-1 is then referred to as an amortization schedule.

As Exhibit 14-1 clearly shows, *the portion of the monthly mortgage payment applied to interest declines each month and the portion that goes to reducing the mortgage balance increases.* The reason for this is that as the mortgage balance is reduced with each monthly mortgage payment, the interest on the mortgage balance declines. Since the monthly mortgage payment is fixed, a larger part of the monthly payment is applied to reduce the principal each month.

It is not necessary to construct an amortization schedule such as Exhibit 14-1 in order to determine the remaining mortgage balance for any month. The following formula can be used:

$$MP_t = MB_0 \left[\frac{[(1 + i)^n - (1 + i)^t]}{[(1 + i)^n - 1]} \right],$$

where

MB_t = Mortgage balance after t months (\$);
n = Original number of months of mortgage;
MB_0 = The original mortgage balance (\$);
i = Simple monthly interest rate (annual interest rate/ 12).

Illustration 14-3. For the mortgage in Illustration 14-1, the mortgage balance after the 210th month is:

t = 210;
n = 360;
MB_0 = \$100,000;
i = .0079167.

$$MB_{210} = \$100,000 \left[\frac{[(1.0079167)^{360} - (1.0079167)^{210}]}{[(1.0079167)^{360} - 1]} \right]$$

$$= \$100,000 \left[\frac{(17.095 - 5.2381)}{(17.095 - 1)} \right]$$

$$= \$73,668.$$

This agrees with the ending mortgage balance for month 210 shown in Exhibit 14-1.

The following formula can be used to determine the amount of the scheduled principal repayment in month t:

$$P_t = MB_0 \left[\frac{[i \, (1 + i)^{t-1}]}{[(1 + i)^n - 1]} \right],$$

where

P_t = Scheduled principal repayment for month t.

Illustration 14-4. The scheduled principal repayment for the 210th month for the mortgage in Illustration 14-1 is

$$\$100,000 \left[\frac{[.0079167 \, (1.0079167)^{210-1}]}{[(1.0079167)^{360} - 1]} \right]$$

$$= \$100,000 \left[\frac{[.0079167 \, (5.19696)]}{[17.095 - 1]} \right]$$

$$= \$255.62.$$

Once again, this agrees with Exhibit 14-1.

To compute the interest paid for month t, the following formula can be used:

$$I_t = MB_0 \left[\frac{i \, [(1 + i)^n - (1 + i)^{t-1}]}{[\, (1 + i)^n - 1 \,]} \right],$$

where

I_t = Interest for month t.

Illustration 14-5. For the 210th month, the interest for the mortgage in Illustration 14-1 is

$$I_{210} = \$100,000 \left[\frac{.0079167 \, [(1.0079167)^{360} - (1.0079167)^{210-1}]}{[(1.0079167)^{360} - 1]} \right]$$

$$= \$100,000 \left[\frac{.0079167 \, (17.095 - 5.19696)}{(17.095 - 1)} \right]$$

$$= \$585.23.$$

Cash Flow and Servicing Fee

For an investor who owns a mortgage, the *scheduled* cash flow is the monthly mortgage payment. A mortgage, however, requires the investor to monitor it to ensure that the borrower complies with the terms of the mortgage. In addition, the investor must periodically supply certain information to the borrower. These activities are referred to as *servicing* the mortgage. More specifically, servicing of the mortgage involves collecting monthly payments from mortgagors, sending payment notices to mortgagors, reminding mortgagors when payments are overdue, maintaining records of mortgage balances, furnishing tax information to mortgagors, administering an escrow account for real estate taxes and insurance purposes, and, if necessary, initiating foreclosure proceedings. Part of the mortgage rate includes the cost of servicing the mortgage. The servicing fee is a fixed percentage of the outstanding mortgage balance.

An investor who acquires a mortgage may service the mortgage or sell the right to service the mortgage. In the former case, the investor's cash flow is the entire cash flow from the mortgage. In the latter case it is the cash flow net of the servicing fee.

The monthly cash flow from the mortgage can therefore be decomposed into three parts:

(1) The amount to service the mortgage;
(2) The interest payment net of the servicing fee;
(3) The scheduled principal repayment.

Illustration 14-6. Consider once again the 30-year mortgage loan for $100,000 with a mortgage rate of 9.5%. Suppose the servicing fee is 0.5% per year. Exhibit 14-2 shows the cash flow for the mortgage with this servicing fee. The monthly mortgage pay-

Exhibit 14-2

Cash Flow for a Mortgage with Servicing Fee

Mortgage loan: $100,000
Mortgage rate: 9.5%
Servicing fee: 0.5%
Monthly payment: $840.85
Term of loan: 30 years (360 months)

Month	Beginning mortgage balance	Monthly mortgage payment	Net interext for month	Servicing fee	Principal repayment	Ending mortgage balance
1	$100,000.00	$840.85	$750.00	$41.67	$49.19	$99,950.81
2	99,950.81	840.85	749.63	41.65	49.58	99,901.24
3	99,901.24	840.85	749.26	41.63	49.97	99,851.27
4	99,851.27	840.85	748.88	41.60	50.37	99,800.90
5	99,800.90	840.85	748.51	41.58	50.76	99,750.14
6	99,750.14	840.85	748.13	41.56	51.17	99,698.97
7	99,698.97	840.85	747.74	41.54	51.57	99,647.40
8	99,647.40	840.85	747.36	41.52	51.98	99,595.42
9	99,595.42	840.85	746.97	41.50	52.39	99,543.03
10	99,543.03	840.85	746.57	41.48	52.81	99,490.23

11	99,490.23	840.85	746.18	41.45	53.22	99,437.00
12	99,437.00	840.85	745.78	41.43	53.64	99,383.36
13	99,383.36	840.85	745.38	41.41	54.07	99,329.29
14	99,329.29	840.85	744.97	41.39	54.50	99,274.79
15	99,274.79	840.85	744.56	41.36	54.93	99,219.86
16	99,219.86	840.85	744.15	41.34	55.36	99,164.50
17	99,164.50	840.85	743.73	41.32	55.80	99,108.70
18	99,108.70	840.85	743.32	41.30	56.24	99,052.45
19	99,052.45	840.85	742.89	41.27	56.69	98,995.77
20	98,995.77	840.85	742.47	41.25	57.14	98,938.63
21	98,938.63	840.85	742.04	41.22	57.59	98,881.04
22	98,881.04	840.85	741.61	41.20	58.05	98,822.99
23	98,822.99	840.85	741.17	41.18	58.51	98,764.49
24	98,764.49	840.85	740.73	41.15	58.97	98,705.52
25	98,705.52	840.85	740.29	41.13	59.44	98,646.08
26	98,646.08	840.85	739.85	41.10	59.91	98,586.18
27	98,586.18	840.85	739.40	41.08	60.38	98,525.80
28	98,525.80	840.85	738.94	41.05	60.86	98,464.94
29	98,464.94	840.85	738.49	41.03	61.34	98,403.60
30	98,403.60	840.85	738.03	41.00	61.83	98,341.77
31	98,341.77	840.85	737.56	40.98	62.32	98,279.46
32	98,279.46	840.85	737.10	40.95	62.81	98,216.65
33	98,216.65	840.85	736.62	40.92	63.31	98,153.34

Exhibit 14-2 continued.

Month	Beginning mortgage balance	Monthly mortgage payment	Net interext for month	Servicing fee	Principal repayment	Ending mortgage balance
34	98,153.34	840.85	736.15	40.90	63.81	98,089.53
35	98,089.53	840.85	735.67	40.87	64.31	98,025.22
36	98,025.22	840.85	735.19	40.84	64.82	97,960.40
: :	......	......	......	......	......	......
: :	......	......	......	......	......	......
: :	......	......	......	......	......	......
98	92,862.54	840.85	696.47	38.69	105.69	92,756.85
99	92,756.85	840.85	695.68	38.65	106.53	92,650.32
100	92,650.32	840.85	694.88	38.60	107.37	92,542.95
101	92,542.95	840.85	694.07	38.56	108.22	92,434.72
102	92,434.72	840.85	693.26	38.51	109.08	92,325.64
103	92,325.64	840.85	692.44	38.47	109.94	92,215.70
104	92,215.70	840.85	691.62	38.42	110.81	92,104.89
105	92,104.89	840.85	690.79	38.38	111.69	91,993.20
106	91,993.20	840.85	689.95	38.33	112.57	91,880.62
107	91,880.62	840.85	689.10	38.28	113.47	91,767.16
108	91,767.16	840.85	688.25	38.24	114.36	91,652.79
109	91,652.79	840.85	687.40	38.19	115.27	91,537.52
110	91,537.52	840.85	686.53	38.14	116.18	91,421.34

111	91,421.34	840.85	685.66	38.09	117.10	91,304.24
112	91,304.24	840.85	684.78	38.04	118.03	91,186.21
113	91,186.21	840.85	683.90	37.99	118.96	91,067.25
114	91,067.25	840.85	683.00	37.94	119.91	90,947.34
115	90,947.34	840.85	682.11	37.89	120.85	90,826.49
:	......	......	......	......	......	......
:	......	......	......	......	......	......
201	76,135.92	840.85	571.02	31.72	238.11	75,897.80
202	75,897.80	840.85	569.23	31.62	240.00	75,657.81
203	75,657.81	840.85	567.43	31.52	241.90	75,415.91
204	75,415.91	840.85	565.62	31.42	243.81	75,172.10
205	75,172.10	840.85	563.79	31.32	245.74	74,926.36
206	74,926.36	840.85	561.95	31.22	247.69	74,678.67
207	74,678.67	840.85	560.09	31.12	249.65	74,429.02
208	74,429.02	840.85	558.22	31.01	251.62	74,177.40
209	74,177.40	840.85	556.33	30.91	253.62	73,923.78
210	73,923.78	840.85	554.43	30.80	255.62	73,668.16
211	73,668.16	840.85	552.51	30.70	257.65	73,410.51
212	73,410.51	840.85	550.58	30.59	259.69	73,150.82
213	73,150.82	840.85	548.63	30.48	261.74	72,889.08
214	72,889.08	840.85	546.67	30.37	263.82	72,625.26
215	72,625.26	840.85	544.69	30.26	265.90	72,359.36

Exhibit 14-2 continued.

Month	Beginning mortgage balance	Monthly mortgage payment	Net interext for month	Servicing fee	Principal repayment	Ending mortgage balance
216	72,359.36	840.85	542.70	30.15	268.01	72,091.35
217	72,091.35	840.85	540.69	30.04	270.13	71,821.22
218	71,821.22	840.85	538.66	29.93	272.27	71,548.95
219	71,548.95	840.85	536.62	29.81	274.43	71,274.52
220	71,274.52	840.85	534.56	29.70	276.60	70,997.93
⋮	⋮	⋮	⋮	⋮	⋮	⋮
⋮	⋮	⋮	⋮	⋮	⋮	⋮
⋮	⋮	⋮	⋮	⋮	⋮	⋮
342	14,778.59	840.85	110.84	6.16	723.86	14,054.73
343	14,054.73	840.85	105.41	5.86	729.59	13,325.15
344	13,325.15	840.85	99.94	5.55	735.36	12,589.78
345	12,589.78	840.85	94.42	5.25	741.19	11,848.60
346	11,848.60	840.85	88.86	4.94	747.05	11,101.55
347	11,101.55	840.85	83.26	4.63	752.97	10,348.58
348	10,348.58	840.85	77.61	4.31	758.93	9,589.65
349	9,589.65	840.85	71.92	4.00	764.94	8,824.71
350	8,824.71	840.85	66.19	3.68	770.99	8,053.72
351	8,053.72	840.85	60.40	3.36	777.10	7,276.63

352	7,276.63	840.85	54.57	3.03	783.25	6,493.38
353	6,493.38	840.85	48.70	2.71	789.45	5,703.93
354	5,703.93	840.85	42.78	2.38	795.70	4,908.23
355	4,908.23	840.85	36.81	2.05	802.00	4,106.24
356	4,106.24	840.85	30.80	1.71	808.35	3,297.89
357	3,297.89	840.85	24.73	1.37	814.75	2,483.14
358	2,483.14	840.85	18.62	1.03	821.20	1,661.95
359	1,661.95	840.85	12.46	0.69	827.70	834.25

ment is unchanged. The amount of the principal repayment is the same as in Exhibit 14-1. The difference is that the interest is reduced by the amount of the servicing fee. The servicing fee, just like the interest, declines each month because the mortgage balance declines.

Summary

In this chapter we have shown how to determine the cash flow of a level-payment fixed-rate mortgage. The cash flow of a mortgage consists of the monthly interest plus the scheduled principal repayment. Each month, the mortgage balance declines, resulting in a lower monthly dollar interest than in the previous month and more of the fixed monthly mortgage payment applied to the reduction of the mortgage balance. The cash flow can be partitioned further by dividing the interest into (1) a servicing fee and (2) interest net of the servicing fee. Exhibit 14-3 summarizes the formulas presented in the chapter.

In illustrating the cash flow from a level payment mortgage, we assumed that the homeowner would not pay off any portion of the mortgage balance prior to the scheduled due date. But homeowners do pay off all or part of their mortgages prior to the maturity date. Payments made in excess of the scheduled principal repayments are called *prepayments*. Thus, the cash flow from the mortgage is uncertain. An investor who purchases the servicing of a mortgage is faced with the same problem of cash flow uncertainty.

Exhibit 14-3
Summary of Formulas for Cash Flow of Level-Payment
Fixed-Rate Mortgages (Assuming No Prepayments)

(1) The monthly mortgage payment:

$$MP = MB_0 \left[\frac{[\, i\, (1+i)^n\,]}{[\, (1+i)^n - 1\,]} \right],$$

where
    MP = Monthly mortgage payment ($);
    n = Number of months;
    MB_0 = Original mortgage balance ($);
    i = Simple monthly interest rate (annual interest rate 12).

(2) The remaining mortgage balance at the end of month t:

$$MP_t = MB_0 \left[\frac{[(1+i)^n - (1+i)^t]}{[\, (1+i)^n - 1\,]} \right],$$

where
    MB_t = Mortgage balance after t months ($);
    n = Original number of months of mortgage;

(3) The scheduled principal repayment in month t:

$$P_t = MB_0 \left[\frac{[i\,(1+i)^{t-1}]}{[(1+i)^n - 1]} \right],$$

where
    P_t = Scheduled principal repayment for month t.

(4) The interest for month t:

$$I_t = MB_0 \left[\frac{i\,[(1+i)^n - (1+i)^{t-1}]}{[\, (1+i)^n - 1\,]} \right],$$

where
    I_t = Interest for month t.

15

Cash Flow Characteristics of Mortgage Pass-Through Securities

A mortgage pass-through security is created when one or more holders of mortgages form a collection (pool) of mortgages and sell shares or participations in the pool. A pool may consist of several thousand mortgages or only one mortgage. There are three major types of mortgage pass-through securities guaranteed by the following organizations: Government National Mortgage Association (GNMA, "Ginnie Mae"), Federal Home Loan Mortgage Corporation (FHLMC, "Freddie Mac"), and Federal National Mortgage Association (FNMA, "Fannie Mae").[1] The

---

[1] For a discussion of mortgage pass-through securities, see Kenneth Sullivan and Linda Lowell, "Mortgage Pass-Through Securities," in *The Handbook of Mortgage-Backed Securities*, Frank J. Fabozzi. ed., 2nd ed. (Chicago: Probus Publishing, 1988), Chapter 5; and Lakhbir S. Hayre and Cyrus Mohebbi, "Mortgage Pass-Through Securities," in *Advances and Innovations in the Bond and Mortgage Markets*, Frank J. Fabozzi, ed., (Chicago: Probus Publishing, 1989).

securities associated with these three entities are known as *agency pass-through* securities. About 98% of all mortgage pass-through securities are agency pass-through securities. The balance are called *conventional mortgage pass-through securities* or *private label mortgage pass-throughs*.[2]

To derive the price or yield of any financial asset, its expected cash flow must be determined. For a mortgage pass-through security, the cash flow depends on the cash flow of the underlying pool of mortgages. The cash flow of a mortgage consists of monthly mortgage payments representing interest, the scheduled repayment of principal, and any prepayments. Because of unpredictable prepayments, the cash flow of a mortgage pass-through security is not known with certainty.

In this chapter we will discuss the various conventions for projecting the cash flow from a mortgage pass-through security. In the next chapter we will use the projected cash flow to show how to price a mortgage pass-through security, determine its yield and evaluate its potential price performance.

The Prepayment Option and the Cash Flow

Since the collateral for a mortgage pass-through security is a pool of mortgages, its cash flow would be simple to compute in the absence of prepayments. However, homeowners do pay off all or part of their mortgages prior to the maturity date. Payments made in excess of the scheduled principal repayments are called *prepayments*. Because of these prepayments, the cash flow pattern of a mortgage pass-through security is not known with certainty.

Effectively, the lender (mortgagee) has granted the homeowner the right to prepay the mortgage balance at any time. Since the cash flow of mortgages will depend on whether the homeowners exercise the option to prepay all or part of the mortgages prior to maturity and, if they do, when those prepayments occur, it is important to understand why prepayments occur.

---

[2] For a discussion of these securities, see Howard Altarescu, Erik Anderson, Michael Asay, and Hal Hinkle, "The Conventional Pass-Through Market," in *The Handbook of Mortgage-Backed Securities*, Chapter 8.

Prepayments occur for one of several reasons. First, home-owners prepay the entire mortgage when they sell their home. The sale of a home may be precipitated by (1) a change of employment that requires relocating, (2) the purchase of a more expensive or less expensive home occasioned by a change in income or net worth, or (3) a divorce in which the settlement requires sale of the marital residence. Second, if interest rates drop substantially after the mortgage is obtained, it may be beneficial for the homeowner to refinance the loan (despite the necessity of paying all refinancing costs) at the lower interest rate. Third, in the case of homeowners who cannot meet their mortgage obligations, the property is repossessed and sold. In the case of a conventional mortgage, the proceeds from the sale are used to pay off the mortgage. For an insured mortgage, the insurer will pay off the mortgage balance. Finally, if the property is destroyed by fire or another insured catastrophe, the insurance proceeds are used to pay off the mortgage.

The risk that homeowners will prepay the mortgage at an inopportune time for the investor (lender) is called *prepayment risk* or *call risk*. The latter term is used because the lender has effectively granted *each* mortgagor a call option, much like the option bondholders grant corporations to call the bonds prior to maturity. An investor in a mortgage pass-through security wants to be compensated for accepting prepayment or call risk. The question is, What is fair compensation for accepting this risk?

When in Chapter 12 we discussed the call option embedded in callable corporate bonds, we advocated a valuation approach based on options theory. The same approach has been advocated for pricing mortgage pass-through securities. While the options theory approach is a useful way of thinking about how a mort-gage pass-through security should be priced, it does have sev-eral limitations.

First, in terms of options theory, homeowners may "irra-tionally" exercise the prepayment option or may not exercise it when it is rational to do so. More specifically, from an options perspective, the rational exercise of the prepayment option by the homeowner should occur when an economic benefit would result from refinancing the mortgage. That is the case when the current market interest rate for mortgages becomes less than the mortgage rate on the loan outstanding by an amount sufficient to cover refinancing costs. In this situation, the option is said to be "in the money." Yet there are homeowners who, for whatever reason, do not exercise this option. Similarly, there are homeowners who prepay their mortgage when the current mortgage rate is considerably above the rate on their mortgage. From an options perspective, such mortgages are "out of the money" and should not be prepaid. For the reasons cited above, the action of these homeowners in prepaying their mortgages may be rational from their point of view. In contrast, consider the position of an investor in a callable corporate bond. The likelihood is low that the corporate issuer will irrationally exercise the call option by calling the issue when the current market yield is higher than the issue's coupon rate. That is, it is highly unlikely that the issuer will exercise an out-of-the-money call option.

The second problem with the options-theory approach is that an investor has not granted a call option to one party but to every homeowner whose mortgage is in the pool. From an options pricing perspective, it is difficult to value a package of call options.

For those money managers who still feel the options-theory approach is appropriate, the call-adjusted yield, call-adjusted duration, and call-adjusted convexity explained in Chapter 12 can be applied to mortgage pass-through securities.

Cash Flow for a Mortgage Pass-Through Security

The cash flow from the pool of mortgages and the cash flow passed through to investors are not identical in amount or in timing. The monthly cash flow for a mortgage pass-through security is less than the monthly cash flow of the underlying mortgages by an amount equal to servicing and other fees.[3] The difference between the mortgage rate and the service fee is called the net coupon rate of the mortgage pass-through security.

The timing of the cash flow is also different. The monthly mortgage payment is due from each mortgagor on the first day

---

[3] The other fees are those charged by the issuer or guarantor of the mortgage pass-through security for guaranteeing the issue. Actually, the servicer pays the guarantee fee to the issuer or guarantor.

of each month. There is a delay in passing through the corresponding monthly cash flow to the security holders. The number of days that the payment is delayed varies by the type of mortgage pass-through security.

Approaches for Estimating the Cash Flow

Estimating the cash flow from a mortgage pass-through security requires forecasting prepayments. Several approaches have been used to make these forecasts. Currently, the three most popular are (1) the constant prepayment rate (or constant prepayment percentage), (2) the Public Securities Association prepayment model, and (3) econometric modeling.[4]

Constant Prepayment Rate (CPR)

One approach to estimating prepayments and the cash flow of a mortgage pass-through security is to assume some fraction of the remaining principal in the pool is prepaid *each* month for the remaining term of the mortgages. The prepayment rate assumed for a pool, called the *constant prepayment rate* (CPR) (or constant prepayment percentage), is based on the characteristics of the pool (including its historic prepayment experience) and the economic environment. The advantage of this approach is its simplicity; what's more, changes in economic conditions that affect prepayment rates and changes in the historical prepayment pattern of a pool can be analyzed quickly.

---

[4] In the early stages of the development of this market, cash flows were calculated by assuming no prepayments for 12 years and in the 12th year, all the mortgages in the pool would prepay. This naive approach was replaced by the "FHA prepayment experience" approach, which is based on the prepayment experience for 30-year mortgages derived from a Federal Housing Administration (FHA) probability table on mortgage survivals. Despite their popularity at one time, prepayment rate forecasts based on FHA experience are not necessarily indicative of the prepayment rate for a particular pool, because FHA experience represents an estimate of prepayments on all FHA-insured mortgages over various interest rate periods. Since prepayment rates are tied to interest rate cycles, an average prepayment rate over various cycles does not have much value for estimating prepayments. In addition, a new FHA table is published periodically, leading to confusion as to which FHA table the estimate of prepayments should be based on.

The CPR is an annual prepayment rate. To estimate monthly prepayments, the CPR must be converted into a monthly prepayment rate, commonly referred to as the *single monthly mortality rate* (SMM). The following formula can be used to determine the SMM for a given CPR:

$$SMM = 1 - (1 - CPR)^{1/12}.$$

Illustration 15-1. Suppose that the CPR used to estimate the prepayments is 6%. The corresponding SMM is

$$\begin{aligned} SMM &= 1 - (1 - .06)^{1/12} \\ &= 1 - (.94)^{.083333} \\ &= .005143. \end{aligned}$$

An SMM of $w\%$ means that approximately $w\%$ of the remaining mortgage balance at the beginning of the month after subtracting the scheduled principal payment will prepay that month. That is,

Prepayment for month = SMM ×
(Beginning monthly mortgage balance – Scheduled monthly principal).

Illustration 15-2. Suppose that an investor owns a mortgage pass-through security in which the remaining mortgage balance at the beginning of some month is $50,525. Assuming that the SMM is 0.5143% and the scheduled principal payment is $67, then the estimated prepayment for the month is

$$.005143 \times (\$50{,}525 - \$67) = \$260.$$

PSA Standard Prepayment Model

Although initially developed for the evaluation of collateralized mortgage obligations, the Public Securities Association (PSA) standard prepayment model has been used to project cash flows for any mortgage-related security. The PSA standard prepayment model is expressed as a monthly series of annual prepayment rates. The basic PSA model assumes that prepayments will occur infrequently for newly originated mortgages but will become more common as the mortgages become seasoned.

More specifically, the PSA model assumes the following prepayment rates for 30-year mortgages:

(1) A CPR of 0.2% for the first month, increasing by 0.2% per annum per month until it reaches 6% per year (after 30 months), and

(2) A 6% CPR for the remaining years.

This benchmark is referred to as "100% PSA" and can be expressed as follows:

$$\text{if } t < 30 \text{ then CPR} = \frac{6\% \; t}{30};$$
$$\text{if } t > 30 \text{ then CPR} = 6\%$$

where t is the number of months since the mortgage originated.

Slower of faster prepayment speeds are then referred to as some percentage of PSA. For example, 50% PSA means one-half the CPR of the PSA prepayment rate; 150% PSA means one and one-half the CPR of the PSA prepayment rate.

We convert the CPR to an SMM by using the formula presented earlier.

Illustration 15-3. The SMM for month 5, month 20, and months 31 through 360, assuming 100% PSA, are calculated as follows:

For month 5:

$$CPR = \frac{6\% \; (5)}{30} = 1\% = .01;$$
$$SMM = 1 - (1 - .01)^{1/12}$$
$$= 1 - (.99)^{083333}$$
$$= .000837.$$

For month 20:

$$CPR = \frac{6\% \ (20)}{30} = 4\% = .04;$$
$$SMM = 1 - (1 - .04)^{1/12}$$
$$= 1 - (.96)^{.083333}$$
$$= .003396.$$

For months 31-360:

$$CPR = 6\%;$$
$$SMM = 1 - (1 - .06)^{1/12}$$
$$= 1 - (.94)^{.083333}$$
$$= .005143.$$

Illustration 15-4.   The SMM for month 5, month 20, and months 31 through 360, assuming 150% PSA, are as follows:

For month 5:

$$CPR = \frac{6\% \ (5)}{30} = 1\% = .01;$$
$$150\% \ PSA = 1.5 \ (.01) = .015;$$
$$SMM = 1 - (1 - .015)^{1/12}$$
$$= 1 - (.985)^{.083333}$$
$$= .001259.$$

For month 20:

$$CPR = \frac{6\% \ (20)}{30} = 4\% = .04;$$
$$150\% \ PSA = 1.5 \ (.04) = .06;$$
$$SMM = 1 - (1 - .06)^{1/12}$$
$$= 1 - (.94)^{.083333}$$
$$= .005143.$$

For months 31-360:

$$CPR = 6\% = .06;$$
$$150\% \text{ PSA} = 1.5 \ (.06) = .09;$$
$$SMM = 1 - (1 - .09)^{1/12}$$
$$= 1 - (.91)^{.083333}$$
$$= .007828.$$

Notice that the SMM assuming 150% PSA is not just 1.5 times the SMM assuming 100% PSA. It is the CPR that is a multiple of the CPR assuming 100% PSA.

Illustration 15-5. The SMM for month 5, month 20, and months 31 through 360, assuming 50% PSA are as follows:

For month 5:

$$CPR = \frac{6\% \ (5)}{30} = 1\% = .01;$$
$$50\% \text{ PSA} = 0.5 \ (.01) = .005;$$
$$SMM = 1 - (1 - .005)^{1/12}$$
$$= 1 - (.995)^{.083333}$$
$$= .000418.$$

For month 20:

$$CPR = \frac{6\% \ (20)}{30} = 4\% = .04;$$
$$50\% \text{ PSA} = 0.5 \ (.04) = .02;$$
$$SMM = 1 - (1 - .02)^{1/12}$$
$$= 1 - (.98)^{.083333}$$
$$= .001682.$$

For months 31-360:

$$CPR = 6\% = .06;$$
$$50\% \text{ PSA} = 0.5 \ (.06) = .03;$$
$$SMM = 1 - (1 - .03)^{1/12}$$
$$= 1 - (.97)^{.083333}$$
$$= .002535.$$

Once again, notice that the SMM assuming 50% PSA is not just half the SMM assuming 100% PSA. It is the CPR that is a multiple of the CPR assuming 100% PSA.

Econometric Modeling

An econometric model of prepayments is a statistical model used to forecast future prepayment rates.[5] The economic factors—and any other factors expected to influence the prepayment rates of a generic mortgage pass-through security or a pool-specific mortgage pass-through security—are incorporated into the model as independent variables.[6] The output of the econometric model is a series of prepayment rates that are then translated into an equivalent CPR or PSA.

Constructing the Projected Cash Flow

To construct a cash flow schedule for a mortgage pass-through security based on some assumed prepayment rate (or rates), the following formulas can be used. First, the formula to obtain the projected monthly mortgage payment for any month is

$$\overline{MP}_t = \overline{MB}_{t-1} \left[\frac{i\,(1 + i)^{n-t+1}}{(1 + i)^{n-t+1} - 1} \right],$$

where

$\overline{MP}_t$ = Projected monthly mortgage payment for month t;

$\overline{MB}_{t-1}$ = Projected mortgage balance at the end of month t given prepayments have occurred in the past (which is the projected mortgage balance at the beginning of month t);

n = Original number of months of mortgage;

i = Simple monthly interest rate (annual interest rate/ 12).

---

[5] For further discussion, see Lakhbir S. Hayre, Kenneth Lauterbach, and Cyrus Mohebbi, "Prepayment Models and Methodologies," in *Advances and Innovations in the Bond and Mortgage Markets*, and David J. Askin, William J. Curtin, and Linda Lowell, "Forecasting Prepayment Rates for Mortgage-Backed Securities," in *The Handbook of Mortgage-Backed Securities*, Chapter 23.

[6] For a discussion of pool-specific mortgage pass-through securities, see Chuck Ramsey and J. Michael Henderson, "Specified Pools," in *The Handbook of Mortgage-Backed Securities*, Chapter 6.

Second, to compute the portion of the projected monthly mortgage payment that is interest, the following formula can be used:

$$\overline{I}_t = \overline{MB}_{t-1}\, i,$$

where

$\overline{I}_t$ = Projected monthly interest for month t.

The above formula states that the projected monthly interest is found by multiplying the mortgage balance at the end of the previous month by the monthly interest rate. The projected monthly interest rate can be divided into two parts: (1) the projected net monthly interest rate after the servicing fee and (2) the servicing fee. The formulas are as follows:

$$\overline{NI}_t = \overline{MB}_{t-1}\, (i - s),$$
$$\overline{S}_t = \overline{MB}_{t-1}\, s,$$

where

$\overline{NI}_t$ = Projected interest net of servicing fee for month t;
$\overline{S}_t$ = Projected servicing fee for month t;
s = Servicing fee rate.

The projected monthly scheduled principal payment is found by subtracting from the projected monthly mortgage payment the projected monthly interest. In terms of our notation,

$$\overline{SP}_t = \overline{MP}_t - \overline{I}_t,$$

where

$\overline{SP}_t$ = Projected monthly scheduled principal payment for month t.

As explained earlier in this chapter, the projected monthly principal prepayment is found by multiplying the SMM by the difference between the outstanding balance at the beginning of the month (the ending balance in the previous month) and the projected scheduled principal payment for the month. That is,

$$\overline{PR}_t = SMM_t \,(\overline{MB}_{t-1} - \overline{SP}_t) \,,$$

where

$\overline{PR}_t$ = Projected monthly principal prepayment for month t;

SMM_t = Assumed single monthly mortality rate for month t.

The cash flow to the investor is then the sum of (1) the projected monthly interest net of the servicing fee, (2) the projected monthly scheduled principal payment, and (3) the projected monthly principal prepayment. That is,

$$\overline{CF}_t = \overline{NI}_t + \overline{SP}_t + \overline{PR}_t \,,$$

where

$\overline{CF}_t$ = Projected cash flow for month t.

Alternatively, this can be expressed as

$$\overline{CF}_t = \overline{I}_t + \overline{SP}_t + \overline{PR}_t - \overline{S}_t \,.$$

The next five illustrations show how to apply the formulas presented above.

Illustration 15-6. Suppose that an investor owns a mortgage pass-through security with an original mortgage balance of $100,000, mortgage rate of 9.5%, a 0.5% servicing fee and 360 months to maturity. Suppose also that the investor believes a CPR of 6% is appropriate.

Thus, using our notation:

$$
\begin{aligned}
MB_0 &= \$100,000; \\
n &= 360; \\
i &= 0.0079167 \ (.095/12); \\
s &= 0.0004167 \ (0.005/12); \\
CPR &= 6\%.
\end{aligned}
$$

From Illustration 15-1, we know that a CPR of 6% is equal to an SMM of 0.5143%. Thus,

$$SMM_t = 0.005143 \ \text{for all } t \ (t = 1, \dots, 360).$$

Exhibit 15-1 shows the projected cash flow for this mortgage pass-through security for selected months. We will explain the meaning of the fourth column in Exhibit 15-1 shortly.

Illustration 15-7. Suppose that for the mortgage pass-through security in the previous illustration the assumed CPR is 8.5% instead of 6%. The SMM is

$$SMM = 1 - (1 - .085)^{1/12}$$
$$= 1 - (.915)^{.083333}$$
$$= .007375.$$

Exhibit 15-2 shows the projected cash flow for selected months.

Illustration 15-8. Suppose that the PSA prepayment model is used to project prepayments for the mortgage pass-through security in Illustration 15-6. In particular, assume that the investor believes that the mortgages will be prepaid at 100% PSA. Exhibit 15-3 shows the cash flow for this mortgage pass-through security for selected months. The SMMs shown in column 3 agree with those computed in Illustration 15-3.

Illustration 15-9. Suppose instead of 100% PSA, 150% PSA is assumed. Exhibit 15-4 shows the cash flow for the mortgage pass-through security for selected months. The SMMs shown in column 3 are the same as those computed in Illustration 15-4.

Illustration 15-10. Suppose the prepayment rate is assumed to be 50% PSA. For selected months, Exhibit 15-5 shows the cash flow.

In the formulas given above, the process begins with a determination of the mortgage balance at the beginning of the month, given prepayments that have occurred in the past. While this balance can be determined by using the procedure shown in Exhibits 15-1 to 15-5, there are formulas that can be used to compute the projected cash flow without knowing the mortgage balance at the beginning of the month. First, it is necessary to introduce the following concept.[7]

---

[7] See the appendix to Hayre and Mohebbi, "Mortgage Pass-Through Securities."

Exhibit 15-1

Projected Cash Flow Assuming a 6% CPR

Original balance $100,000
Mortgage rate 9.5%
Servicing fee 0.5%
Term 360 months

(1) t	(2) MB_{t-1}	(3) SMM_t	(4) $\bar{b}_{t-1}$	(5) MP_t	(6) SP_t	(7) $\bar{I}_t$	(8) $\overline{PR}_t$	(9) $\bar{S}_t$	(10) CF_t	(11) MB_t
1	100,000	0.005143	1.00000	841	49	792	514	41	1,313	99,437
2	99,437	0.005143	0.99486	837	49	787	511	41	1,306	98,876
3	98,876	0.005143	0.98974	832	49	783	508	40	1,300	98,319
4	98,319	0.005143	0.98465	828	50	778	505	40	1,293	97,764
5	97,764	0.005143	0.97959	824	50	774	503	39	1,286	97,211
6	97,211	0.005143	0.97455	819	50	770	500	39	1,280	96,662
7	96,662	0.005143	0.96954	815	50	765	497	39	1,273	96,115
8	96,115	0.005143	0.96455	811	50	761	494	38	1,266	95,571
9	95,571	0.005143	0.95959	807	50	757	491	38	1,260	95,029
10	95,029	0.005143	0.95465	803	50	752	488	37	1,253	94,490
11	94,490	0.005143	0.94974	799	51	748	486	37	1,247	93,954

12	93,954	0.005143	0.94486	794	51	744	483	36	1,240	93,420
13	93,420	0.005143	0.94000	790	51	740	480	36	1,234	92,889
14	92,889	0.005143	0.93517	786	51	735	477	36	1,228	92,361
15	92,361	0.005143	0.93036	782	51	731	475	35	1,221	91,835
16	91,835	0.005143	0.92557	778	51	727	472	35	1,215	91,312
17	91,312	0.005143	0.92081	774	51	723	469	35	1,209	90,791
18	90,791	0.005143	0.91608	770	52	719	467	34	1,202	90,273
19	90,273	0.005143	0.91136	766	52	715	464	34	1,196	89,757
20	89,757	0.005143	0.90668	762	52	711	461	33	1,190	89,244
21	89,244	0.005143	0.90201	758	52	707	459	33	1,184	88,733
22	88,733	0.005143	0.89737	755	52	702	456	33	1,177	88,225
23	88,225	0.005143	0.89276	751	52	698	453	32	1,171	87,719
24	87,719	0.005143	0.88817	747	52	694	451	32	1,165	87,216
25	87,216	0.005143	0.88360	743	53	690	448	32	1,159	86,715
26	86,715	0.005143	0.87906	739	53	686	446	31	1,153	86,217
27	86,217	0.005143	0.87453	735	53	683	443	31	1,147	85,721
28	85,721	0.005143	0.87004	732	53	679	441	31	1,141	85,228
29	85,228	0.005143	0.86556	728	53	675	438	30	1,135	84,736
30	84,736	0.005143	0.86111	724	53	671	436	30	1,129	84,248
31	84,248	0.005143	0.85668	720	53	667	433	30	1,123	83,761
32	83,761	0.005143	0.85228	717	54	663	431	29	1,117	83,277
33	83,277	0.005143	0.84789	713	54	659	428	29	1,112	82,795
34	82,795	0.005143	0.84353	709	54	655	426	29	1,106	82,316

Exhibit 15-1 continued.

(1) t	(2) $\overline{MB}_{t-1}$	(3) SMM_t	(4) $\overline{b}_{t-1}$	(5) $\overline{MP}_t$	(6) $\overline{SP}_t$	(7) $\overline{I}_t$	(8) $\overline{PR}_t$	(9) $\overline{S}_t$	(10) $\overline{CF}_t$	(11) $\overline{MB}_t$
35	82,316	0.005143	0.83919	706	54	652	423	28	1,100	81,839
36	81,839	0.005143	0.83488	702	54	648	421	28	1,094	81,364
37	81,364	0.005143	0.83058	698	54	644	418	28	1,088	80,892
38	80,892	0.005143	0.82631	695	54	640	416	27	1,083	80,422
39	80,422	0.005143	0.82206	691	55	637	413	27	1,077	79,954
40	79,954	0.005143	0.81783	688	55	633	411	27	1,071	79,488
41	79,488	0.005143	0.81363	684	55	629	409	26	1,066	79,025
42	79,025	0.005143	0.80944	681	55	626	406	26	1,060	78,564
43	78,564	0.005143	0.80528	677	55	622	404	26	1,055	78,105
:	......	......	......	:	:	:	:	:	:	......
98	56,315	0.005143	0.60643	510	64	446	289	14	785	55,962
99	55,962	0.005143	0.60332	507	64	443	287	14	781	55,610
100	55,610	0.005143	0.60021	505	64	440	286	13	776	55,260
101	55,260	0.005143	0.59713	502	65	437	284	13	772	54,911
102	54,911	0.005143	0.59405	500	65	435	282	13	768	54,564
103	54,564	0.005143	0.59100	497	65	432	280	13	764	54,219
104	54,219	0.005143	0.58796	494	65	429	279	13	760	53,875
:										......

t	$\overline{MB}_{t-1}$	SMM_t	$\overline{b}_{t-1}$	$\overline{MP}_t$	$\overline{SP}_t$	$\overline{I}_t$	$\overline{PR}_t$	$\overline{S}_t$	$\overline{CF}_t$	$\overline{MB}_t$
205	26,256	0.005143	0.34928	294	86	208	135	3	424	26,036
206	26,036	0.005143	0.34748	292	86	206	133	3	422	25,816
207	25,816	0.005143	0.34570	291	86	204	132	3	419	25,598
208	25,598	0.005143	0.34392	289	87	203	131	3	417	25,380
209	25,380	0.005143	0.34215	288	87	201	130	3	414	25,163
210	25,163	0.005143	0.34039	286	87	199	129	3	412	24,947
211	24,947	0.005143	0.33864	285	87	197	128	3	409	24,732
⋮	⋯⋯	⋯⋯	⋯⋯	⋮	⋮	⋮	⋮	⋮	⋯⋯	⋯⋯
353	1,057	0.005143	0.16284	137	129	8	5	0	142	924
354	924	0.005143	0.16200	136	129	7	4	0	140	791
355	791	0.005143	0.16117	136	129	6	3	0	139	658
356	658	0.005143	0.16034	135	130	5	3	0	137	526
357	526	0.005143	0.15951	134	130	4	2	0	136	394
358	394	0.005143	0.15869	133	130	3	1	0	135	262
359	262	0.005143	0.15788	133	131	2	1	0	133	131
360	131	0.005143	0.15706	132	131	1	0	0	132	0

Key:

$\overline{MB}_{t-1}$ = Projected mortgage balance at the end of month $t-1$.

SMM_t = Single monthly mortality.

$\overline{b}_{t-1}$ = $(1 - SMM_{t-1})(1 - SMM_{t-1})(1 - SMM_{t-2}) \dots (1 - SMM_1)$.

$\overline{MP}_t$ = Projected monthly mortgage payment for month t.

$\overline{SP}_t$ = Projected monthly scheduled principal payment for month t.

$\overline{I}_t$ = Projected monthly interest for month t.

$\overline{PR}_t$ = Projected monthly principal prepayment for month t.

$\overline{S}_t$ = Projected servicing fee for month t.

$\overline{CF}_t$ = Projected cash flow for month t.

Exhibit 15-2

Projected Cash Flow Assuming an 8.5% CPR*

Original balance $100,000
Mortgage rate 9.5%
Servicing fee 0.5%
Term 360 months

(1) t	(2) $\overline{MB}_{t-1}$	(3) SMM_t	(4) $\overline{b}_{t-1}$	(5) $\overline{MP}_t$	(6) $\overline{SP}_t$	(7) $\overline{I}_t$	(8) $\overline{PR}_t$	(9) $\overline{S}_t$	(10) $\overline{CF}_t$	(11) $\overline{MB}_t$
1	100,000	0.007375	1.00000	841	49	792	737	41	1,536	99,214
2	99,214	0.007375	0.99262	835	49	785	731	41	1,525	98,433
3	98,433	0.007375	0.98530	828	49	779	726	40	1,514	97,658
4	97,658	0.007375	0.97804	822	49	773	720	39	1,502	96,889
5	96,889	0.007375	0.97082	816	49	767	714	39	1,491	96,126
6	96,126	0.007375	0.96366	810	49	761	709	38	1,480	95,368
7	95,368	0.007375	0.95656	804	49	755	703	38	1,469	94,615
8	94,615	0.007375	0.94950	798	49	749	697	37	1,458	93,869
9	93,869	0.007375	0.94250	793	49	743	692	36	1,448	93,127
10	93,127	0.007375	0.93555	787	49	737	686	36	1,437	92,391
11	92,391	0.007375	0.92865	781	49	731	681	35	1,426	91,661

12	91,661	0.007375	0.92180	775	49	726	676	35	1,416	90,936
13	90,936	0.007375	0.91500	769	49	720	670	34	1,405	90,216
14	90,216	0.007375	0.90825	764	49	714	665	34	1,395	89,501
15	89,501	0.007375	0.90155	758	50	709	660	33	1,384	88,792
16	88,792	0.007375	0.89490	752	50	703	655	33	1,374	88,088
17	88,088	0.007375	0.88830	747	50	697	649	32	1,364	87,389
18	87,389	0.007375	0.88175	741	50	692	644	32	1,353	86,696
19	86,696	0.007375	0.87525	736	50	686	639	31	1,343	86,007
20	86,007	0.007375	0.86879	731	50	681	634	31	1,333	85,323
21	85,323	0.007375	0.86239	725	50	675	629	30	1,323	84,645
22	84,645	0.007375	0.85603	720	50	670	624	30	1,314	83,971
23	83,971	0.007375	0.84971	714	50	665	619	29	1,304	83,302
24	83,302	0.007375	0.84345	709	50	659	614	29	1,294	82,639
25	82,639	0.007375	0.83723	704	50	654	609	28	1,284	81,980
26	81,980	0.007375	0.83105	699	50	649	604	28	1,275	81,326
27	81,326	0.007375	0.82492	694	50	644	599	27	1,265	80,677
28	80,677	0.007375	0.81884	689	50	639	595	27	1,256	80,032
29	80,032	0.007375	0.81280	683	50	634	590	27	1,246	79,392
30	79,392	0.007375	0.80680	678	50	629	585	26	1,237	78,757
31	78,757	0.007375	0.80085	673	50	623	580	26	1,228	78,127
32	78,127	0.007375	0.79495	668	50	619	576	25	1,218	77,501
33	77,501	0.007375	0.78908	664	50	614	571	25	1,209	76,880
34	76,880	0.007375	0.78326	659	50	609	567	25	1,200	76,263

Exhibit 15-2 continued.

(1) t	(2) $\overline{MB}_{t-1}$	(3) SMM_t	(4) $\overline{b}_{t-1}$	(5) $\overline{MP}_t$	(6) $\overline{SP}_t$	(7) $\overline{I}_t$	(8) $\overline{PR}_t$	(9) $\overline{S}_t$	(10) $\overline{CF}_t$	(11) $\overline{MB}_t$
35	76,263	0.007375	0.77749	654	50	604	562	24	1,191	75,651
36	75,651	0.007375	0.77175	649	50	599	558	24	1,182	75,044
37	75,044	0.007375	0.76606	644	50	594	553	23	1,173	74,440
38	74,440	0.007375	0.76041	639	50	589	549	23	1,164	73,842
39	73,842	0.007375	0.75480	635	50	585	544	23	1,156	73,247
40	73,247	0.007375	0.74924	630	50	580	540	22	1,147	72,657
41	72,657	0.007375	0.74371	625	50	575	535	22	1,138	72,072
42	72,072	0.007375	0.73822	621	50	571	531	22	1,130	71,490
43	71,490	0.007375	0.73278	616	50	566	527	21	1,121	70,913
:	......	......	......	:	:	:	:	:	:	......
98	45,289	0.007375	0.48770	410	52	359	334	9	735	44,904
99	44,904	0.007375	0.48410	407	52	355	331	9	729	44,522
100	44,522	0.007375	0.48053	404	52	352	328	8	723	44,142
101	44,142	0.007375	0.47699	401	52	349	325	8	717	43,765
102	43,765	0.007375	0.47347	398	52	346	322	8	712	43,391
103	43,391	0.007375	0.46998	395	52	344	320	8	706	43,020
104	43,020	0.007375	0.46651	392	52	341	317	8	701	42,651
:	......	......	......	:	:	:	:	:	:	......

205	16,604	0.007375	0.22088	186	54	131	122	1	306	16,428
206	16,428	0.007375	0.21925	184	54	130	121	1	304	16,253
207	16,253	0.007375	0.21764	183	54	129	119	1	301	16,079
208	16,079	0.007375	0.21603	182	54	127	118	1	298	15,906
209	15,906	0.007375	0.21444	180	54	126	117	1	296	15,735
210	15,735	0.007375	0.21286	179	54	125	116	1	293	15,565
211	15,565	0.007375	0.21129	178	54	123	114	1	291	15,396
:	....	....	....	:	:	:	:	:	......	......
353	480	0.007375	0.07385	62	58	4	3	0	65	418
354	418	0.007375	0.07331	62	58	3	3	0	64	357
355	357	0.007375	0.07276	61	58	3	2	0	63	297
356	297	0.007375	0.07223	61	58	2	2	0	62	236
357	236	0.007375	0.07170	60	58	2	1	0	62	177
358	177	0.007375	0.07117	60	58	1	1	0	61	117
359	117	0.007375	0.07064	59	58	1	0	0	60	58
360	58	0.007375	0.07012	59	58	0	0	0	59	0

* See Key to Exhibit 15-1

Exhibit 15-3

Projected Cash Flow Assuming 100% PSA*

Original balance $100,000
Mortgage rate 9.5%
Servicing fee 0.5%
Term 360 months

(1) t	(2) $\overline{MB}_{t-1}$	(3) SMM_t	(4) $\overline{b}_{t-1}$	(5) $\overline{MP}_t$	(6) $\overline{SP}_t$	(7) $\overline{I}_t$	(8) $\overline{PR}_t$	(9) $\overline{S}_t$	(10) $\overline{CF}_t$	(11) $\overline{MB}_t$
1	100,000	0.000166	1.00000	841	49	792	17	41	816	99,934
2	99,934	0.000333	0.99983	841	50	791	33	41	832	99,851
3	99,851	0.000501	0.99950	840	50	790	50	41	849	99,751
4	99,751	0.000669	0.99900	840	50	790	67	41	865	99,634
5	99,634	0.000837	0.99833	839	51	789	83	41	881	99,500
6	99,500	0.001005	0.99749	839	51	788	100	41	897	99,349
7	99,349	0.001174	0.99649	838	51	787	117	41	913	99,181
8	99,181	0.001343	0.99532	837	52	785	133	41	929	98,996
9	98,996	0.001512	0.99398	836	52	784	150	41	944	98,795
10	98,795	0.001682	0.99248	835	52	782	166	40	960	98,576

11	98,576	0.001852	0.99081	833	53	780	182	40	975	98,341
12	98,341	0.002022	0.98898	832	53	779	199	40	990	98,089
13	98,089	0.002192	0.98698	830	53	777	215	40	1,005	97,821
14	97,821	0.002363	0.98481	828	54	774	231	40	1,019	97,536
15	97,536	0.002535	0.98248	826	54	772	247	39	1,033	97,235
16	97,235	0.002706	0.97999	824	54	770	263	39	1,047	96,917
17	96,917	0.002878	0.97734	822	55	767	279	39	1,061	96,584
18	96,584	0.003050	0.97453	819	55	765	294	39	1,075	96,235
19	96,235	0.003223	0.97155	817	55	762	310	38	1,088	95,870
20	95,870	0.003396	0.96842	814	55	759	325	38	1,101	95,489
21	95,489	0.003569	0.96513	812	56	756	341	38	1,114	95,093
22	95,093	0.003742	0.96169	809	56	753	356	38	1,126	94,681
23	94,681	0.003916	0.95809	806	56	750	371	37	1,138	94,255
24	94,255	0.004090	0.95434	802	56	746	385	37	1,150	93,813
25	93,813	0.004265	0.95043	799	56	743	400	37	1,162	93,357
26	93,357	0.004440	0.94638	796	57	739	414	36	1,173	92,886
27	92,886	0.004615	0.94218	792	57	735	428	36	1,184	92,400
28	92,400	0.004790	0.93783	789	57	732	442	36	1,195	91,901
29	91,901	0.004966	0.93334	785	57	728	456	35	1,205	91,387
30	91,387	0.005143	0.92870	781	57	723	470	35	1,215	90,860
31	90,860	0.005143	0.92392	777	58	719	467	34	1,209	90,336
32	90,336	0.005143	0.91917	773	58	715	464	34	1,203	89,814
33	89,814	0.005143	0.91444	769	58	711	462	34	1,196	89,294

Exhibit 15-3 continued.

(1) t	(2) $\overline{MB}_{t-1}$	(3) SMM_t	(4) $\overline{b}_{t-1}$	(5) $\overline{MP}_t$	(6) $\overline{SP}_t$	(7) $\overline{I}_t$	(8) $\overline{PR}_t$	(9) $\overline{S}_t$	(10) $\overline{CF}_t$	(11) $\overline{MB}_t$
34	89,294	0.005143	0.90974	765	58	707	459	33	1,190	88,777
35	88,777	0.005143	0.90506	761	58	703	456	33	1,184	88,263
36	88,263	0.005143	0.90041	757	58	699	454	33	1,178	87,751
37	87,751	0.005143	0.89578	753	59	695	451	32	1,171	87,241
38	87,241	0.005143	0.89117	749	59	691	448	32	1,165	86,734
39	86,734	0.005143	0.88659	745	59	687	446	32	1,159	86,229
40	86,229	0.005143	0.88203	742	59	683	443	31	1,153	85,727
41	85,727	0.005143	0.87749	738	59	679	441	31	1,147	85,228
42	85,228	0.005143	0.87298	734	59	675	438	31	1,141	84,730
43	84,730	0.005143	0.86849	730	59	671	435	30	1,135	84,235
⋮	⋯	⋯	⋯	⋮	⋮	⋮	⋮	⋮	⋯	⋯
98	60,735	0.005143	0.65403	550	69	481	312	16	845	60,354
99	60,354	0.005143	0.65067	547	69	478	310	16	841	59,975
100	59,975	0.005143	0.64732	544	70	475	308	16	836	59,597
101	59,597	0.005143	0.64399	542	70	472	306	15	832	59,221
102	59,221	0.005143	0.64068	539	70	469	304	15	827	58,847
103	58,847	0.005143	0.63739	536	70	466	302	15	823	58,475
104	58,475	0.005143	0.63411	533	70	463	300	15	818	58,104

:	......	......	:	:	:	:	:	......	......
205	28,317	0.005143	0.37670	317	93	224	145	4	457	28,079
206	28,079	0.005143	0.37476	315	93	222	144	4	455	27,842
207	27,842	0.005143	0.37283	313	93	220	143	4	452	27,607
208	27,607	0.005143	0.37091	312	93	219	142	4	449	27,372
209	27,372	0.005143	0.36901	310	94	217	140	4	446	27,138
210	27,138	0.005143	0.36711	309	94	215	139	4	444	26,905
211	26,905	0.005143	0.36522	307	94	213	138	4	441	26,673
:	......	......	:	:	:	:	:	......	......
353	1,140	0.005143	0.17562	148	139	9	5	0	153	997
354	997	0.005143	0.17471	147	139	8	4	0	151	853
355	853	0.005143	0.17382	146	139	7	4	0	150	710
356	710	0.005143	0.17292	145	140	6	3	0	148	567
357	567	0.005143	0.17203	145	140	4	2	0	147	425
358	425	0.005143	0.17115	144	141	3	1	0	145	283
359	283	0.005143	0.17027	143	141	2	1	0	144	141
360	141	0.005143	0.16939	142	141	1	0	0	142	0

*See Key to Exhibit 15-1

Exhibit 15-4

Projected Cash Flow Assuming 150% PSA*

Original balance $100,000
Mortgage rate 9.5%
Servicing fee 0.5%
Term 360 months

(1) t	(2) $\overline{MB}_{t-1}$	(3) SMM_t	(4) $\overline{b}_{t-1}$	(5) $\overline{MP}_t$	(6) $\overline{SP}_t$	(7) $\overline{I}_t$	(8) $\overline{PR}_t$	(9) $\overline{S}_t$	(10) $\overline{CF}_t$	(11) $\overline{MB}_t$
1	100,000	0.000250	1.00000	841	49	792	25	41	824	99,926
2	99,926	0.000501	0.99975	841	50	791	50	41	849	99,826
3	99,826	0.000753	0.99925	840	50	790	75	41	874	99,701
4	99,701	0.001005	0.99850	840	50	789	100	41	898	99,551
5	99,551	0.001258	0.99749	839	51	788	125	41	923	99,375
6	99,375	0.001512	0.99624	838	51	787	150	41	947	99,174
7	99,174	0.001767	0.99473	836	51	785	175	41	970	98,947
8	98,947	0.002022	0.99297	835	52	783	200	40	994	98,695
9	98,695	0.002278	0.99096	833	52	781	225	40	1,017	98,419
10	98,419	0.002535	0.98871	831	52	779	249	40	1,040	98,117

11	98,117	0.002792	0.98620	829	52	777	274	40	1,063	97,791
12	97,791	0.003050	0.98345	827	53	774	298	40	1,085	97,440
13	97,440	0.003309	0.98045	824	53	771	322	39	1,107	97,065
14	97,065	0.003569	0.97720	822	53	768	346	39	1,128	96,665
15	96,665	0.003829	0.97371	819	53	765	370	39	1,150	96,242
16	96,242	0.004090	0.96998	816	54	762	393	38	1,170	95,794
17	95,794	0.004352	0.96602	812	54	758	417	38	1,190	95,324
18	95,324	0.004615	0.96181	809	54	755	440	38	1,210	94,830
19	94,830	0.004878	0.95737	805	54	751	462	37	1,230	94,313
20	94,313	0.005143	0.95270	801	54	747	485	37	1,248	93,774
21	93,774	0.005407	0.94780	797	55	742	507	37	1,267	93,213
22	93,213	0.005673	0.94268	793	55	738	529	36	1,285	92,629
23	92,629	0.005940	0.93733	788	55	733	550	36	1,302	92,025
24	92,025	0.006207	0.93176	783	55	729	571	35	1,319	91,399
25	91,399	0.006475	0.92597	779	55	724	592	35	1,335	90,752
26	90,752	0.006744	0.91998	774	55	718	612	34	1,351	90,085
27	90,085	0.007014	0.91377	768	55	713	632	34	1,366	89,399
28	89,399	0.007284	0.90736	763	55	708	651	33	1,380	88,693
29	88,693	0.007556	0.90075	757	55	702	670	33	1,394	87,968
30	87,968	0.007828	0.89395	752	55	696	688	32	1,407	87,224
31	87,224	0.007828	0.88695	746	55	691	682	32	1,396	86,487
32	86,487	0.007828	0.88001	740	55	685	677	31	1,385	85,755
33	85,755	0.007828	0.87312	734	55	679	671	31	1,374	85,028

Exhibit 15-4 continued.

(1) t	(2) $\overline{MB}_{t-1}$	(3) SMM_t	(4) $\overline{b}_{t-1}$	(5) $\overline{MP}_t$	(6) $\overline{SP}_t$	(7) $\overline{I}_t$	(8) $\overline{PR}_t$	(9) $\overline{S}_t$	(10) $\overline{CF}_t$	(11) $\overline{MB}_t$
34	85,028	0.007828	0.86628	728	55	673	665	30	1,363	84,308
35	84,308	0.007828	0.85950	723	55	667	660	30	1,352	83,593
36	83,593	0.007828	0.85277	717	55	662	654	29	1,341	82,884
37	82,884	0.007828	0.84610	711	55	656	648	29	1,331	82,180
38	82,180	0.007828	0.83947	706	55	651	643	28	1,320	81,482
40	80,789	0.007828	0.82638	695	55	640	632	27	1,299	80,102
41	80,102	0.007828	0.81991	689	55	634	627	27	1,289	79,420
42	79,420	0.007828	0.81349	684	55	629	621	26	1,278	78,743
43	78,743	0.007828	0.80712	679	55	623	616	26	1,268	78,072
:	......	......	......	:	:	:	:	:	......	......
98	48,647	0.007828	0.52386	440	55	385	380	10	810	48,211
99	48,211	0.007828	0.51976	437	55	382	377	10	804	47,779
100	47,779	0.007828	0.51569	434	55	378	374	10	797	47,350
101	47,350	0.007828	0.51165	430	55	375	370	10	790	46,924
102	46,924	0.007828	0.50765	427	55	371	367	9	784	46,502
103	46,502	0.007828	0.50367	424	55	368	364	9	777	46,083
104	46,083	0.007828	0.49973	420	55	365	360	9	771	45,667
:	......	......	......	:	:	:	:	:	......	......

205	16,985	0.007828	0.22594	190	56	134	133	1	321	16,797
206	16,797	0.007828	0.22417	188	56	133	131	1	318	16,610
207	16,610	0.007828	0.22242	187	56	131	130	1	315	16,425
208	16,425	0.007828	0.22068	186	56	130	128	1	312	16,241
209	16,241	0.007828	0.21895	184	56	129	127	1	309	16,059
210	16,059	0.007828	0.21724	183	56	127	125	1	306	15,878
211	15,878	0.007828	0.21554	181	56	126	124	1	304	15,699
⋮	......	......	......	::	::	::	::	:	::	......
353	458	0.007828	0.07061	59	56	4	3	0	63	400
354	400	0.007828	0.07005	59	56	3	3	0	62	341
355	341	0.007828	0.06951	58	56	3	2	0	61	283
356	283	0.007828	0.06896	58	56	2	2	0	60	226
357	226	0.007828	0.06842	58	56	2	1	0	59	169
358	169	0.007828	0.06789	57	56	1	1	0	58	112
359	112	0.007828	0.06735	57	56	1	0	0	57	56
360	56	0.007828	0.06683	56	56	0	0	0	56	0

*See Key to Exhibit 15-1.

Exhibit 15-5

Projected Cash Flow Assuming 50% PSA

Original balance $100,000
Mortgage rate 9.5%
Servicing fee 0.5%
Term 360 months

(1) t	(2) MB_{t-1}	(3) SMM_t	(4) b_{t-1}	(5) MP_t	(6) SP_t	(7) I_t	(8) PR_t	(9) S_t	(10) CF_t	(11) MB_t
1	100,000	0.000083	1.00000	841	49	792	8	41	808	99,942
2	99,942	0.000166	0.99992	841	50	791	17	41	816	99,876
3	99,876	0.000250	0.99975	841	50	791	25	41	824	99,801
4	99,801	0.000333	0.99950	840	50	790	33	41	832	99,718
5	99,718	0.000417	0.99917	840	51	789	42	41	840	99,625
6	99,625	0.000501	0.99875	840	51	789	50	41	848	99,524
7	99,524	0.000585	0.99825	839	51	788	58	41	856	99,415
8	99,415	0.000669	0.99766	839	52	787	66	41	864	99,296
9	99,296	0.000753	0.99700	838	52	786	75	41	872	99,169
10	99,169	0.000837	0.99625	838	53	785	83	41	880	99,034

11	99,034	0.000921	0.99541	837	53	784	91	41	887	98,890
12	98,890	0.001005	0.99449	836	53	783	99	40	895	98,737
13	98,737	0.001089	0.99349	835	54	782	108	40	902	98,576
14	98,576	0.001174	0.99241	834	54	780	116	40	909	98,406
15	98,406	0.001258	0.99125	833	54	779	124	40	917	98,227
16	98,227	0.001343	0.99000	832	55	778	132	40	924	98,041
17	98,041	0.001427	0.98867	831	55	776	140	40	931	97,846
18	97,846	0.001512	0.98726	830	56	775	148	40	938	97,642
19	97,642	0.001597	0.98576	829	56	773	156	40	945	97,431
20	97,431	0.001682	0.98419	828	56	771	164	39	951	97,211
21	97,211	0.001767	0.98253	826	57	770	172	39	958	96,982
22	96,982	0.001852	0.98080	825	57	768	180	39	965	96,746
23	96,746	0.001937	0.97898	823	57	766	187	39	971	96,501
24	96,501	0.002022	0.97708	822	58	764	195	39	977	96,249
25	96,249	0.002107	0.97511	820	58	762	203	39	984	95,988
26	95,988	0.002192	0.97305	818	58	760	210	38	990	95,719
27	95,719	0.002278	0.97092	816	59	758	218	38	996	95,443
28	95,443	0.002363	0.96871	815	59	756	225	38	1,001	95,158
29	95,158	0.002449	0.96642	813	59	753	233	38	1,007	94,866
30	94,866	0.002535	0.96405	811	60	751	240	38	1,013	94,566
31	94,566	0.002535	0.96161	809	60	749	240	37	1,010	94,267
32	94,267	0.002535	0.95917	807	60	746	239	37	1,008	93,968
33	93,968	0.002535	0.95674	804	61	744	238	37	1,005	93,669

Exhibit 15-5 continued.

(1) t	(2) $\overline{MB}_{t-1}$	(3) SMM_t	(4) $\bar{b}_{t-1}$	(5) $\overline{MP}_t$	(6) $\overline{SP}_t$	(7) $\bar{I}_t$	(8) $\overline{PR}_t$	(9) $\bar{S}_t$	(10) $\overline{CF}_t$	(11) $\overline{MB}_t$
34	93,669	0.002535	0.95431	802	61	742	237	37	1,002	93,371
35	93,371	0.002535	0.95189	800	61	739	237	37	1,000	93,073
36	93,073	0.002535	0.94948	798	62	737	236	36	997	92,776
37	92,776	0.002535	0.94707	796	62	734	235	36	995	92,479
38	92,479	0.002535	0.94467	794	62	732	234	36	992	92,182
39	92,182	0.002535	0.94228	792	63	730	234	36	990	91,886
40	91,886	0.002535	0.93989	790	63	727	233	35	987	91,590
41	91,590	0.002535	0.93751	788	63	725	232	35	985	91,295
42	91,295	0.002535	0.93513	786	64	723	231	35	982	91,000
43	91,000	0.002535	0.93276	784	64	720	231	35	979	90,706
:	......	......	......	:	:	:	:	:	......	......
98	75,332	0.002535	0.81122	682	86	596	191	25	847	75,056
99	75,056	0.002535	0.80917	680	86	594	190	25	845	74,779
100	74,779	0.002535	0.80711	679	87	592	189	25	843	74,503
101	74,503	0.002535	0.80507	677	87	590	189	24	841	74,228
102	74,228	0.002535	0.80303	675	88	588	188	24	838	73,952
103	73,952	0.002535	0.80099	674	88	585	187	24	836	73,677
104	73,677	0.002535	0.79896	672	89	583	187	24	834	73,402

...	......	......	......	...	...	...	...	...	......	......
205	46,478	0.002535	0.61828	520	152	368	117	11	625	46,208
206	46,208	0.002535	0.61672	519	153	366	117	11	623	45,939
207	45,939	0.002535	0.61515	517	154	364	116	11	622	45,669
208	45,669	0.002535	0.61359	516	154	362	115	11	620	45,399
209	45,399	0.002535	0.61204	515	155	359	115	11	618	45,129
210	45,129	0.002535	0.61049	513	156	357	114	11	616	44,859
211	44,859	0.002535	0.60894	512	157	355	113	11	614	44,589
...	......	......	......	...	...	...	...	...	......	......
353	2,757	0.002535	0.42466	357	335	22	6	0	363	2,416
354	2,416	0.002535	0.42358	356	337	19	5	0	361	2,074
355	2,074	0.002535	0.42251	355	339	16	4	0	359	1,731
356	1,731	0.002535	0.42144	354	341	14	4	0	358	1,386
357	1,386	0.002535	0.42037	353	342	11	3	0	356	1,041
358	1,041	0.002535	0.41930	353	344	8	2	0	354	695
359	695	0.002535	0.41824	352	346	6	1	0	352	348
360	348	0.002535	0.41718	351	348	3	0	0	351	0

*See Key to Exhibit 15-1.

Let

$$\overline{b}_t = (1 - \text{SMM}_t)\, (1 - \text{SMM}_{t-1}) \,.....\, (1 - \text{SMM}_2)\, (1 - \text{SMM}_1),$$

where

$\overline{b}_t$ = Projected mortgage balance in month t per \$1 of the original mortgage, given prepayments through month t.

Then, the projected monthly mortgage payment in month t is

$$\overline{\text{MP}}_t = \overline{b}_{t-1}\text{MP},$$

where

MP = Monthly mortgage payment on the original principal, assuming no prepayments.

The projected scheduled principal payment is found as follows:

$$\overline{\text{SP}}_t = \overline{b}_{t-1}\text{P}_t,$$

where

P_t = Scheduled principal payment on the original balance, assuming no prepayments.

Once MP and P_t are computed, the other values necessary to compute the projected cash flow can be easily determined.

How do we obtain MP and P_t? The formula for each was given in the previous chapter.

Illustration 15-11. Consider the mortgage pass-through security we have been using in all previous illustrations. Assuming a CPR of 6%, the projected monthly mortgage payment for month 210 is

$$\overline{\text{MP}}_{210} = \overline{b}_{209}\text{MP}.$$

In Illustration 14-1 of the previous chapter, we showed that the monthly mortgage payment assuming no principal prepayments is \$840.85. Since the SMM is 0.005143 for each month, then

$$\overline{b}_{209} = (1 - .005143)\, (1 - .005413) \,....\, (1 - .005143).$$

The product above contains the same factor 209 times and therefore can be expressed as

$$\bar{b}_{209} = (1 - .005143)^{209} = .34039.$$

So,

$$\overline{MP}_{209} = (.34039)\ \$840.85 = \$286.$$

The projected scheduled principal payment is

$$\overline{SP}_{210} = \bar{b}_{209}P_{210}.$$

In Illustration 14-4 of the previous chapter, we showed that scheduled principal payment in month 210 assuming no prepayments is \$255.62. The projected scheduled principal payment is then

$$\overline{SP}_{210} = (.34039)\ \$255.62 = \$87.$$

Notice that both of the values computed here agree with the values for month 210 shown in Exhibit 15-1.

Obtaining Prepayment Estimates

The major dealers in mortgage pass-through securities (and independent vendors) have developed models that estimate prepayment rates. These models take into account the economic factors that influence prepayment rates. Recently, the major dealers have made access to their projected prepayment rates (not their forecasting model) easier by supplying them to services used by investors. For example, Exhibit 15-6 shows the projected prepayment rate in terms of PSA by major dealers as reported on the Knight-Ridder MoneyMarket Center.

Summary

In this chapter we showed how to construct the projected cash flow for a mortgage pass-through security. The cash flow depends on the cash flow of the underlying pool of mortgages, which in turn depends on prepayments. Thus, an estimate of the future prepayments must be made. The three common approaches for estimating prepayments are (1) the constant prepayment rate, (2) the PSA standard prepayment model, and (3) econometric models.

Exhibit 15-7 summarizes the formulas presented in this chapter.

Exhibit 15-6*

Mortgage Prepayment Rate Tables - Public Securities Association

The following tables contain projected prepayment rates as formulated and
reported by each dealer listed.   These projections represent individual dealer's
views of future prepayment rates, as of the date specified.   Projections may
change without notice and provide no assurance as to actual prepayment
experience.   Each dealer must be consulted about the timeliness of its
projections and the underlying assumptions.   Historical prepayment information
reflects the arithmetic mean of historical prepayment rates for the preceding
three months, as reported by listed dealers.   The median information reflects
the median of projected prepayment rates and the low/high information reflects
the lowest and highest projected prepayment rates, as reported by listed
dealers.   All rates are reported as percentages of PSA. PSA, the Public
Securities Association prepayment model, is an industry developed reference
standard that neither reflects historical nor predicts future rates.   Although
PSA has received the information contained in the tables from sources PSA
believes to be reliable, PSA has not verified such information and assumes no
responsibility for its accuracy.   The information contained in the tables may be
revised or corrected at any time and does not constitute a basis for the
valuation of pricing of any security.   (Continued on page 291.)

* Page references in this exhibit refer to pages on the Knight-Ridder MoneyCenter System.

Exhibit 15-6 continued.

Mortgage Prepayment Rate Tables
Public Securities Association

Quoting or publishing information from the tables is prohibited without the express written consent of PSA.

Abbreviations:

BS	= Bear Stearns		KP	= Kidder Peabody
CITI	= Citicorp		ML	= Merrill Lynch
DBL	= Drexel Burnham Lambert		MS	= Morgan Stanley
DW	= Dean Witter		PW	= Paine Webber
FBC	= First Boston Corp.		PB	= Prudential Bache
GS	= Goldman Sachs & Co.		SAL	= Salomon Brothers
			SL	= Shearson Lehman

N = New = Final Maturity >330 months (GNMA); WAM >330 months (FHLMC/FNMA).
Otherwise pools are classified as seasoned (S).
GNMA I 30Y-SF = GNMA I 30 Year Single-Family.
FHLMC 30Y-GU = FHLMC 30 year Guarantor.
FNMA 30Y = FNMA 30 Year

(See tables on pages 292-299.)

PSA: Mortgage Prepayment Rate Tables

GNMA I:3M-PSA: 4/21/88

30Y-SF:	4/88:MED	LOW-HIGH:	DW	DBL	FBC	GS	KP	ML
7.5 S:	74 : 93	80-120	90	80-85	110-120	93	105	85
8.0 N:	39 : 83	70-110	70	80-85	100-110	82	75	85
8.0 S:	84 :100	85-130	90	85-90	125-130	97	105	90
8.5 N:	54 : 90	75-115	80	90-95	110-115	87	75	85
8.5 S:	93 :105	90-135	195	90-100	130-135	102	105	90
9.0 N:	60 : 95	75-120	195	100-105	115-120	95	75	95
9.0 S:	89 :110	100-135	110	105-110	130-135	110	105	100
9.5 N:	89 :113	75-130	100	110-115	120-130	105	75	105
9.5 S:	94 :120	100-135	110	110-115	130-135	120	100	105
10.0 N:	135 :130	80-150	120	120-130	130-135	122	80	130
10.0 S:	108 :135	90-150	130	120-130	135-140	137	90	130
10.5 N:	185 :153	105-200	140	140-165	135-150	150	105	160
Update:		4/19/88	4/19/88	4/15/88	4/19/88	4/15/88	4/15/88	4/05/88

*See notes on pages 290-291.

*Tables continued on page 293.

Exhibit 15-6 continued.

293   Fixed Format Page   KNIGHT-RIDDER MoneyCenter   2-May-88 12:47P

PSA: Mortgage Prepayment Rate Tables — Cont.

GNMA I:3M-PSA :   4/21/88

30Y-SF:	4/88:	MS :	PU :	PB :	SAL :	SL :	BS :	CITI
7.5 S:	74 :	95 :	110 :	93 :	105 :	90 :	85-95 :	95
8.0 N:	39 :	85 :	85 :	78 :	90 :	80 :	75-85 :	90
8.0 S:	84 :	100 :	115 :	96 :	110 :	90 :	95-105:	105
8.5 N:	54 :	90 :	95 :	82 :	100 :	80 :	85-95 :	100
8.5 S:	93 :	105 :	125 :	99 :	115 :	90 :	105-115:	110
9.0 N:	60 :	95 :	110 :	90 :	115 :	95 :	95-105:	105
9.0 S:	89 :	110 :	125 :	105 :	120 :	100 :	115-125:	115
9.5 N:	89 :	110 :	120 :	100 :	125 :	120 :	110-120:	115
9.5 S:	94 :	120 :	135 :	117 :	125 :	120 :	125-135:	125
10.0 N:	135 :	130 :	135 :	126 :	130 :	150 :	130-140:	125
10.0 S:	108 :	135 :	145 :	126 :	130 :	150 :	135-145:	135
10.5 N:	185 :	167 :	165 :	156 :	140 :	200 :	170-200:	145
Updated:	:	4/04/88:	4/07/88:	4/19/88:	4/15/88:	4/15/88:	4/04/88:	4/15/88

*See notes on pages 290-291.
*Tables continued on page 294.

PSA: Mortgage Prepayment Rate Tables – Cont.

GNMA I:3M-PSA :   4/21/88

30Y-SF:	4/88:MED	LOW-HIGH:	DW :	DBL :	FBC :	GS :	KP :	ML
11.0 S:	161 :220	160-250 :	200	:195-245:	175-210 :	202 :	160 :	230
11.5 S:	231 :280	215-375 :	260	:245-305:	250-305 :	285 :	220 :	350
12.0 S:	286 :340	285-500 :	360	:355-435:	370-435 :	362 :	285 :	425
12.5 S:	311 :375	325-620 :	400	:430-465:	500-560 :	407 :	345 :	440
13.0 S:	318 :432	345-655 :	410	:445-460:	615-645 :	432 :	395 :	450
Update:	:	4/19/88	:4/19/88:	4/15/88:	4/19/88	:4/15/88:	4/05/88	

*See notes on pages 290-291.

*Tables continued on page 295.

Exhibit 15-6 continued.

295 Fixed Format Page   KNIGHT-RIDDER MoneyCenter   2-May-88 12:48P

PSA: Mortgage Prepayment Rate Tables - Cont.

GNMA I:3M-PSA :   4/21/88

30Y-SF:	4/88:	MS	:	PW	:	PB	:	SAL	:	SL	:	BS	:	CITI
11.0 S:	161 :	225	:	225	:	199	:	160	:	250	:	210-230:	185
11.5 S:	231 :	300	:	280	:	243	:	215	:	300	:	250-275:	240
12.0 S:	286 :	350	:	325	:	324	:	285	:	340	:	285-315:	320
12.5 S:	311 :	400	:	335	:	351	:	325	:	360	:	350-400:	375
13.0 S:	318 :	450	:	345	:	382	:	360	:	410	:	415-465:	410
Updated:	:	4/04/88:		4/07/88:		4/19/88		:4/15/88		:4/15/88:		4/04/88:	4/15/88

*See notes on pages 290-291.

*Tables continued on page 296.

PSA: Mortgage Prepayment Rate Tables - Cont.

FHLMC : 3M-PSA: 4/21/88

30Y-GU:	4/88:MED	LOW-HIGH:	DW	: DBL	: FBC	: GS	: KP	: ML
8.0 N:	99 :130	110-150 :	130	:145-150	:135-140	: 118	: 145	: 125
8.0 S:	106 :140	115-160 :	140	:140-145	:140-150	: 133	: 135	: 125
8.5 N:	102 :135	120-150 :	135	:145-150	:135-145	: 127	: 145	: 125
8.5 S:	105 :145	124-165 :	145	:145-150	:150-160	: 142	: 135	: 135
9.0 N:	106 :145	134-160 :	145	:150-155	:150-155	: 138	: 145	: 135
9.0 S:	115 :155	136-180 :	150	:150-160	:170-180	: 153	: 140	: 145
9.5 N:	116 :155	145-180 :	150	:160-175	:155-160	: 155	: 145	: 155
9.5 S:	114 :165	145-195 :	155	:160-170	:185-195	: 170	: 145	: 165
10.0 N:	155 :180	145-230 :	175	:180-195	:165-175	: 184	: 145	: 175
10.0 S:	145 :200	150-230 :	190	:190-200	:205-215	: 199	: 150	: 200
10.5 S:	184 :248	150-320 :	230	:195-220	:230-265	: 236	: 200	: 290
11.0 S:	214 :325	165-410 :	300	:280-320	:305-365	: 327	: 315	: 410
11.5 S:	249 :400	235-530 :	370	:320-395	:390-460	: 432	: 400	: 530
12.0 S:	272 :485	325-650 :	430	:425-520	:560-650	: 500	: 490	: 645
Update:	:	4/19/88	: 4/19/88:	4/15/88:	4/19/88:	4/15/88:	4/15/88 :	4/05/88

*See notes on pages 290-291.   *Tables continued on page 297.

Exhibit 15-6 continued.

PSA: Mortgage Prepayment Rate Tables - Cont.

4/21/88

FHLMC : 3M-PSA:

30Y-GU:	4/88:	MS	PU	PB	SAL	SL	BS	CITI
8.0 N:	99 :	130	140	110	140	130	125-135:	135
8.0 S:	106 :	155	140	115	140	135	135-145:	160
8.5 N:	102 :	135	150	120	140	135	130-140:	135
8.5 S:	105 :	158	150	124	140	140	145-150:	165
9.0 N:	106 :	140	160	134	145	155	145-155:	145
9.0 S:	115 :	160	160	136	145	155	150-160:	175
9.5 N:	116 :	150	170	150	145	180	160-170:	155
9.5 S:	114 :	165	170	151	145	180	165-175:	190
10.0 N:	155 :	180	200	173	155	230	185-200:	185
10.0 S:	145 :	217	200	172	150	230	195-210:	210
10.5 S:	184 :	263	250	216	150	320	235-270:	250
11.0 S:	214 :	350	325	275	165	390	310-350:	325
11.5 S:	249 :	417	360	353	235	445	385-435:	385
12.0 S:	272 :	517	395	400	325	500	460-510:	455
Updated:	:	4/04/88 :	4/07/88 :	4/19/88 :	4/15/88:	4/15/88:	4/04/88:	4/15/88

PSA: Mortgage Prepayment Rate Tables — Cont.

| FNMA | 3M-PSA: | | | | | | | | 4/21/88 |
30Y : 4/88:MED	LOW-HIGH:	DJ :	DBL :	FBC :	GS :	KP :	ML
8.0 N: 98 :130	110-145 :	130	:140-150:	125-130 :	118 :	140 :	120
8.0 S: 102 :140	114-160 :	140	:140-150:	140-145 :	133 :	135 :	125
8.5 N: 107 :135	120-150 :	135	:145-150:	135-140 :	127 :	140 :	125
8.5 S: 115 :145	125-165 :	145	:150-155:	160-165 :	142 :	135 :	135
9.0 N: 115 :145	133-160 :	145	:150-165:	145-155 :	138 :	140 :	135
9.0 S: 120 :153	135-180 :	150	:155-165:	170-180 :	153 :	135 :	145
9.5 N: 122 :155	145-180 :	150	:160-180:	155-160 :	155 :	145 :	155
9.5 S: 129 :165	140-200 :	155	:175-190:	190-200 :	170 :	140 :	165
10.0 N: 152 :175	145-230 :	175	:180-190:	165-175 :	184 :	145 :	175
10.0 S: 148 :199	145-230 :	190	:190-210:	200-215 :	199 :	145 :	200
10.5 S: 197 :248	150-320 :	230	:190-220:	240-280 :	236 :	180 :	290
11.0 S: 200 :325	165-410 :	300	:270-352:	295-350 :	327 :	270 :	410
11.5 S: 272 :400	235-530 :	370	:310-450:	390-470 :	432 :	370 :	530
12.0 S: 286 :470	325-660 :	430	:420-560:	570-660 :	500 :	460 :	645
Update: : 4/19/88	:4/19/88:		4/15/88:	4/19/88:	4/15/88:	4/15/88:	4/05/88

*See notes on pages 290-291.   *Tables continued on page 299.

Exhibit 15-6 continued.

PSA: Mortgage Prepayment Rate Tables - Cont.

FNMA : 3M-PSA: 4/21/88

30Y	4/88:	MS	PU	PB	SAL	SL	BS :	CITI
8.0 N:	98 :	130	140	110	140	130	125-135:	130
8.0 S:	102 :	155	140	114	140	135	135-145:	160
8.5 N:	107 :	135	150	120	140	135	130-140:	135
8.5 S:	115 :	158	150	125	140	140	140-150:	165
9.0 N:	115 :	140	160	133	145	155	140-150:	145
9.0 S:	120 :	160	160	136	145	155	145-155:	175
9.5 N:	122 :	150	170	149	145	180	150-160:	160
9.5 S:	129 :	165	170	151	145	180	155-165:	190
10.0 N:	152 :	175	200	173	155	230	175-190:	185
10.0 S:	148 :	200	200	172	150	230	185-200:	210
10.5 S:	197 :	250	260	217	150	320	235-260:	250
11.0 S:	200 :	333	335	286	165	390	310-350:	325
11.5 S:	272 :	400	375	359	235	445	375-425:	400
12.0 S:	286 :	500	400	406	325	500	450-500:	470
Updated:	4/04/88	4/04/88	4/07/88	4/19/88	4/15/88	4/15/88	4/04/88:	4/15/88

*See notes on pages 290-291.

Exhibit 15-7

Summary of Formulas

To convert from CPR to SMM:

$$SMM = 1 - (1 - CPR)^{1/12}.$$

Benchmark PSA prepayment model:

$$\text{if } t < 30 \text{ then CPR} = \frac{6\% \, t}{30},$$
$$\text{if } t > 30 \text{ then CPR} = 6\%,$$

where t is the number of months since the mortgage originated.

Constructing the Cash Flow:

Let

$\overline{MP}_t$	=	Projected monthly mortgage payment for month t;
$\overline{MB}_{t-1}$	=	Projected mortgage balance at the end of month $t-1$ given prepayments have occurred in the past (which is the projected mortgage balance at the beginning of month t);
n	=	Original number of months of mortgage;
i	=	Simple monthly interest rate (annual interest rate/ 12);
$\overline{I}_t$	=	Projected monthly interest for month t;
$\overline{NI}_t$	=	Projected interest, net of servicing fee, for month t;
$\overline{S}_t$	=	Projected servicing fee for month t;
s	=	Servicing fee rate;
$\overline{SP}_t$	=	Projected monthly scheduled principal payment for month t;
$\overline{PR}_t$	=	Projected monthly principal prepayment for month t;
$\overline{CF}_t$	=	Projected cash flow for month t.

Exhibit 15-7 continued.

$$\overline{MP}_t = \overline{MB}_{t-1} \left[\frac{i(1+i)^{n-t+1}}{(1+i)^{n-t+1}-1} \right],$$

Then

$$\overline{I}_t = \overline{MB}_{t-1} i;$$
$$\overline{NI}_t = \overline{MB}_{t-1}(i-s);$$
$$\overline{S}_t = \overline{MB}_{t-1} s;$$
$$\overline{SP}_t = \overline{MP}_t - \overline{I}_t;$$
$$\overline{PR}_t = SMM_t(\overline{MB}_{t-1} - \overline{SP}_t);$$
$$\overline{CF}_t = \overline{NI}_t + \overline{SP}_t + \overline{PR}_t$$
$$\text{or } \overline{CF}_t = \overline{I}_t + \overline{SP}_t + \overline{PR}_t - \overline{S}_t.$$

Alternatively, let

$\overline{b}_t$ = The projected mortgage balance in month t per $1 of the original mortgage given prepayments through month t;

SMM_t = Assumed single monthly mortality rate for month t;

MP = Monthly mortgage payment on the original principal, assuming no prepayments;

P_t = Scheduled principal payment on the original balance assuming no prepayments.

Then,

$$\overline{b}_t = (1 - SMM_t)(1 - SMM_{t-1}) \ldots (1 - SMM_2)(1 - SMM_1);$$

$$\overline{MP}_t = b_{t-1} \overline{MP};$$

$$\overline{SP}_t = b_{t-1} \overline{P}_t.$$

16

Cash Flow Yield, Price and Performance of Mortgage-Backed Securities

In this chapter we will explain (1) how to compute the yield on mortgage pass-through securities, (2) the drawbacks of the yield measure quoted, (3) how to compute the price of mortgage pass-through securities, (4) how to use the horizon return framework to assess their performance over a specified investment horizon, and (5) their price performance characteristics. In addition, we look at the price performance characteristics of stripped mortgage-backed securities.

Cash Flow Yield

Given the projected cash flow and the price of a pass-through security, its yield can be determined. Recall from Chapter 4 that the yield is the interest rate that will make the present value of the expected cash flow equal to the price. A yield computed in this manner is known as a *cash flow yield*.

Bond Equivalent Yield

The problem we face is how to obtain an annual yield, given that the interest rate that makes the present value of the cash flow equal to the price is a monthly interest rate. To compare the yield for a pass-through security to that of a Treasury or corporate bond, the yield of a pass-through security cannot be computed by just multiplying the monthly yield by 12. The reason is that a Treasury bond and a corporate bond pay interest semiannually, while a mortgage pass-through security has a monthly cash flow. This gives the investor of a pass-through security the opportunity to generate more interest by reinvesting monthly cash flows compared to a bond investor, who receives coupon payments semiannually and reinvests them. Therefore, the yield on a pass-through security must be calculated so as to make it comparable to the yield to maturity for a bond.

This is accomplished by computing the *bond equivalent yield* for a mortgage pass-through security, assuming that the monthly cash flows are reinvested at the cash flow yield until the end of each semiannual period. The formula used is:

$$\text{Bond equivalent yield} = 2\,[(1 + i_M)^6 - 1]$$

where

i_M = Monthly interest rate that will equate the present value of the projected monthly cash flow to the price of the mortgage pass-through security.

The bond equivalent semiannual yield on the monthly pass-through is

$$[(1 + i_M)^6 - 1].$$

Illustration 16-1. Suppose that a pass-through security with a mortgage rate of 9.5%, a servicing fee of 0.5%, 360 months remaining to maturity (new pass-through security), and an original mortgage balance of $100,000 can be purchased for $94,521. To compute the cash flow yield, a prepayment assumption must be made. Assuming that the prepayment rate is 100% PSA, the cash flow would be as shown in Exhibit 15-3 of Chapter 15. Assuming that the first monthly cash flow will occur 30 days from now, the interest rate that will make the present value of the cash flow, assuming 100% PSA, equal to the price of $94,521 is 0.8333% (0.008333). The bond equivalent yield is then 10.21%, as shown below:

$$i_M = 0.008333$$
$$\text{Bond equivalent yield} = 2\,[(1.008333)^6 - 1] = .1021 = 10.21\%.$$

Illustration 16-2. Suppose that the pass-through security in the previous illustration can be purchased for $105,985. Assuming a prepayment rate of 200% PSA, the interest rate that will make the present value of the cash flow equal to $105,985 is 0.006667 (0.6667%). The bond equivalent yield is found as follows:

$$i_M = 0.006667$$
$$\text{Bond equivalent yield} = 2\,[(1.006667)^6 - 1] = .0813 = 8.13\%.$$

Drawbacks of the Cash Flow Yield Measure

In Chapter 4 we illustrated the two shortcomings of the yield to maturity as a measure of a bond's potential return: (1) the coupon payments must be reinvested at a rate equal to the yield to maturity, and (2) the bond must be held to maturity. These same shortcomings apply to the cash flow yield measures for pass-through securities: (1) the projected cash flows are assumed to be reinvested at the cash flow yield and (2) the pass-through is assumed to be held until all the mortgages in the pool pay off. The importance of reinvestment risk, the risk that the cash flow will be reinvested at a rate less than the cash flow yield, is particularly important for pass-through securities because they make payments monthly.

In addition, the cash flow yield is dependent on the realization of the cash flow projected on the basis of some prepayment rate. If the prepayment experience is different from the prepayment rate assumed, the cash flow yield will not be realized.

The proper context in which to evaluate the relative attractiveness of a mortgage pass-through security is that of the horizon return. This will be discussed after we illustrate how to compute the price of a mortgage pass-through security.

Price

Given the required yield for a pass-through security, the price is simply the present value of the projected cash flow. Care must be taken, however, in determining the monthly interest rate that should be used to compute the present value of each monthly cash flow.

To convert a bond equivalent yield to a monthly interest rate, the following equation can be used:

$$i_M = [1 + (0.5) \text{ Bond equivalent yield}]^{1/6} - 1 .$$

Illustration 16-3.   Once again, consider the pass-through security in Illustration 16-1. Suppose that the investor (1) requires an 8.13% yield on a bond equivalent basis, and (2) assumes a prepayment rate of 150% PSA. The corresponding monthly interest rate for a bond equivalent yield of 8.13% is 0.6667% (0.006667), as shown below:

$$
\begin{aligned}
i_M &= [1 + (0.5) .0813]^{1/6} - 1 \\
&= [1.04065]^{.16667} - 1 \\
&= 0.006667.
\end{aligned}
$$

The projected cash flow, based on 150% PSA, would be the same as Exhibit 15-4 in Chapter 15. Discounting the projected cash flow at 0.6667% gives a price of $106,710.

Illustration 16-4.   Suppose that instead of 8.13%, the investor wants a yield of 12.30%. Also assume that the investor believes that a 25% PSA rate is appropriate to project the cash flow. The monthly interest rate is determined as follows:

$$
\begin{aligned}
i_M &= [1 + (0.5) .1230]^{1/6} - 1 \\
&= [1.0615]^{.16667} - 1 \\
&= 0.01.
\end{aligned}
$$

Discounting the cash flow projected on the basis of 25% PSA would give a price of $79,976.

Horizon Return

The horizon return framework can be used to assess the relative attractiveness of a mortgage pass-through security over some investment horizon period. The total receipts resulting from investing in a mortgage pass-through security consist of:

(1) The projected cash flow of the pass-through security from:
   (a) the projected interest payments (net of servicing fee),
   (b) the projected principal repayment (scheduled plus prepayments),
(2) The interest earned on the reinvestment of the projected interest payments and the projected principal repayments, and
(3) The projected price of the pass-through security at the end of the investment horizon.

To obtain (1), a prepayment rate over the investment horizon must be assumed. To calculate (2), a reinvestment rate must be assumed. Finally, to calculate (3) the investor must make two assumptions. First, the investor must project what the bond equivalent yield will be for the pass-through security at the end of the investment horizon. Second, the investor must project what prepayment rate the market will assume at the end of the investment horizon. Obviously, the first and second assumptions are not independent. The projected prepayment rate will depend on the projected yield in the market.

As we have stressed throughout this book, an investor should not use one set of projections to determine the horizon return. Instead, an investor should assess the performance of a security over a range of likely assumptions.

The monthly horizon return is then found by using the following formula:

$$\left[\frac{\text{Total future amount}}{\text{Price of the pass-through}} \right]^{1/\text{Number of months}} - 1$$

The monthly horizon return can be annualized on the basis of the bond equivalent yield given earlier or by computing the effective annual yield as follows:

$$(1 + \text{Monthly horizon return})^{12} - 1$$

Illustration 16-5. Suppose a portfolio manager is considering investing in a mortgage pass-through security with a 9.5% mortgage rate, 0.5% servicing fee, 360 months remaining to maturity, and an original mortgage balance of $100,000. The price of this security is $94,521. The cash flow yield, assuming 100% PSA, is 10.21% (see Illustration 16-1). The portfolio manager has a six-month investment horizon and believes the following:

(1) For the next six months the prepayment rate will be 100% PSA,

(2) The projected cash flow can be reinvested at 0.5% per month,

(3) The pass-through security will sell to yield 7.62% at the end of the investment horizon, and

(4) The projected PSA prepayment rate at the end of the investment horizon will be 185% PSA.

On the basis of the first assumption, the projected cash flow (projected interest net of servicing fee, projected scheduled principal, and projected principal prepayment) for the first six months is:

End of month	Projected cash flow
1	$816
2	832
3	849
4	865
5	881
6	897

The projected cash flow is obtained from Exhibit 15-3 of Chapter 15.

The projected cash flow, plus interest from reinvesting the cash flow at 0.5% per month, is shown below:

End of month	Projected cash flow	Projected cash flow plus reinvestment income
1	$816	$ 837
2	832	849
3	849	862
4	865	874
5	881	885
6	897	897
	Total	$5,204

At the end of the investment horizon, our original pass-through security would have a remaining mortgage balance of $99,379 (see Exhibit 15-3 of Chapter 15) and remaining maturity of 354 months. Assuming a required yield of 7.62% and a pre-payment rate of 185% PSA, the projected price of this pass-through security would be $106,210.

The total future amount is then:

Projected cash flow plus reinvestment income	$ 5,204
Projected price	106,210
Total	= $111,414

The monthly horizon return is

$$\left[\frac{\$111,414}{\$94,521}\right]^{1/6} - 1 = .02778.$$

On a bond equivalent basis, the horizon return is

$$2\,[(1.02778)^6 - 1] = .3574 = 35.74\%.$$

On an effective annual yield basis, the horizon return is

$$(1.02778)^{12} - 1 = .3893 = 38.93\%.$$

Illustration 16-6. Suppose that a portfolio manager wants to assess the performance of the pass-through security in the previous illustration over a six month investment horizon on the basis of the following assumptions:

(1) For the next six months the prepayment rate will be 100% PSA,
(2) The projected cash flow can be reinvested at 0.75% per month,
(3) The pass-through security will sell to yield 12.30% at the end of the investment horizon, and
(4) The projected PSA prepayment rate at the end of the investment horizon will be 50% PSA.

Based on the first assumption, the projected cash flow for the first six months is the same as in the previous illustration. The projected cash flow plus interest from reinvesting the cash flow at 0.75% per month is computed below:

End of month	Projected cash flow	Projected cash flow plus reinvestment income
1	$816	$ 847
2	832	857
3	849	868
4	865	878
5	881	888
6	897	897
Total		$5,235

At the end of the investment horizon, our original pass-through security would have a remaining balance of $99,174 and remaining maturity of 354 months. Assuming a required yield of 12.30% and a prepayment rate of 50% PSA, the projected price of this pass-through security would be $78,757.

The total future amount is then

Projected cash flow plus reinvestment income	$ 5,235
Projected price	78,757
Total	$ 83,992

The monthly horizon return is

$$\left[\frac{\$\,83{,}992}{\$\,94{,}521}\right]^{1/6} - 1 = -.019491.$$

On a bond equivalent basis, the horizon return is

$$2\,[(0.98051)^6 - 1] = -0.2228 = -22.28\%.$$

On an effective annual yield basis, the horizon return is

$$(0.98051)^{12} - 1 = -0.2104 = -21.04\%.$$

Yield Spread to Treasuries

It should be clear that it is not possible to determine an exact yield for a pass-through security; the yield depends on the actual prepayment experience of the mortgages in the pool. Nevertheless, it is often stated that pass-through securities offer a higher yield than Treasury securities. Typically, Ginnie Mae pass-through securities and are compared with Treasuries, since both are free of default risk. The difference between the two yields should therefore primarily represent prepayment risk. The question is whether the amount of the premium the investor receives in terms of higher yield for bearing prepayment risk is adequate. This is where option pricing models have been applied to pass-through securities.[1] By using an option pricing model, it is possible to determine whether the pass-through security is offering the proper compensation for accepting prepayment risk.

---

[1] See David J. Askin, Woodward C. Hoffman and Steven Meyer, "Evaluation of the Option Component of Mortgages," in *The Handbook of Mortgage-Backed Securities*, Frank J. Fabozzi, ed., 2nd ed. (Chicago, Probus Publishing, 1988), Chapter 28; Gifford Fong, Ki-Young Chung, and Eric M. P. Tang, "The Valuation of Mortgage-Backed Securities: A Contingent Claims Approach," in *The Handbook of Mortgage-Backed Securities*, Chapter 30; and David P. Jacob, Graham Lord and James A. Tilley, "Price, Duration and Convexity of Mortgage-Backed Securities," in *Mortgage-Backed Securities: New Strategies, Applications and Research*, Frank J. Fabozzi, ed. (Chicago: Probus Publishing, 1987).

In evaluating the yield of a mortgage pass-through security versus that of a comparable Treasury, what does "comparable" mean? The stated maturity of a mortgage pass-through security is inappropriate because of prepayments. Instead, market participants have used two measures: Macaulay duration and average life.

Macaulay Duration

In Chapter 10 we stressed the role of Macaulay duration as a measure of the interest-rate sensitivity of a fixed income security, not as some measure of its life. As we will explain in the next section, Macaulay duration is not a good measure of the interest-rate sensitivity of a pass-through security, but it is commonly used as a measure of the life of a pass-through.

Calculating the Macaulay duration requires a projection of the cash flow, which, in turn, requires a prepayment rate assumption. From the projected cash flow, the price of the pass-through security, and the monthly interest rate (computed from the yield on a bond equivalent basis), Macaulay duration can be computed, as illustrated in Chapter 10. Macaulay duration is converted into years by dividing the Macaulay duration in months by 12.

Illustration 16-7. For the pass-through security in Illustration 16-1, selling for $94,521 and yielding 10.21% (assuming 100% PSA), Macaulay duration is 6.17, as shown below.

The numerator of the Macaulay duration is the present value of the projected cash flow using a monthly interest rate of 0.8333% times the time period (the month). For our pass-through security, the numerator is $6,998,347. Macaulay duration is then found by dividing by the price of the pass-through security. Thus,

$$\text{Macaulay duration (in months)} = \frac{\$6,998,347}{\$94,521} = 74.04.$$

To convert the Macaulay duration in months to Macaulay duration in years:

$$\text{Macaulay duration (in years)} = \frac{74.04}{12} = 6.17.$$

Average Life

A second measure commonly used to compare Treasury securities and pass-through securities is the average life, which is the average time to receipt of principal payments (projected scheduled principal and projected principal prepayments), weighted by the amount of principal expected divided by the total principal to be repaid.

Mathematically, the average life is expressed as follows:

$$\text{Average life} = \frac{1}{12} \sum_{t=1}^{n} \frac{t \, (\text{Principal received at time } t)}{\text{Total principal received}},$$

where n is the number of months remaining.

Illustration 16-8. For the pass-through security in the previous illustration, assuming the same prepayment rate (100% PSA), the principal payments are shown in columns (6) and (8) of Exhibit 15-3 of Chapter 15. Adding the principal payments in these two columns and applying the above formula, the average life is 12.18 years.

Duration, Convexity, and Price Performance for a Pass-Through Security

As explained in Chapter 10, duration is a measure of the interest-rate sensitivity of a bond. Macaulay duration is a measure of price volatility if the cash flow does not change with interest rates. In Chapter 13 we saw that Macaulay duration is not an appropriate measure for callable corporate bonds because the projected cash flow changes as interest rates change.

The same is true for mortgage pass-through securities. The reason is that the projected cash flow changes as the interest rate changes. When interest rates decline (rise), prepayments are expected to rise (fall). As a result, when interest rates decrease (increase), Macaulay duration and modified duration may decrease (increase) rather than increase (decrease). As we explained in Chapter 13, this property is referred to as negative convexity.

To illustrate this characteristic, consider the Macaulay duration for the 9.5% pass-through security (assuming 100% PSA) selling to yield 10.21%. If the required yield decreases to 8.14% instantaneously and the prepayment rate is assumed not to change, Macaulay duration would increase from 6.17 to 6.80. Suppose, however, that when the yield declines to 8.14%, the assumed prepayment rate changes to 150% PSA. The Macaulay duration would decline to 5.91 rather than increase.

The effect of negative convexity on the price performance of a pass-through security is the same as for callable corporate bonds. When interest rates decline, a fixed-income security with an embedded call option will not perform as well as an option-free fixed-income security. For example, if the required yield decreases instantaneously from 10.21% to 8.14%, the price would increase from \$94,521 to \$107,596. If the prepayment rate increases to 150% PSA, however, the price will rise to only \$106,710.

Formulas for Approximating Duration and Convexity

While Macaulay duration and modified duration are inappropriate as measures of interest-rate sensitivity, there are two approaches that can be taken to estimate interest-rate sensitivity. One approach is to use the call-adjusted duration discussed in Chapter 13. The other is to use the following formula to approximate the duration:

$$\text{Duration} = \frac{P_- - P_+}{(P_0)\,(y_+ - y_-)},$$

where
P_0 = Initial price;
P_- = Price if yield is decreased by x basis points;
P_+ = Price if yield is increased by x basis points;
y_- = Initial yield minus x basis points;
y_+ = Initial yield plus x basis points.

When computing duration by using the above formula, the price at the higher and lower interest rates will depend on the prepayment rate assumed. A lower prepayment rate is typically assumed at the lower interest rate than at the higher interest rate.

Illustration 16-9. Consider the mortgage pass-through security in Illustration 16-1. The price assuming 100% PSA and a yield of 10.21% is $94,521. Let's look at what would happen to the price if the yield changes by 50 basis points. Suppose that if the yield decreases by 50 basis points to 9.71%, the prepayment rate is unchanged at 100% PSA. If the yield increases by 50 basis points to 10.71%, however, the prepayment rate is assumed to decrease to 75% PSA. The prices at 9.71% and 10.71% would be $97,520 and $90,992, respectively. Therefore,

$$P_0 = \$94,521$$
$$P_- = \$97,520$$
$$P_+ = \$90,992$$
$$y_- = .0971 \ (.1021 - .005)$$
$$y_+ = .1071 \ (.1021 + .005)$$

$$\text{Duration} = \frac{\$97,520 - \$90,992}{\$94,521 \ (.1071 - .0971)},$$

$$= 6.91.$$

For convexity, one approach is to compute a call-adjusted convexity, as explained in Chapter 13. Alternatively, the following formula can be used to approximate convexity:

$$\text{Convexity} = \frac{P_+ + P_- - 2 \ (P_0)}{(P_0) \ [0.5 \ (y_+ - y_-)]^2}$$

Illustration 16-10. Given the assumptions in the previous illustration, the approximate convexity is:

$$\text{Convexity} = \frac{\$90,992 + \$97,520 - 2 \ (\$94,521)}{(\$94,521) \ [0.5 \ (.1071 - .0971)]^2}$$

$$= \frac{-\$530}{\$94,521 \ (0.005)^2} = -224.29.$$

Notice that the convexity of this mortgage pass-through security is negative.

Price and Price Performance
of IO/PO Stripped Mortgage-Backed Securities

In early 1987, stripped mortgage-backed securities were introduced in which all of the interest from a pass-through security is paid to one class and all of the principal to the other class. These securities are referred to as the IO security and PO security, respectively.

The cash flows of IO and PO securities depend on the cash flow of the underlying mortgage pass-through security, which, in turn, depends on the cash flow of the underlying pool of mortgages. Thus, to determine the price of an IO or PO security, a prepayment rate must be assumed. The price of an IO is the present value of the projected interest payments net of the servicing fee. The price of a PO is the present value of the projected principal payments (projected scheduled principal payments and projected principal prepayments).

Illustration 16-11. For the 9.5% pass-through security with a 0.5% servicing fee and 360 months to maturity, the projected interest payments net of the servicing fee and the projected principal payments assuming 100% PSA are shown in Exhibit 15-3 for selected months. Assuming a required yield of 10.21%, then:

Price of pass-through security	$ 94,521
Price of IO security	55,548
Price of PO security	38,973

Illustration 16-12. Assuming that the required yield is 12.30% rather than 10.21% and the prepayment rate is 25% PSA rather than 100% PSA, then:

Price of pass-through security	$ 79,976
Price of IO security	61,010
Price of PO security	18,966

Notice what has happend to the price of the IO security in Illustration 16-11 compared to Illustration 16-12. As interest rates increased from 10.21% to 12.30%, the price of the IO increased. This is to be expected since the holder of an IO security benefits by the slowing of prepayments — that is, the longer the mortgages are outstanding because of the reduced prepayments, the longer will the IO receive interest. The PO portion decreases as interest rates increase.

Illustration 16-13. Assuming that the required yield is 8.14% rather than 10.21% and the prepayment rate is 200% PSA rather than 100% PSA, then:

Price of pass-through security	$105,985
Price of IO security	47,875
Price of PO security	58,110

The price of the IO in Illustration 16-13 has decreased as a result of both a lower required yield and a higher prepayment rate compared to Illustration 16-11. The opposite is true for the PO.

From the last two illustrations we can see that IOs move in the same direction as interest rates while POs move inversely with interest rates.

Summary

Once the cash flow of a mortgage pass-through security is projected and the price is known, the yield can be determined. The yield, which is simply the internal rate of return of the projected cash flow, is called a cash flow yield. To compare mortgage pass-through securities, which have monthly cash flows, to Treasury and corporate bonds, which have semiannual cash flows, requires that the monthly interest rate be computed on a bond equivalent basis.

Given the projected cash flow and the required yield on a bond equivalent basis, the price of a mortgage pass-through security can be computed. The interest rate for discounting the monthly cash flows must be properly determined.

As a measure of potential performance, cash flow yield suffers from all the shortcomings of the yield to maturity measure, and more. A better measure is horizon return. In addition to requiring assumptions about the reinvestment rate and bond equivalent yield at the end of the investment horizon, the horizon return framework requires an assumption about the prepayment rate at the end of the investment horizon.

Mortgage pass-through securities share the price performance characteristics of callable corporate bonds. As interest rates change, the cash flow of a mortgage pass-through security changes. When the current mortgage rate declines below the mortgage rate for the underlying pool, the mortgage pass-through security will exhibit negative convexity (price compression).

Because the cash flow of a pass-through security changes with interest rates, Macaulay duration is not an appropriate measure of its interest-rate sensitivity. Despite its shortcomings, it is common to use Macaulay duration as a risk measure to compare Treasury securities and mortgage pass-through securities. Average life is also used as a risk measure for such comparisions. The duration and convexity for a mortgage pass-through security can be approximated.

For a stripped mortgage-backed security, the cash flow is redirected so that one group of bondholders receives only the interest payments and another only the principal payments. Given the projected cash flow for a mortgage pass-through security and its required yield, the price of the IO and PO can be determined. The price of the PO moves inversely with interest rates. In contrast, the price of the IO moves in the same direction as interest rates — increasing when interest rates increase and decreasing when interest rates decrease.

Exhibit 16-1 summarizes the formulas presented in this chapter.

Exhibit 16-1

Summary of Formulas

Bond equivalent yield for a mortgage pass-through security:

$$\text{Bond equivalent yield} = 2\,[(1 + i_M)^6 - 1]$$

where

i_M = Monthly interest rate that will equate the present value of the projected monthly cash flow to the price of the mortgage pass-through security.

Conversion of a bond equivalent yield to a monthly interest rate:

$$i_M = [1 + (0.5)\,\text{Bond equivalent yield}]^{1/6} - 1.$$

Monthly horizon return for a mortgage pass-through security:

$$\left[\frac{\text{Total future amount}}{\text{Price of the pass-through}}\right]^{1/\text{Number of months}} - 1.$$

Annualized effective horizon return:

$$(1 + \text{Monthly horizon return})^{12} - 1.$$

Average life:

$$\text{Average life} = \frac{1}{12} \sum_{t=1}^{n} \frac{t\,(\text{Principal received at time } t)}{\text{Total principal received}},$$

where n is the number of months remaining.

Approximate duration:

$$\text{Duration} = \frac{P_- - P_+}{(P_0)\,(y_+ - y_-)}$$

Exhibit 16-1 continued.

where

P_0 = Initial price;
P_- = Price if yield is decreased by x basis points;
P_+ = Price if yield is increased by x basis points;
y_- = Initial yield minus x basis points;
y_+ = Initial yield plus x basis points.

Approximate convexity:

$$\text{Convexity} = \frac{P_+ + P_- - 2(P_0)}{(P_0)[0.5(y_+ - y_-)]^2}.$$

Appendices

Appendix A

Derivation of Duration and Convexity for Option-Free Bonds and Callable Bonds

In Chapters 10 and 11 we showed how to measure the duration and convexity of an option-free bond and their relationship to bond price volatility. In Chapter 13, we extended the duration and convexity measures to callable bonds. The purpose of this appendix is to derive the formulas for duration and convexity and their relationship to bond price volatility. To understand the derivations, the reader must be familiar with differential calculus. We begin with a discussion of a Taylor series.

Taylor Series to Approximate a Function

Suppose that we have any mathematical function, say,

$$P = f(y).$$

This means that the variable P depends on (is a function of) some variable y. If y changes, P will change. How much will P change if y changes by a small amount? The Taylor series is a tool of calculus that allows us to find an approximate answer to this question. Specifically, the Taylor series states the following:

Approximate change in P =

$$\frac{\text{(First derivative of } P \text{ with respect to } y) \times \text{(change in } y)^1}{1}$$

$$+ \frac{\text{(Second derivative of } P \text{ with respect to } y) \times \text{(change in } y)^2}{2 \times 1}$$

$$+ \frac{\text{(Third derivative of } P \text{ with respect to } y) \times \text{(change in } y)^3}{3 \times 2 \times 1}$$

$$+ \frac{\text{(Fourth derivative of } P \text{ with respect to } y) \times \text{(change in } y)^4}{4 \times 3 \times 2 \times 1}$$

etc.

Each fraction represents a term of the Taylor series. The more terms included, the better the approximation of the change in P.

Application of Taylor Series to Bond Price Volatility

Why is the Taylor series important? Think about what our objective is. In the case of an option-free bond, the price of a bond depends on the required yield. We want to approximate the change in price for a small change in yield; we can do so by using the Taylor series.

Let P equal the price of the bond and y the required yield. If we take only the first two terms of the Taylor series, then

Approximate change in P =

$$\frac{\text{(First derivative of } P \text{ with respect to } y) \times \text{(Change in } y)^1}{1}$$

$$+ \frac{\text{(Second derivative of } P \text{ with respect to } y) \times \text{(Change in } y)^2}{2 \times 1}$$

The price of an option-free bond (the price function) can be expressed as[1]

$$P = \frac{c}{(1+y)^1} + \frac{c}{(1+y)^2} + \cdots + \frac{c}{(1+y)^n} + \frac{M}{(1+y)^n} \,, \qquad (1)$$

where

P = Price;
c = Semiannual coupon interest ($);
M = Maturity value ($);
n = Number of semiannual periods (number of years times 2);
y = One-half the yield to maturity or required yield.

In the standard notation for derivatives from calculus, the first two terms of the Taylor series are

$$\Delta P = \frac{dP}{dy} (\Delta y) + \frac{1}{2} \frac{d^2P}{dy^2} (\Delta y)^2 \,, \qquad (2)$$

where

ΔP = Change in price;
Δy = Change in required yield;
$\dfrac{dP}{dy}$ = First derivative of the price function with respect to a change in the required yield;
$\dfrac{d^2P}{dy^2}$ = Second derivative of the price function with respect to a change in the required yield.

Divide both sides of Equation (2) by P, so that:

$$\frac{\Delta P}{P} = \frac{dP}{dy} \frac{1}{P} (\Delta y) + \frac{1}{2} \frac{d^2P}{dy^2} \frac{1}{P} (\Delta y)^2 \,. \qquad (3)$$

---

[1] Equation (1) assumes that the next coupon payment is due exactly six months from now and that there is no accrued interest. It is not difficult to extend the model to account for the possibility that the first coupon payment will occur less than six months from the valuation date and to adjust the price to include accrued interest.

Let's examine each term of the Taylor series.

First Term of Taylor Series and Duration

The first derivative of the price function is:

$$\frac{dP}{dy} = \frac{(-1)c}{(1+y)^2} + \frac{(-2)c}{(1+y)^3} + \cdots + \frac{(-n)c}{(1+y)^{n+1}} + \frac{(-n)M}{(1+y)^{n+1}} , \quad (4)$$

Rearranging Equation (4), we obtain

$$\frac{dP}{dy} = -\frac{1}{(1+y)}\left[\frac{1c}{(1+y)^1} + \frac{2c}{(1+y)^2} + \cdots + \frac{nc}{(1+y)^n} + \frac{nM}{(1+y)^n}\right] \quad (5)$$

Dividing Equation (5) by P gives

$$\frac{dP}{dy}\frac{1}{P} = -\frac{1}{(1+y)}\left[\frac{1c}{(1+y)^1} + \frac{2c}{(1+y)^2} + \right.$$

$$\left. \cdots + \frac{nc}{(1+y)^n} + \frac{nM}{(1+y)^n}\right]\frac{1}{P} \quad (6)$$

The expression in the brackets, divided by the price (or multiplied by the reciprocal of the price), is

$$\frac{\left[\frac{1c}{(1+y)^1} + \frac{2c}{(1+y)^2} + \cdots + \frac{nc}{(1+y)^n} + \frac{nM}{(1+y)^n}\right]}{P}$$

Look at the numerator of the above expression. It is the time period weighted by the present value of the cash flow to be received. This quantity, divided by the price, is something we've seen before—it's nothing more than Macaulay duration.[2] To get Macaulay duration in terms of years, the above expression must be divided by 2.

Substituting Macaulay duration into Equation (6) gives

---

[2] See page 171 of Chapter 10.

$$\frac{dP}{dy}\frac{1}{P} = -\frac{1}{(1+y)} \text{ (Macaulay duration).} \qquad (7)$$

Recall from Chapter 10 that

$$\text{Modified duration} = \frac{\text{Macaulay duration}}{(1+y)} \qquad (8)$$

Substituting Equation (8) into Equation (7) gives

$$\frac{dP}{dy}\frac{1}{P} = -\text{Modified duration}. \qquad (9)$$

From Equation (3), the first term of the Taylor series is

$$\frac{\Delta P}{P} = \frac{dP}{dy}\frac{1}{P}(\Delta y). \qquad (10)$$

Substituting Equation (9) into Equation (10) gives

$$\frac{\Delta P}{P} = -\text{Modified duration}(\Delta y). \qquad (11)$$

We can translate Equation (11) as

Approximate percentage change in price =
− Modified duration × Yield change

This is precisely the relationship we showed in Chapter 10.[3] Thus, by using modified duration to approximate the percentage price change, we are using the first term of a Taylor series as an approximation of the percentage price change of a bond for a small change in yield.

---

[3] See page 179. Technically, the equation gives the *fractional* change in price, not the *percentage* change, multiplying by 100 gives the percentage change.

Second Term of the Taylor Series and Convexity

The second derivative of the price function [Equation (1)] is

$$\frac{d^2P}{dy^2} = \left[\frac{1}{(1+y)^2}\ \frac{1\,(2)\,c}{(1+y)^1} + \frac{2\,(3)\,c}{(1+y)^2} + \right.$$

$$\left. \cdots + \frac{(n-1)\,n\,c}{(1+y)^n} + \frac{(n-1)\,n\,M}{(1+y)^n}\right]. \tag{12}$$

Dividing Equation (12) by P, we have:

$$\frac{d^2P}{dy^2}\ \frac{1}{P} = \left[\frac{1}{(1+y)^2}\ \frac{1\,(2)\,c}{(1+y)^1} + \frac{2\,(3)\,c}{(1+y)^2} + \right.$$

$$\left. \cdots + \frac{(n-1)\,n\,c}{(1+y)^n} + \frac{(n-1)\,n\,M}{(1+y)^n}\right]\frac{1}{P}. \tag{13}$$

Notice that the term on the right-hand side is the convexity measure that we presented in Chapter 11.[4] Thus,

$$\frac{d^2P}{dy^2}\ \frac{1}{P} = \text{Convexity.} \tag{14}$$

From Equation (3), the second term of the Taylor series to approximate the percentage change in price is

$$\frac{\Delta P}{P} = \frac{1}{2}\ \frac{d^2P}{dy^2}\ \frac{1}{P}\ (\Delta y)^2. \tag{15}$$

Substituting Equation (14) into Equation (15),

$$\frac{\Delta P}{P} = \frac{1}{2}\ (\text{Convexity})\ (\Delta y)^2. \tag{16}$$

Equation (16) states that the percentage change in price based on the second term of the Taylor series, is

---

[4] See page 209.

$$(0.5) \times (\text{Convexity}) \times (\text{Yield change})^2$$

Notice that this is the formula presented in Chapter 11 to approximate the percentage price change due to convexity.[5] Thus, approximating the percentage change in price due to convexity corresponds to using the second term of the Taylor series.

Adding the percentage price change due to duration and the percentage price change due to convexity is just making use of the first two terms of the Taylor series. Why not use more terms? Looking back at Exhibit 11-8 of Chapter 11 (page 214), you can see that using just the first two terms explains most of the percentage change in the price of a bond.

The Importance of the Assumption
of a Flat Yield Curve and Parallel Shifts

The formulas presented in Chapters 10 and 11 for duration and convexity can be used to approximate the percentage price change for small changes in the required yield, assuming (1) the yield curve is flat and (2) any change in yield results in a parallel shift in the yield curve. Where did these assumptions come from?

Look back at the price function, Equation (1). There is only one yield to discount each cash flow; that is, the yield used to discount each cash flow is independent of the timing of the cash flow. This is equivalent to saying that the yield curve is flat — the same for each maturity. When we take the derivative of Equation (1) with respect to y, we assume that the change in yield is the same for each maturity — that is, there is a parallel shift of the yield curve.

These two assumptions may seem to limit the value of duration as a measure of bond price volatility. Several researchers have formulated more complex measures of duration based on different assumptions about how the yield curve will shift. Studies comparing the predictive value of these more complex meas-

---

[5] See page 218. As noted in footnote 3, technically the equation gives the fractional change.

ures with the simple Macaulay (modified) duration, however, have shown that the latter performs just as well.[6]

Call-Adjusted Duration

In Chapter 13, we explained that the price of a callable bond can be expressed as follows:

Price of a callable bond =
Price of a noncallable bond − Call option price

or

$$P_{cb} = P_{ncb} - P_{co} \, , \qquad (17)$$

where

P_{cb} = Price of a callable bond;
P_{ncb} = Price of a noncallable bond;
P_{co} = Price of a call option.

Taking the first derivative of Equation (17) with respect to yield (y), we have

$$\frac{dP_{cb}}{dy} = \frac{dP_{ncb}}{dy} - \frac{dP_{co}}{dy} \, . \qquad (18)$$

Dividing both sides by the price of the callable bond,

$$\frac{dP_{cb}}{dy} \frac{1}{P_{cb}} = \frac{dP_{ncb}}{dy} \frac{1}{P_{cb}} - \frac{dP_{co}}{dy} \frac{1}{P_{cb}} \, .$$

Multiplying the numerator and denominator of the right-hand side by the price of a noncallable bond;

$$\frac{dP_{cb}}{dy} \frac{1}{P_{cb}} = \frac{dP_{ncb}}{dy} \frac{1}{P_{ncb}} \frac{P_{ncb}}{P_{cb}} - \frac{dP_{co}}{dy} \frac{1}{P_{ncb}} \frac{P_{ncb}}{P_{cb}} \, .$$

---

[6] See Gerald O. Bierwag, *Duration Analysis* (Cambridge, MA: Ballinger Publishing, 1987), Chapter 11 for a discussion of alternative duration measures and Chapter 12 for the empirical evidence of the relative performance of Macaulay duration and the more complex duration measures.

Let's look at each of the components.

$$\frac{dP_{cb}}{dy} \frac{1}{P_{cb}} = \text{Modified duration of callable bond} = \text{Dur}_{cb}.$$

The above relationship can be seen by looking at Equation (9).[7]

$$\frac{dP_{ncb}}{dy} \frac{1}{P_{ncb}} = \text{Duration of a noncallable bond} = \text{Dur}_{ncb}.$$

Thus, we have

$$\text{Dur}_{cb} = \text{Dur}_{ncb} \frac{P_{ncb}}{P_{cb}} - \frac{dP_{co}}{dy} \frac{1}{P_{ncb}} \frac{P_{ncb}}{P_{cb}}. \qquad (19)$$

The change in the value of the call option for a change in yield is

$$\frac{dP_{co}}{dy}. \qquad (20)$$

The change in the value of the call option, however, depends on the change in the price of the noncallable bond for a given change in yield. That is,

$$P_{co} = f(P_{ncb}) \text{ and } P_{ncb} = g(y).$$

Using the function-of-a-function rule from calculus, Equation (20) can be expressed as

$$\frac{dP_{co}}{dy} = \frac{dP_{co}}{dP_{ncb}} \frac{dP_{ncb}}{dy}. \qquad (21)$$

The first term on the right-hand side of Equation (21) is the change in the value of the call option for a change in the price of

---

[7] Actually, it is equal to $-\text{Dur}_{cb}$, but because we will be omitting the negative sign for the durations on the right-hand side, this will not affect our derivation.

the noncallable bond. As explained in Chapter 12, this is the *delta* of an option. Thus,

$$\frac{dP_{co}}{dy} = \text{Delta} \times \frac{dP_{ncb}}{dy} \, . \tag{22}$$

Substituting Equation (22) into Equation (21) and rearranging terms,

$$\text{Dur}_{cb} = \text{Dur}_{ncb} \times \frac{P_{ncb}}{P_{cb}} \times (1 - \text{Delta}). \tag{23}$$

The duration for the callable bond given by Equation (23) is the same as the call-adjusted duration presented in Chapter 13.

Call-Adjusted Convexity

From Equation (14), convexity is equal to the second derivative multiplied by the reciprocal of the price. Equation (18) gives the first derivative for the price of a callable bond. Once again, since the price of the call option depends on the price of the underlying noncallable bond and, in turn, the price of the noncallable bond depends on its yield, the function-of-a-function rule allows Equation (18) to be expressed as

$$\frac{dP_{cb}}{dy} = \frac{dP_{ncb}}{dy} - \frac{dP_{co}}{dP_{ncb}} \frac{dP_{ncb}}{dy} \, . \tag{24}$$

The second derivative of Equation (24) is:

$$\frac{d^2P_{cb}}{dy^2} = \frac{d^2P_{ncb}}{dy^2} - \left[\frac{d^2P_{co}}{dP^2_{ncb}} \left(\frac{dP_{ncb}}{dy} \right)^2 + \frac{dP_{co}}{dP_{ncb}} \frac{d^2P_{ncb}}{dy^2} \right]. \tag{25}$$

Let's look at each of the components on the right-hand side of Equation (25). First consider the second derivative of the price of the noncallable bond with respect to yield, i.e.,

$$\frac{d^2P_{ncb}}{dy^2} \, .$$

Multiplying the numerator and denominator by the price of the noncallable bond gives

$$\frac{d^2 P_{ncb}}{dy^2} \times \frac{P_{ncb}}{P_{ncb}} \, ,$$

which is equivalent to the convexity of the noncallable bond times the price of the noncallable bond:

$$\mathrm{Con}_{ncb} \times P_{ncb} \, . \tag{26}$$

Next let's look at

$$\frac{d^2 P_{co}}{dP^2_{ncb}} \left(\frac{dP_{ncb}}{dy} \right)^2 .$$

The first term is the rate of change of the delta of the call option with respect to a change in the price of the noncallable bond. As explained in Chapter 12, this is the gamma of the call option. Thus, we have

$$\mathrm{Gamma} \times \left(\frac{dP_{ncb}}{dy} \right)^2 ,$$

which can also be expressed as

$$\mathrm{Gamma} \times \left(\frac{dP_{ncb}}{dy} \right)^2 \times \frac{P^2_{ncb}}{P^2_{ncb}} \, ,$$

which is equivalent to

$$\mathrm{Gamma} \times (\mathrm{Dur}_{ncb})^2 \times P^2_{ncb} \, . \tag{27}$$

Now look at

$$\frac{dP_{co}}{dP_{ncb}} \frac{d^2 P_{ncb}}{dy^2} \, ,$$

The first term is the delta of the call option, so

$$\text{Delta} \times \frac{d^2 P_{ncb}}{dy^2}.$$

Multiplying the numerator and denominator by the price of the noncallable bond, we have

$$\text{Delta} \times \frac{d^2 P_{ncb}}{dy^2} \times \frac{P_{ncb}}{P_{ncb}},$$

but recall that the second derivative of the price of a noncallable bond times the reciprocal of its price is the convexity of the noncallable bond. Therefore, the term becomes

$$\text{Delta} \times \text{Con}_{ncb} \times P_{ncb}. \tag{28}$$

Substituting Equations (26), (27), and (28) into Equation (25),

$$\frac{d^2 P_{cb}}{dy^2} = \text{Con}_{ncb} \times P_{ncb}$$

$$- [\text{Gamma} \times (\text{Dur}_{ncb})^2 \times P^2_{ncb} + \text{Delta} \times \text{Con}_{ncb} \times P_{ncb}] \tag{29}$$

Multiplying the left-hand side of Equation (29) by the reciprocal of the price of the callable bond gives the convexity of the callable bond. Multiplying the right-hand side of equation (29) by the reciprocal of the price of the callable bond and rearranging terms gives

$$\text{Con}_{cb} = \frac{P_{ncb}}{P_{cb}} [\text{Con}_{ncb} \times (1 - \text{Delta}) - P_{ncb} \times \text{Gamma} \times (\text{Dur}_{ncb})^2] \tag{30}$$

This is the equation presented in Chapter 13 for the call-adjusted convexity of a callable bond.

Appendix B
Screens from Fabozzi's *Fixed Income Calculator*

U. S. Treasury Note and Bond Analysis

Bonds	Mny Mkt	Options	Analysis	Yld Crv	Misc	Info	Quit
TRSY	TBILL	BSEQU	BNEQU	YC	SWAP	TUTOR	QUIT
AGCY	CP	BSFUT	BNFUT	ALTYC	FOREX	NEWS	
MUNI	BA	BSCOM			CSHFL	SPECT	
CORP	EUDS	BSCUR			FINAN	FABOZ	
ZERO	CD				CALEN	ACKNO	
FRGN	EUCD				PARAM		

```
| Fabozzi's Fixed Income Calculator |
```

Copyright (C) 1987, 1988 by SpectraSoft, Inc.
11 Harrison Street, New York, NY 10013, (212) 219-0404
All Rights Reserved. Release 2.0

All calculations, while not guaranteed, are based
upon information which we believe to be reliable.
Cursor keys or first few letters of page name to highlight then ↵ to select

Foreign Bond Analysis

Bonds	Mny Mkt	───── Foreign Bonds ─────	Info	Quit
Bonds	Mny Mkt	EUR - Eurodollar Bond	Info	Quit
TRSY	TBILL	AUD - Australian Government Bond	TUTOR	QUIT
AGCY	CP	BEF - Belgian Government Bond	NEWS	
MUNI	BA	CAD - Canadian Government Bond	SPECT	
CORP	EUDS	CHF - Swiss Government Bond	FABOZ	
ZERO	CD	DEM - West German Government Bund	ACKNO	
FRGN	EUCD	DKK - Danish Government Bond		
		FRN - French Government Bond		
		GBP - United Kingdom Gilt		
		JPY - Japanese Government Bond		
		NLG - Netherlands Government Bond		
	Cop	NZD - New Zealand Government Bond	c.	
	11 Harri	SEK - Sweden Government Bond	9-0404	

All calculations, while not guaranteed, are based
upon information which we believe to be reliable.
Cursor keys or first few letters of page name to highlight then ↵ to select

9.125 of 05/15/2018

Settlement date 06/03/1988

Coupon	9.125	Current yield	9.085
Maturity	05/15/2018	Yield value of a 1/32 (BP)	0.304
Price	100.140 / 32	Price value of an 01	0.103
Yield	9.081	dP/dY	-10.282
Issue date	/ /	Duration (years)	10.652
Redemption value	100.000	Modified duration	10.189
Price (decimal)	100.43750000	Convexity	180.354

Face amount (1M)	1000	Redemption value	1,000,000.00
Principal	1,004,375.00	Coupon payments	2,737,500.00
Accrued interest	4,711.28	Interest on interest	10,685,557.00
Total payment	1,009,086.28	Total income	14,423,057.00

F1-Help, F2-Calculate, PgUp-Prev Page, PgDn-Next Page or Esc-Menu

---

9.125 of 05/15/2018

Settlement date	06/03/1988	Horizon date	05/15/2018
Price	100.140 / 32	Horizon price	100.000
Yield	9.081	Horizon yield	9.125
Re-investment rate	9.081		
Principal	1,004,375.00		
Accrued interest	4,711.28		
Total payment	1,009,086.28		
Redemption value	1,000,000.00		
Coupon income	2,737,500.00		
Re-investment income	10,685,557.00		
Total income	14,423,057.00		
Total return	9.081		

F1-Help, F2-Calculate, PgUp-Prev Page, PgDn-Next Page or Esc-Menu

9.125 of 05/15/2018

Face amount (1M)   1000

Price		Yield		P/L
100.070		9.103		-2187.50
100.080		9.100		-1875.00
100.090		9.097		-1562.50
100.100		9.094		-1250.00
100.110		9.090		-937.50
100.120		9.087		-625.00
100.130		9.084		-312.50
100.140	1/ 32	9.081	1/100	0.00
100.150		9.078		312.50
100.160		9.075		625.00
100.170		9.072		937.50
100.180		9.069		1250.00
100.190		9.066		1562.50
100.200		9.063		1875.00
100.210		9.060		2187.50

Sell settlement	06/03/1988		Buy settlement	06/03/1988
Coupon	8.875 ·		Coupon	9.125
Maturity	08/15/2017		Maturity	05/15/2018
Price	96.220	/ 32	Price	100.140	/ 32
Yield	9.200		Yield	9.081
Issue date	/ /		Issue date	/ /
Redemption value	100.000000		Redemption value	100.000000
Price (decimal)	96.68750000		Price (decimal)	100.43750000
F4-List of bond types			F4-List of bond types	
Type	1		Type	1
Duration	10.318		Duration	10.652
Mod. Duration	9.865		Mod. Duration	10.189
dP/dY	-9.801		dP/dY	-10.282
YV 32	0.319		YV 32	0.304

F1-Help, F2-Calculate, F4-Choice, PgUp-Prev, PgDn-Next or Esc-Menu

Sell settlement	06/03/1988		Buy settlement	06/03/1988
Coupon	8.875		Coupon	9.125
Maturity	08/15/2017		Maturity	05/15/2018
Price	96.220	/ 32	Price	100.140	/ 32
Yield	9.201		Yield	9.081
Mod. duration	9.864		Mod. duration	10.189
dP/dY	-9.799		dP/dY	-10.282
YV 32	0.319		YV 32	0.304
Accrued int.	2.658		Accrued int.	0.471

Swap Forms	Amt (M)	Market	Amt (M)	Market	Pay Up	Ratio	Ratio
Par for Par	1000	988.78	1000	1006.11	17.34	1.00	1.02
$ for $	1000	988.78	982	988.00	-0.77	0.98	1.00
YV/32 Hedge	1000	988.78	953	958.82	-29.95	0.95	0.97
Mod. Dur.	1000	988.78	953	958.82	-29.95	0.95	0.97

F1-Help, F2-Calculate, PgUp-Prev Page, PgDn-Next Page or Esc-Menu

Horizon Date	08/15/2017		Re-investement Rate	9.201	
Sell Settlement	06/03/1988		Buy Settlement	06/03/1988	
Price	96.220	/ 32	Price	100.140	/ 32
Yield	9.201		Yield	9.081	
Horizon Price	96.220		Horizon Price	100.140	
Horizon Yield	16.031		Horizon Yield	8.477	
Sell	1000		Buy	1000	

In: Principal	966,875.00	1,004,375.00		
Accrued Interest	26,576.24	4,711.28		
Pay Up/Take Out	15,635.04	0.00		
Present Value	1,009,086.28	1,009,086.28	Difference	
Out:Interest Income	2,618,125.00	2,669,062.50		50,937.50
Principal Paid	966,875.00	1,004,375.00		37,500.00
Re-investment Income	10,121,013.44	9,890,129.52		-230,883.92
Future Value	13,706,013.44	13,563,567.02		-142,446.42
Total Return	9.193	9.099		-9.334

F1-Help, F2-Calculate, PgUp-Prev Page, PgDn-Next Page or Esc-Menu

Date 1: 06/03/1988   Date 2: 06/25/1988

         Friday   Saturday

```
┌─────── June 1988 ───────┐    ┌─────── June 1988 ───────┐
│ Su Mo Tu We Th Fr Sa │    │ Su Mo Tu We Th Fr Sa │
│           1  2  3  4 │    │           1  2  3  4 │
│  5  6  7  8  9 10 11 │    │  5  6  7  8  9 10 11 │
│ 12 13 14 15 16 17 18 │    │ 12 13 14 15 16 17 18 │
│ 19 20 21 22 23 24 25 │    │ 19 20 21 22 23 24 25 │
│ 26 27 28 29 30       │    │ 26 27 28 29 30       │
│                      │    │                      │
└──────────────────────┘    └──────────────────────┘
```

Days between Date 1 and Date 2 (Actual):   22
Days between Date 1 and Date 2 (30/360):   22

                    F2-Calculate or Esc-Menu

Number of cash flows   15   Remember to add cash flow 0 to this number.

Discount rate   10.000   Per period rate used to calculate npv.

Cash flow 0: -57,259.00   Initial cash outflow or inflow.

1: 2,300.00	11: 1,050.00	21: 0.00	31: 0.00	41: 0.00
2: 2,300.00	12: 1,050.00	22: 0.00	32: 0.00	42: 0.00
3: 2,300.00	13: 1,050.00	23: 0.00	33: 0.00	43: 0.00
4: 2,300.00	14: 21,050.00	24: 0.00	34: 0.00	44: 0.00
5: 2,300.00	15: 0.00	25: 0.00	35: 0.00	45: 0.00
6: 32,300.00	16: 0.00	26: 0.00	36: 0.00	46: 0.00
7: 1,400.00	17: 0.00	27: 0.00	37: 0.00	47: 0.00
8: 1,400.00	18: 0.00	28: 0.00	38: 0.00	48: 0.00
9: 1,400.00	19: 0.00	29: 0.00	39: 0.00	49: 0.00
10: 11,400.00	20: 0.00	30: 0.00	40: 0.00	50: 0.00

Net present value = -17397.37   Internal rate of return =   4.77

                    F2-Calculate or Esc-Menu

Series	Coupon	Maturity	Price	Settlement Issue	03/30/1987 Yield	Page 1 of 4 Duration
3 Mo	5.620	05/26/1988	93.397		0.000	0.000
6 Mo	5.870	08/25/1988	91.619		0.000	0.000
1 Yr	6.160	02/16/1989	88.210		0.000	0.000
2 Yr	7.125	02/15/1990	100.000	/ /	0.000	0.000
3 Yr	7.375	02/15/1991	100.050	/ /	0.000	0.000
4 Yr	8.250	12/15/1991	102.150	/ /	0.000	0.000
5 Yr	7.625	05/15/1993	99.260	/ /	0.000	0.000
7 Yr	8.625	01/15/1995	103.200	/ /	0.000	0.000
10 Yr	8.125	02/15/1998	99.260	/ /	0.000	0.000
20 Yr	9.375	02/15/2006	108.240	/ /	0.000	0.000
30 Yr	8.875	08/15/2017	105.250	/ /	0.000	0.000

F1-Help, F2-Calculate, F3-Graph, F4-Choice, PgUp-Prev, PgDn-Next or Esc-Menu

Increment 1 / 32   Page 2 of 4

3 Mo			6 Mo			1 Yr		
5.560	93.467	5.931	5.810	91.705	6.296	6.100	88.325	6.831
5.570	93.455	5.942	5.820	91.690	6.307	6.110	88.306	6.843
5.580	93.444	5.954	5.830	91.676	6.319	6.120	88.287	6.855
5.590	93.432	5.965	5.840	91.662	6.331	6.130	88.268	6.868
5.600	93.420	5.976	5.850	91.648	6.342	6.140	88.249	6.880
5.610	93.408	5.987	5.860	91.633	6.354	6.150	88.230	6.893
5.620	93.397	5.999	5.870	91.619	6.365	6.160	88.210	6.905
5.630	93.385	6.010	5.880	91.605	6.377	6.170	88.191	6.917
5.640	93.373	6.021	5.890	91.590	6.389	6.180	88.172	6.930
5.650	93.361	6.032	5.900	91.576	6.400	6.190	88.153	6.942
5.660	93.349	6.044	5.910	91.562	6.412	6.200	88.134	6.955
5.670	93.338	6.055	5.920	91.548	6.423	6.210	88.115	6.967
5.680	93.326	6.066	5.930	91.533	6.435	6.220	88.096	6.980

F1-Help, F2-Calculate, F3-Graph, PgUp-Prev Page, PgDn-Next Page or Esc-Menu

2 Yr		3 Yr		4 Yr		5 Yr	
99.26	7.194	99.31	7.381	102.09	7.659	99.20	7.700
99.27	7.182	100.00	7.371	102.10	7.651	99.21	7.694
99.28	7.169	100.01	7.362	102.11	7.643	99.22	7.687
99.29	7.157	100.02	7.353	102.12	7.636	99.23	7.681
99.30	7.145	100.03	7.343	102.13	7.628	99.24	7.674
99.31	7.133	100.04	7.334	102.14	7.620	99.25	7.668
100.00	7.121	100.05	7.324	102.15	7.612	99.26	7.661
100.01	7.108	100.06	7.315	102.16	7.604	99.27	7.655
100.02	7.096	100.07	7.306	102.17	7.596	99.28	7.648
100.03	7.084	100.08	7.296	102.18	7.588	99.29	7.642
100.04	7.072	100.09	7.287	102.19	7.580	99.30	7.635
100.05	7.060	100.10	7.278	102.20	7.572	99.31	7.629
100.06	7.048	100.11	7.268	102.21	7.565	100.00	7.622

7 Yr		10 Yr		20 Yr		30 Yr	
103.14	8.020	99.20	8.176	108.18	8.457	105.19	8.363
103.15	8.014	99.21	8.171	108.19	8.454	105.20	8.361
103.16	8.009	99.22	8.167	108.20	8.451	105.21	8.358
103.17	8.004	99.23	8.162	108.21	8.448	105.22	8.355
103.18	7.998	99.24	8.158	108.22	8.445	105.23	8.352
103.19	7.993	99.25	8.154	108.23	8.442	105.24	8.350
103.20	7.988	99.26	8.149	108.24	8.438	105.25	8.347
103.21	7.982	99.27	8.145	108.25	8.435	105.26	8.344
103.22	7.977	99.28	8.140	108.26	8.432	105.27	8.342
103.23	7.972	99.29	8.136	108.27	8.429	105.28	8.339
103.24	7.966	99.30	8.132	108.28	8.426	105.29	8.336
103.25	7.961	99.31	8.127	108.29	8.423	105.30	8.334
103.26	7.956	100.00	8.123	108.30	8.420	105.31	8.331

Settlement date 06/03/1988

Strike	100.000	Call price	2.713	Put price	2.713
Expiration	07/15/1988	Delta	0.510	Delta	-0.483
Underlying price	100.000	Gamma	0.058	Gamma	0.058
Volatility	20.000	Theta	0.031	Theta	0.031
Risk free rate	6.500	Vega	0.134	Vega	0.134
Early excercise (Y/N)	N				
Number of periods	25				
Number of options	1,000	Value	2,712.56	Value	2,712.56
Days to expiration	42				

F1-Help, F2-Calculate, PgUp-Prev Page, PgDn-Next Page or Esc-Menu

Settlement date	06/03/1988	Horizon date	07/15/1988
Expiration	07/15/1988		
Strike price	100.000		
Underlying price	100.000	Underlying price	100.000
Volatility	20.000	Volatility	20.000
Risk free rate	6.500	Risk free rate	6.500
Call price	2.713	Call price	0.000
Put price	2.713	Put price	0.000

Number of options	1,000	Number of options		
Value of call	2,712.56	Value of call	0.00	-2,712.56
Value of put	2,712.56	Value of put	0.00	-2,712.56
Days to exp.	42	Days to exp.	0	

F1-Help, F2-Calculate, PgUp-Prev Page, PgDn-Next Page or Esc-Menu

Underlying	Volatility	Call Prc	Call P&L	Call Dlt	Put Prc	Put P&L	Put Dlt
99.30	20.000	2.36	-0.36	0.469	3.05	0.34	-0.524
99.40	20.000	2.41	-0.31	0.475	3.00	0.29	-0.518
99.50	20.000	2.46	-0.25	0.480	2.95	0.24	-0.512
99.60	20.000	2.51	-0.20	0.486	2.91	0.19	-0.506
99.70	20.000	2.56	-0.15	0.492	2.86	0.14	-0.500
99.80	20.000	2.61	-0.10	0.498	2.81	0.10	-0.495
99.90	20.000	2.66	-0.05	0.504	2.76	0.05	-0.489
100.00 1/ 10	20.000 1/ 10	2.71	0.00	0.510	2.71	0.00	-0.483
100.10	20.000	2.76	0.05	0.516	2.66	-0.05	-0.477
100.20	20.000	2.81	0.10	0.521	2.62	-0.10	-0.471
100.30	20.000	2.87	0.15	0.527	2.57	-0.14	-0.465
100.40	20.000	2.92	0.20	0.533	2.52	-0.19	-0.460
100.50	20.000	2.97	0.25	0.539	2.47	-0.24	-0.454
100.60	20.000	3.02	0.31	0.545	2.42	-0.29	-0.448
100.70	20.000	3.07	0.36	0.550	2.3r	-0.34	-0.442

F1-Help, F2-Calculate, F3-Graph, PgUp-Prev Page, PgDn-Next Page or Esc-Menu

Index